THE ART OF

Mexican Cooking

THE ART OF

Mexican Cooking

JAN AARON

&

GEORGINE SACHS SALOM

Drawings by Deirdre Stanforth

CASTLE

This edition published in the United States of America in 1985 by
Castle, a division of Book Sales, Inc., 110 Enterprise Ave.,
Secaucus, N.J. 07094, by arrangement with Doubleday & Company
and Galahad Books, Inc.

Library of Congress Catalog Card Number: 81-81158
ISBN: 0-89009-924-3

Printed in the United States of America

To Miguel Aleman
President of the Mexican National Tourist Council
and the many Mexicans
who helped us with this book.

Table of Contents

❖

Introduction

❖

A happy combination of work and pleasure introduced us to the delights of Mexican cookery about ten years ago. The work that each of us did in Mexico was so different that we had the opportunity to meet different kinds of people and to sample and learn about different varieties of food. While Jan Aaron was writing about chic restaurants and shops in Mexico City as a free lancer, Georgine Salom was writing about rural people in remote villages for an American voluntary agency. We have exchanged recipes with Mexicans in rambling haciendas and in adobe huts. We have consulted with chefs, government officials, society women, businesswomen, and farm women. We have eaten at outdoor stalls, country hotels, and fashionable Mexico City restaurants. We have made eating forays into Mexican restaurants in New York and have spent many delightful hours preparing Mexican food in our own kitchens.

Our experience with Mexican food is wide and varied and, therefore, we are eager to share our joy with the many

Americans who believe that Mexican food is one big *tortilla* surrounded by chili peppers. One look at the Table of Contents of this book will prove that Mexican food is one of the most varied and exotic cuisines in the world.

Our travels led us through the many regions of Mexico, and we discovered that the food of the country is as much a blend as the people themselves. In a land which has been trod upon at one time or another by the Spanish, the French, the English, and the Americans, their influences are naturally felt in the food. Yet it is still distinctly and deliciously Mexican despite all intrusions.

Foreign intervention in Mexico introduced the typical Danish pastry of the blond and blue-eyed person in a Northern country to the beautiful brown-eyed brunette of the Yucatán. The food in this region is said to be highly derivative of the Danish and the French because early settlers in this area sent their cooks back to Europe to learn the fine art of cooking and baking. The result is fantastic: Indian women in the long white native huipiles (dresses of the Yucatán) bake bread in their own style in charcoal ovens and it turns out to be crusty, delicious, and undeniably French. Danish pastry is served in the morning along with some of the most extraordinary honey in the world, produced in the Yucatán through the courtesy of imported Italian bees.

To really understand Mexican food, it is necessary to go back to its beginnings. The cuisine of the country is one of the oldest in the world. French cooking, which is so highly revered today, is about four hundred years old. Mexico started out with a great many staples with which to create a varied and interesting style of cooking as far back as 300 to 900 A.D. when the Maya civilization was at its peak. The Spanish introduced some of their favorite recipes around 1520, but the Indians were, by that time, already known for their elegant and sumptuous repasts.

The Journals of Bernal Díaz del Castillo, a soldier in the Cortés army, mentioned the miraculous Mexico City of 1519. "When I beheld the scene around me, I thought that this was the garden of the world." He was quite impressed with the table of Moctezuma: "His cooks had upwards of thirty different ways of dressing meats and had earthenware vessels so contrived as to keep them always hot. For the table of Moctezuma, himself, above three hundred dishes were dressed; and for his guards, above a thousand."

He continued listing some of the menu: pheasants, geese, partridge, quail, venison, Indian hogs, pigeons, hares, rabbits, and a host of other animals—enough to fill a native Noah's ark. He described Moctezuma as being the type of host who checked on the food himself when it was served. When it came to eating, however, the soldier noted that the Emperor ate little, but preferred to drink foaming chocolate and feast his eyes on the antics of the jesters and buffoons. Moctezuma also enjoyed lemonade, the early records say. In fact, he used to dispatch runners to snow-capped Popocatepetl for ice because he liked his lemonade cold. We assume that by the time they reached the city the ice was melted, but the story is a rich one anyway.

Although this book is about eating and cooking, it might not be too out of order to mention an after dinner pleasure loved today and adored by the great Moctezuma. That treat is tobacco, which the Emperor used to smoke in highly ornamented little canes.

In the early days, the Mexican-Iberian food marriage changed European eating habits more than the influence of Spain altered Mexican cuisine. Europeans got acquainted with such foods as tomatoes, beans, vanilla, chilies, maize, avocados, eggplants, potatoes, cashews, peanuts, and chocolate from the early Aztecs. The potato, that mainstay of the Irish diet, supposedly traveled to the Emerald Isle via Spain, and came there originally from Mexico or South America.

The earliest Spanish visitors to Mexico also noticed that all kinds of breads and little wafers were traditionally served with meals. The wafers were probably tortillas, little corncakes, which are so much a part of the Mexican table today that we've included them in the chapter, "Enchiladas, Tacos, Tamales, Tostadas, Empanadas," showing just how they can be used to highlight meals in many different ways.

Just to give you some idea: there's the Taco,* which is made either with a "soft" tortilla which is just baked, or a "hard" tortilla which is fried. With the soft tortilla, you fill your own little envelope with anything at hand, such as meat, chicken, beans, or any hot sauce (Salsa Rapida*). With a hard tortilla, any filling is acceptable, but the tortilla is fried into a hot, stiff cylinder before it is eaten. There are Enchiladas,* tortillas fried hard and smothered in a sauce; Tostadas,* open-faced tortilla sandwiches; and Gorditas,* tortillas which are rather thick and whose borders are pinched up to hold the filling used in them and then spread with sausages or pepper sauce—to name only a few of the dishes which depend upon tortillas as their base. The chapter, "A Guide to the Art of Mexican Cooking" clearly explains the different kinds of tortillas.

The Indians ground their own maize or corn to make the tortillas. The maize, which grows in about a dozen glowing colors, has played a great role in the history of Mexico. It was believed that this vegetable was invented by the great god Quetzalcoatl, who brought civilization from the Huaxteca region. Legend has it that Quetzalcoatl turned himself into a black ant and accompanied a red ant to bring corn, the food of the gods, to the people. Quetzalcoatl carried the corn to Tamoanchan, a mythical Mayan place of creation, and the story continues that the gods chewed upon the corn and put it into the mouths of humans to strengthen them.

The *Popol Vuh,* a holy Maya book, says that corn was so important that humans were constructed of it. "They made their flesh of the yellow and white ears of corn . . . then, they husked and ground the yellow and white ears, and Ixmucane [another holy figure] made nine drinks, these elements belonging to the substances destined to give life, force, and energy to the people. The tzite [corn] was the flesh of man," the Maya text continues. The ancient ruins around the Yucatán show extraordinary corn designs believed to be designs representing old, feared, and revered gods, either made of maize or carrying ears of corn.

History also shows, however, that gods, whether made of corn or sterner stuff, can fail and poor Quetzalcoatl supposedly died of drink and debauchery in disgrace. The unfortunate Moctezuma mistook Cortés for the returning Quetzalcoatl and so the Spanish moved right in and brought some of their eating habits along with them.

It is interesting that the Mexicans can prepare rice as well as the Chinese. They coat it with oil and fry it with spices and add tender succulent bits of meat and fish to create Arroz Clásico* or Paella,* which is sea food and rice

Chocolate is used in different ways in Mexican food. It flavors Champurrado,* a special drink. It is used in the classic Mole de Guajolote* (turkey *mole*), which calls for twenty-nine different ingredients, including chocolate, and the patience of an Indian woman to make it in its most famous way. In our recipes for Turkey Mole* we tell the classic method and give short cuts. It is interesting, also, that chocolate was so highly valued at one time in Mexico that it was used as money. In the very early days, counterfeiters managed to remove the sweet and edible portion of the cacao bean and fill it with mud, thus making it dud money . . . or the first "hot" chocolate.

Beans, another staple of the Mexican diet, come in more than a half dozen high-fashion shades . . . red, purple, and multi-colored varieties included. By this time, it should be no surprise to you to learn that beans were well known to the Mexicans long before Boston even existed North of the border. Mexican beans can be prepared in a variety of ways . . . *alubias* are kidney beans cooked with different kinds of sausage and flavored with spices; *frijoles* are dried kidney beans or black or natural-colored dried beans; but when they are *refritos,* they are twice fried and garnished with cheese and tortillas.

To the unschooled, chili is just another hot spice, but in Mexico there are ninety-two different kinds of chilies. What most people do not realize is that they not only "heat" the food, but offer some benefit to the digestive system. As we understand it, they start important digestive glands working. We have included a section in the following guide on the many varieties of chilies for those purists who are able to find different types of chilies in their communities. However, chili powder may be used satisfactorily in most of the recipes in this book.

Vegetables are to be found on almost every Mexican table. Many of them are native to the country, such as *nopales,* the tender green leaves of the nopal cactus. They are served stewed, fried, or fresh in salads, and for any of you who can obtain cactus leaves in the United States of America, we've included directions for serving them in this book.

There are a number of root vegetables cultivated in Mexico. We sampled one of the most interesting in the Yucatán. It is called "jicama" and resembles a plump turnip, but has a flavor which is a cross between an apple and potato. Jicama is delicious and is usually eaten raw.

As to fruit, the many species in the country make it a veritable paradise for fruit lovers. Bananas—take your choice of five colors: pink, purple, orange, peach, and yellow, if you will—grow as small as your little finger and others much larger than you would expect from a banana. Pineapples are much bigger in Mexico than those usually seen in the States. There are mangoes, mammee fruits, *chirimoya,* which is used in the making of a special custard, *papaya, guayaba* (guava), and *tunas*—not fish at all, but the fruit of a cactus. As to coconuts, they grow in abundance; and experienced Mexican cooks (even devotees who have never set foot inside a kitchen) say that you can tell how close a coconut tree grows to the sea by the taste of its meat.

Fruit is served at almost every meal in a Mexican home. In luxurious resort hotels, such as the de luxe Las Brisas in Acapulco, hotels stock your personal room refrigerator with a rich variety of fruits. You will find Mexican fruit desserts and tips on how to serve fresh fruit Mexican style in the dessert and sweet section of this book.

For a long time, Mexican food represented the blend of two different systems of cooking—Spanish and native—both applied to foods raised in Mexico. International overtones really caught on during the days of President Porfirio Diaz (1876–1911). His term lasted thirty-five years and during that time the President, the government, and its loyal followers took their cues in terms of manners from France. Cooks were, therefore, imported not only from France, but from Italy, Spain, and Germany. Many of these people stayed on to add their distinctive touches to the pot on the Mexican stove.

During the Revolution in 1910, international cuisine and manners went into decline. Interest returned to the establishment of a national cuisine of a high order. As peace brought tourists once more, many of whom stayed to live in the beautiful country, international dishes became popular side by side with Mexican and remain so today.

One of the best ways to see just how many different kinds of cookery exist in the country today is to spend some weeks traveling around the various states eating in different restaurants. In Mexico, as the capital is called by those who "know," the chic Ambassadeurs features French cookery complete with Louis XV *décor*. The Focolare, created by the talented Cesar Balsa, is a replica of an Italian patio and the menu lists the pastas that go with the decoration. Delmonico's, in modern Mexican style, includes waterfalls and fountains. The menu features flaming giant shrimps and barbecued spareribs. Mauna Loa, a tropical paradise with roving flamingos, offers Island food. Spanish is the word for the food and handsome decoration at El Parador.

Travel to Guadalajara and eat at La Copa de Leche. This restaurant offers drinks on the street level, omelettes and other quick dishes on another floor, roast suckling pig in the Spanish dining room, and thick American-style steaks in its rooftop night club.

In Puerta Vallarta, a remote beach resort, Americans will find their favorite flapjacks and bacon and eggs on the breakfast menu at the Hotel Océano.

For the traveler in search of native foods, the Hotel Mérida in Mérida has a dish called "Fish a La Cubana" and the only thing Cuban about it is its name, for it is a specialty of the Yucatán. The tiny tiled dining patio at the Hotel Colón in Mérida features "Pollo Pibil," a regional specialty which consists of chicken baked in banana leaves. The Hotel Mayaland near the ruins of Chichén Itzá makes good use of sweet potatoes and coconut for a fabulous dessert.

In Mexico City, at the Loredo, where the owner, Jose Inés Loredo, has dedicated his life to maintaining the *haute cuisine* of Mexico, there is a "fountain of youth" platter of sea food which contains abalone, shrimp, and turtle's eggs, to name only a few of the delicacies heaped upon it. El Refugio, a quaint restaurant featuring regional dishes in the capital city, has a menu completely written in Spanish, even for foreign visitors, and a specialty of the house is *bistec* (beefsteak) prepared with peppers.

In Tampico, we found absolutely poetic sea food stews and soups. Tamales are a specialty in Oaxaca. There are banana dishes in the humid Tabasco region and famous broiled, roasted, and barbecued beef in the lush green region of Huaxteca. Almost every region's specialty and those of some famous restaurants are represented in the recipe section of this book.

There is another thing to be said about dining out in Mexico. No matter what kind of food delights your palate, the eye will get its fill as well. How much more delicious everything tastes when served on silver plates from Taxco, woven mats or colorful cloths from Oaxaca, and glassware from Guadalajara. The Mexicans have a great sense of showmanship; so whether you go out for French, Italian, or Chinese food, expect it to be served with a flourish which might include a paper snowstorm confected in a large glass-enclosed tropical garden at Jacarandá, or chafing dishes and cart service at the lovely Continental, an "Alice in Wonderland"-type setting in the capital city. You can have your food with a view on the rooftop of the Alameda and take your cocktails right in the swimming pool from little tables dotted at the shallow end. You can enjoy the glittering city by night while eating and drinking on the roof restaurant at the Del Paseo. From there, the world looks like a Christmas card no matter the season of the year. You'll have music—*mariachis* (strolling players)—everywhere you go.

Dining out is of interest to the traveler, but the reader of this book who wants to prepare these dishes at home will be interested in the typical Mexican kitchen. There are always strings of herbs. No cook in the country would be without *epazote*, often used in the preparation of black beans. Coriander is used in almost everything. To the Mexican cook, it is more important to the mashed avocado dish, Guacamole,* than the vegetable itself. The endless varieties of chilies, leaves, and berries in a native kitchen make it a thing of aromatic and visual delight. Many of the strangest looking leaves are thought to be love potions. We had no time to test them and can only report here what we have been told.

Another fairly common object in the Mexican kitchen is the soup pot, which is almost always simmering. The Mexicans are expert soup makers. *Pozole*—the fire soup of the middle country—takes about eleven hours to prepare. But other soups, many described in this book, are easier to prepare and just as tasty.

Aside from herbs and spices which add flavor to foods all over the world, there is a great deal of purely Mexican creativity applied to the best dishes in the country. Nowhere is this so apparent as in an excursion to one of the country's wonderful bakeries. Such a trip is almost like going to a great art museum—the aromas are the things from which culinary masterpieces are made; the names of sweets and breads are pictures in themselves. For example: *cuernos* (horns), *orejas* (ears), and *ojos de Pancha* (Pancha's eyes) are all tasty and pretty breads. There are also *corbatas* and *conchas* (neckties and shells), *piedras* (stones), and *chilindrinas,* which literally means joke but, like the others mentioned above, is a kind of sweetbread with a special shape and topping.

To show again how the foreign influence affected Mexican food, one need only know a few other names of sweets found at the pastry shop. *Chus* comes from the French *chou* and means, just as it does in France, cream puff; doughnuts are *donas* and poundcake is *panque. Bistec* and *rosbif* are beefsteak and roast beef, other Anglo-Saxon additions to the Mexican menu.

Mexico is also a country where festivals have their own foods. Go back to that bakery again around the Yuletide and you'll find Rosca de Reyes,* ring-shaped cakes with a tiny porcelain figure of a child hidden in them. This is cut open on January 6, the Coming of the Kings, and culminates the series of *posadas* (Christmas fiestas which begin December 16). The little doll represents the Christ child and the person who finds it must give a party on February 2, which is the date that the Christ child is taken up from the crèche and put away for the following year.

As to those *posadas,* they are to be found only in Mexico. They represent, strangely enough, the early Mexican custom of blending church rites with pagan Aztec ceremonies. We've attended a number of *posadas* in Mexico at one time or another during the holiday season and found them to be as colorful and fascinating as their origin.

It seems that certain pagan customs were tolerated by the first friars who regarded it as convenient to allow the Indians to preserve some of their fiestas and dances, changing them only as devotion to a special saint rather than an Aztec god. So, before the conquest, the advent of the god Huitzilopochtli was observed with great pomp at the season now known as Christmas. During the nights and days around this time, there were parties in homes; and guests were given small figures of gods made out of dough. They were called *tzotl.* To give this festival a Christian character, Fra Diego de Soria, Prior of the San Agustin Acolman convention, obtained permission from Pope Sixtus V, in 1578, to celebrate masses known as *Aguinaldo* masses in New Spain between December 16 and 24 each year. *Aguinaldo* is the word for Christmas gift.

Actually, these colorful parties that go on every night for the nine days before Christmas are a re-enactment of Joseph and Mary looking for an inn. The *peregrinos* (pilgrims) made of clay and cardboard are carried on litters at the head of the procession made up of the invited guests, who march double file, carrying candles as they chant the litany. The procession halts in front of a door and the voices of Mary and Joseph are heard asking for shelter. The people inside the house at first refuse but finally relent, and the doors are opened wide.

Everyone rejoices in the living room and *piñatas* (vessels of clay or papier-mâché) in fantastic shapes filled with candies and fruits are hung above the room and broken open. Gifts and sweetmeats are distributed all around and everyone joins in eating typical holiday foods such as Buñuelos,* crisp, fried doughnut-type cake covered with syrup, and Torrejas,* sweetened fried bread or cake somewhat like French toast. There are all kinds of hard and soft drinks and brilliant dancing which usually brings the fiesta to a close.

In Mexico a gay holiday celebrated in November has the solemn-sounding name of Day of the Dead. It is comparable to All Saints' Day, and in Mexico it is a time that lovers of sweets look forward to with great anticipation. It is not gruesome to nibble a skull or buy a skeleton which grins ridiculously from the candy store window. Crumbs and pumpkin, with brown sugar, properly spiced, of course, are placed on brightly colored altars in some homes so that the spirits may dine. In Mexico the soul is fed with delicacies not only of the spirit but of the kitchen as well.

And there are other sweets to be had throughout the year. There is Flan,* a melt-in-your-mouth custard; the famous Cocada,* which is made of fresh coconut, milk, and eggs; and Queso de Almendras,* (Almond Cheese), which is not a cheese at all, but a sweet to be eaten as cheese with apples and crackers. One dessert uses fragrant orchids as flavoring; others use plain vanilla with delicious results.

No cookbook on Mexico would be complete without some information on the drinks of the country. Agua de Tamarindo* is a refreshing lemonade. Pulque* is produced from the lowly cactus, but was described in 1838 in the Journals of Madame Calderón de la Barca, the wife of the first Spanish Ambassador to the country since its independence in 1810, as a drink worthy of "the nectar of Olympus." "Pluto must have cultivated the maguey, the plant from which pulque is derived," said the lovely lady.

Mexicans produce an excellent assortment of beers. Tequila, a strong liquor, is drunk straight with lime and salt on the side or mixed with other ingredients; Puebla produces Sidra, a great apple cider, sometimes called a champagne. Fruit cordials come from Campeche, and Xtabentum is a liquor from the Yucatán produced by bees who feed on anisette-flavored clover. There are experts in the field of wine and spirits who claim that the best rum in the world comes from Mexico.

In fact, at this point, it might be handy to have a glass of Mexican Sidra champagne so that we could toast the many people who have helped us with this book. The names are almost too numerous to list if you think of the times we've been to Mexico and the people we've met who have given us advice and tips on cooking. However, there are some names which call to mind such appreciation on our part that they must be mentioned.

We thank Miguel Aleman, President of the Mexican National Tourist Council, for the co-operation of his organization; and special appreciation to Mrs. Blanca Griffin in the Council's New York office for finding time to translate many of the complicated recipes in this book and for answering questions on Mexican cookery which went beyond our knowledge of this fine cuisine. We are also grateful to the many Mexican women who contributed some of the best recipes we've included. Some of these women permitted us to put their names beside their recipes; others preferred to remain anonymous. La Fonda del Sol in New York and restaurateurs in Mexico and New York are also high on our "thank you" list.

To you, the readers of this introduction, we can only say that we hope you find the many culinary surprises and treats in cooking these dishes which we discovered when we made them over the years. Writing this book has helped us to recapture many of the great moments we've had in Mexico where cookery and food are associated with fun. We hope a touch of that fiesta feeling comes with these recipes and with the "olés" you get when you serve them.

A Guide to the Art of
Mexican Cooking

❖

Mexican food is rich and exciting to the palate not only because it is seasoned subtly, but because of its special method of preparation. To help you master the art of Mexican cookery, here are a few pointers:

Chilies: As indicated in the introduction, these members of the pepper family figure importantly in the art of Mexican cookery. Mexicans toast their chilies, peel them, remove their seeds and membranes, and soak the peppers in milk or warm water until they are softened enough for cooking. The seeds are frequently toasted and ground, too, and they are used to impart a distinctive flavor to certain dishes.

Many specialty food stores—and, of course, those markets which specialize in Mexican cooking ingredients—stock many different kinds of chilies. But it takes time and patience to deal with these whole chilies, so we've designed most of the recipes in this book to be prepared with chili powder. However, there are a few recipes where real chilies are needed, such as the classic Turkey Mole,* which calls for several different kinds of chili peppers. We have indicated throughout this book when chili peppers are definitely needed, so for best results do not substitute powders in those dishes. And, not to sound contradictory, but as a further help, there are certain cases where a different kind of pepper can be substituted for the pepper indicated in a recipe and no appreciable loss of flavor will result. For the purists, who may want to use real chilies, for the plain curious, and for those who may have to use substitutions where real chilies are called for, here is a partial list of chili peppers used by Mexican cooks and the easy-to-find substitutes for them.

Poblano Chilies – are the peppers most frequently used in Mexico. If a recipe calls for a *poblano* chili and you have to make a substitute for it, no great harm will result from using canned green peppers or bell peppers. *Poblanos* can be stuffed whole or cut up to season sauces, as the recipes indicate.

Serrano and Jalapeño Chilies – any variety of small red or green hot pepper can be used, if the genuine article is not available. *Serrano* and *Jalapeño* chilies can often be found in cans in Mexican and other specialty food stores.

Pimientos – use any kind of canned pimiento, or use sweet red or green pepper, as indicated in the recipes, if absolutely necessary.

Ancho, Pasilla, and Mulato Chilies – are used in sauces and *moles* and are sometimes hard to find whole in the United States, so you can substitute chili powder for them.

Chili Powder – freshly ground chili powder is the best; but the easiest to use is ready-made powder, which is also quite successful in cooking and available in virtually every market. Be sure to keep your chili powder well sealed after using it, so that its strength will not be altered through contact with the air. Do not use chili powder which you've had for a year or more, for its strength and effectiveness will change as it stands, and cause loss of flavor to the foods you are preparing.

Tomatoes and Onions: Both tomatoes and onions are used a great deal by Mexican cooks. Tomatoes are frequently toasted over an open flame, skinned, and puréed. It is easy to purée tomatoes at home with an electric blender, but, as a real short cut, which will cause no harm to the dish at hand, you can substitute canned tomato purée. We've used canned tomato purée often in the recipes which follow to make them as easy as possible to prepare.

In some of the recipes in this book, tomato-onion purée is listed as an ingredient. It is prepared with fresh or canned tomato purée and fresh or bottled onion juice. As to quantity, follow the directions in the recipes.

Sometimes when using tomatoes, Mexicans add a dash of sugar. They claim that this not only sweetens the pot but aids the digestion. In some of the recipes in this book, in keeping with the Mexican style, we suggest some sugar along with the tomatoes, and directions for adding both ingredients are listed with these various recipes.

Chives: Cebollinos, or chives, are also used in Mexican cookery, as you will see when you prepare some of the dishes in this book.

Beans: Beans are so much a part of the Mexican diet, that we've included a special section on them in this book. The most popular bean is the *bayo gordo.* You can substitute the pinto or red kidney bean for it.

Chorizo: Chorizo is a special type of pork sausage with a delicious and distinctly Mexican flavor. It is called for in a number of the following recipes. Many specialty food stores carry *chorizos,* but if they are not available you can substitute pork sausage at the expense of some of the authentic flavor. You can also make your own *chorizos,* and the recipe for this has been included in the meat section of this book.

Spices: Pumpkin seeds, sesame seeds, *epazote* (called *pazote* in some places in the United States), and a host of other spices used in Mexican cooking can be found in Mexican and other food markets. In Mexico, orange blossom water and vanilla beans are used rather than their extracts. We have simplified throughout this book by using extracts.

Cooking Oils: Lard is specified in a few of our recipes as a means of preserving the authenticity of the dish. But, if you prefer a vegetable shortening or cooking oil, it can be substituted without altering the flavor of the dish too much. Quantities specified in the recipes which follow apply to lard or vegetable shortening, unless otherwise indicated. When making substitutions, increase the fat if butter is used; decrease slightly if you use bacon or chicken fat. We also recommend using sweet butter for best results in cooking these dishes.

Tortillas, Tostadas, Tostaditas, Totopos, Tacos, Enchiladas, Tamales: It is sometimes confusing for a North American to tell the difference between tortilla, tostada, tostadita, totopos, tacos, enchilada, and tamales without a little guide. Actually, nothing could be easier, as you will see as you go through this book. Of the seven, four are basically tortillas. These are tostadas, tostaditas, totopos, and enchiladas. A tamale is an altogether different dish, but its basic ingredient is corn, as is true of all of them. In making classic tortillas and tamales, you should use masa or *nixtamalina,* special fine-grade Mexican corn flours which are available at specialty and Mexican food stores. There is also an American version of this Mexican flour. It is actually a fine white corn meal. Use it instead of masa or *nixtamalina,* if necessary, but do not use yellow corn meal unless the recipe calls for it. Here are the specifics when it comes to telling a tortilla from other similar foods, and how to identify a tamale as well.

Tortilla—a basic and staple of the Mexican table, tortillas are made from corn-meal dough, pounded into thin patties and cooked on an ungreased hot surface. You can make tortillas at home according to a recipe in this book, or better yet, when it comes to simplicity, you can buy them precooked in cans or packages at most stores. *Tortillas de harina* are made with flour and are popular in northern Mexico. They tend to be larger and thicker than those made with corn meal.

Tostada—this is a toasted tortilla covered with other ingredients such as cheese, chopped meat, mashed beans, lettuce, chopped tomatoes, *etc.*

Tostaditas and Totopos—tostaditas are wedges of tortilla which have been fried until crisp in deep hot fat. Totopos are basically the same as tostaditas, except that they are round instead of wedge-shaped. Both are used to accompany appetizers and other dishes.

Tacos—are tortillas which are wrapped around some meat, chicken, or other kind of filling, and most usually fried before they are eaten.

Enchiladas—are tortillas which are rolled around a filling which might be made from meat or chicken or some other ingredients, and baked in a sauce, or fried and dipped in a sauce.

Tamales—are made of masa dough spread on a cornhusk and filled with a number of different things including chopped meat. Tamales are rolled, tied, and steamed before they are eaten. The word *tamale* supposedly comes from the Aztec language, Nahuatl, and was originally *tamalli*.

Finally, an asterisk (*) following the name of a dish means that a recipe is given for it in the book, and you can find it listed in the Index.

Aperitivos

❖

(APPETIZERS)

North Americans are credited with introducing the *coctel,* or cocktail party, to Mexico. But, as usual, the Mexicans have added their own special touches to these gatherings and that distinctive quality has a lot to do with the appetizers as well as the drinks.

At a typical cocktail party in Mexico, the guests gather on the patio around seven and the party goes on until nine or ten when everyone goes off for a light supper. A handsome Indian woman in a beautiful regional costume, half-hidden by a cascade of bougainvillaea, sits near a charcoal brazier and prepares tasty tacos. The *mariachis* stroll among the guests, playing and singing, and the ice in the bartender's shaker adds a staccato beat to the music as he concocts Mexican tequila, rum, or American-style drinks.

There are Panuchos* (little crisp, stuffed pancakes), the famous Guacamole* (avocado dip), and Camarón de Cortés* (Cortés' Shrimp), to name only a few.

There are always bowls of *pepitas,* tiny succulent squash seed. Indeed, they are as much a part of any cocktail party in Mexico as the guests themselves. Be sure to include *pepitas* with your Mexican appetizers. They are readily available in markets all over the United States.

We've included the recipes for appetizers in the section following; the drinks to go with them are in the beverage section. And, when preparing appetizers, be sure and check the recipes for Empanadas,* or turnovers. Although the Mexicans frequently serve these as main dishes at light supper meals or as side dishes at other times, we think they make wonderful accompaniments with drinks when prepared in miniature.

GUACAMOLE (*Avocado Appetizer*)
Yield: 3 cups of spread

Most North Americans use Guacamole as a dip, but it is also delicious as a side dish for meat or fish and as a filling for tacos. It can also be used on crispy toasted bread rounds, but we like it best when accompanied by Tostaditas* (little chips of fried tortilla) or plain salted crackers. There are probably as many ways of making this dish as there are states in Mexico, but here is our favorite, followed by some delicious variations:

2 medium-sized, very ripe avocados
2 medium-sized ripe tomatoes
1 small onion, grated very fine
2 small Serrano *or any hot chilies, chopped, or 2 tablespoons chili powder*

1 tablespoon olive oil
2 teaspoons (1 each) lime and lemon juice
Dash of paprika
2 teaspoons salt (more or less)
Freshly ground pepper to taste
½ teaspoon coriander (or more to taste)

Mash avocados with fork. Add the other ingredients and stir into a paste that has texture and is not too smooth. This dish is best if made immediately before serving. But if you want to make it a bit ahead of time, be sure to put avocado seed in the spread and wrap the dish tightly with foil or cellophane wrap so it will not darken. Serve with Tostaditas* or crackers.

VARIATIONS

1. Add bits of crisp diced bacon.

2. Add 2 teaspoons of freshly chopped parsley.

3. Use dry white wine instead of lime and lemon juice.

4. Mix a 3-ounce package of cream cheese with the ingredients.

5. Use ½ cup of chopped leftover turkey in the spread.

6. Add a dash of curry powder.

MEJILLONES RELLENOS FRIOS
(*Mussels in Sweet Chili Vinaigrette*)   Serves 6

These are featured at La Fonda del Sol, one of New York's most attractive eating spots.

36 large mussels	*1 cup plus 2 tablespoons*
3 medium-sized sweet	*vinegar*
green peppers	*1½ cups salad oil*
3 medium-sized sweet red	*Salt to taste*
peppers	
3 medium-sized red or	
Spanish onions	

Wash and scrub the mussels until clean. Steam a few minutes to open and set aside to cool. Dice the green and red peppers and the onion in very fine pieces. Place in a large bowl and add vinegar and oil. Mix well and season with salt.

Open mussels, discard one-half of the shell, be sure there is no sand inside of the shell. Pry mussel from shell.

With a teaspoon, place enough pepper and onion mixture on mussel to cover the entire opening of the shell and the fish.

Refrigerate until serving time.

COCTEL DE ABULON O CAMARON
(*Abalone or Shrimp Cocktail*)

Canned abalone may be used for this dish because the fresh variety is usually hard to find. If the canned abalone is used, drain well before going on with the recipe. We prefer fresh shrimp or prawns to the canned varieties and suggest that they be prepared according to your favorite method. Either fish should be seasoned lightly with lemon juice and allowed to stand under refrigeration for a few hours before the following sauce is added.

For sauce (enough for about 1 pound of shrimp):

Combine:

2–3 *tablespoons dark prepared hot mustard*	1 *teaspoon toasted sesame seed*
¾ *cup olive oil*	*Salt and freshly ground pepper to taste*
½ *cup white wine vinegar*	

Marinate the fish for several hours until serving time and serve in cocktail glasses. This sauce can also be served on the side. Let your guests dip abalone cubes or whole shrimp into it. Just serve the fish on a platter, the sauce in the middle, and lots of toothpicks for the dunkers.

SEVICHE (*Pickled Fish*) Serves 6

At Acapulco, Mexico's most beautiful resort, and, indeed, in other places throughout the country, Seviche is very popular. It makes a delicious light luncheon or supper dish as well as a tangy appetizer. The "cooking," by the way, is done by the lemon reacting with the fish. We've had this dish made with clams and oysters, but somehow pompano, haddock, and whitefish rate highest, as far as we are concerned, for the basic ingredients. Do not substitute chili powder in this recipe. The chilies are needed to provide the proper texture.

1 pound pompano,
 haddock, or whitefish
Juice of 5 good-sized
 lemons (or about 1
 cup freshly squeezed
 lemon juice)
1 cup tomatoes, peeled
 and diced (or 1
 8-ounce can)
3–4 small hot green or
 red chilies

¼ cup salad oil
1 tablespoon dry white
 wine
1 teaspoon orégano
½ teaspoon basil
1 teaspoon epazote (or
 coriander)
Salt and pepper, freshly
 ground, to taste

FOR GARNISHES

2 avocados, sliced thin

1 Spanish onion (prepare rings and soak in ice water with a little salt so they'll be very crisp)

Wash the filleted fish, remove the skin, and cut into small squares. Put the fish in a glass dish and pour the lemon juice over it. Let stand for 3 or 4 hours, turning occasionally with a wooden spoon or two wooden forks used as tongs. Add the tomatoes, sliced chilies, oil, wine, and seasonings. Refrigerate for several hours before serving. Serve very cold in cocktail glasses or on the "half shell." Garnish with avocado slices and Spanish onion rings, sliced very thin.

VARIATIONS

1. Add 3 or 4 teaspoons of capers to spices. If so, cut down on the amount of salt used.

2. Green olive rings can be used instead of capers. Black olives, pitted and sliced, can also be used. Watch the salt if green olives are used.

CAMARON DE CORTES (*Cortes' Shrimp*)
Serves 6–8

1 cup white wine vinegar
1 teaspoon prepared
horse-radish
2 tablespoons prepared
mustard
2 tablespoons tomato
purée
½ teaspoon chili powder
(more or less, but taste
before you add more)
Salt to taste

1 cup salad oil
Dash of orégano
1 pound cooked, cleaned
shrimp
2 tomatoes, sliced very
thin
Spanish onion rings, sliced
very thin (soak them in
cold water to get them
extra crisp)

Combine all ingredients except the shrimp, tomatoes, and onions, and stir until well blended. Pour over shrimp and let the shrimp stand in the marinade for about 5 hours before serving. When ready to serve, arrange shrimps on tomato slices and top with thin onion rings. Pour dressing over all.

PANUCHOS (*Filled Tortillas*) Makes 30

Some people make Panuchos with hot little biscuits which they slit open and fill as soon as they come from the oven. The best *panuchos* we've eaten were in Mérida and they were made with tortillas as follows:

30 extra-small, rather
thick Tortillas*
1 pound red kidney or
pinto beans (prepare
them as you would for
Refried Beans*)

6 hard-cooked eggs, sliced
2 cups chicken meat,
cooked (or ham or
turkey can be used)

SAUCE

4 medium onions, chopped
3 small hot green chilies,
    chopped, or 2 or more
    tablespoons chili powder
    to taste
½ cup vinegar
½ cup water
10 whole peppercorns,
    slightly bruised

10 cumin seeds
3 cloves garlic, crushed
1 bay leaf
1 large tomato, peeled
    and chopped
Salt to taste

To prepare Panuchos, make a slit in each warm tortilla to create a pocket and fill each pocket with some refried beans, slices of hard-cooked egg, and a bit of the chicken, ham, or turkey. Fasten the tortilla flap with toothpicks to close the pocket and fry the tortillas in deep hot fat (365°). Drain on absorbent paper. Top with additional shredded chicken (ham or turkey) and the sauce, which is served hot.

For sauce: Combine all ingredients and simmer until thickened.

NOTE: Cold shredded lettuce is sometimes served on top of these. It makes a good crisp, cool contrast.

TORTITAS COMPUESTAS (*Filled Rolls*)
Makes 12

12 very small rolls
1 cup or a little more
    Mexican Refried Beans*
¾–1 cup shredded lettuce
    or chopped watercress
    (tossed with dressing)
2 tablespoons sharp
    French dressing

1 cup chopped chicken or
    chopped salmon,
    sardines, or tuna
12 slices mild cheese,
    sliced thin
1 avocado, sliced very
    thin
Chili powder to taste

Cut rolls in half and hollow out the bottom parts to form little boats, taking care not to damage the shell of the roll. Spread some bean paste on each roll; top this with a layer of the lettuce mixed with the dressing; add a layer of chopped chicken (or salmon, sardines, or tuna). Put cheese slice on after that, then avocado, and a dash of chili powder. Top with the other half of the roll. (Fasten with toothpicks for easy eating.)

CANAPES

Lots of people in Mexico use bread as a base for their canapés just as we do at home. But to us, a base of tortillas seems more delicious and typical. You can use canned tortillas to make the following Tostadas* (Toasted Tortillas). These toasted tortillas, when broken into chips, are frequently served with Guacamole,* or served alone like ever-lovin' potato chips.

TORTILLAS TOSTADAS (*Toasted Tortillas*)

Use about 1 tablespoon of salt and dissolve it in ½ cup of water and sprinkle over both sides of the tortillas. Cut each tortilla into 4 pie-shaped pieces and allow to stand until almost dry. In deep fat which registers 365° on your thermometer, cook the tortilla pieces until well browned. Drain on absorbent paper and use as a base for the following canapés:

ACEITUNAS Y QUESO (*Olive and Cheese*) – spread the tortilla wedges with cream cheese softened with a few drops of milk. Top with pimiento-stuffed olives which have been sliced into rings or chopped well.

FRIJOLES (*Beans*) – spread with Mexican bean paste (Refried Beans*) and garnish with freshly grated mild Cheddar cheese, topped with a dash of cayenne pepper. Toast briefly in oven until cheese puffs.

JAIBA (*Crab*) – spread fried tortilla squares with a little prepared mustard and top with crab flakes (canned or frozen, well drained). Top with freshly grated mild cheese and a dash of paprika, and toast under broiler for a few minutes or until cheese melts.

GUACAMOLE – put a dab of Guacamole* on each square. Garnish with one-half of a pitted ripe olive.

JICARA (*Black Caviar*) – spread toasted tortilla pieces with black caviar; top with minced onion and a thin slice of hard-cooked egg.

APERITIVOS CON CHILES
(*Appetizers with Chilies*)

Here are three quick tricks that you can do with canned chili peppers.

1. Use any variety of small canned red or green hot peppers. Peel the peppers; remove the seeds. Stuff the peppers with cream cheese which has been seasoned lightly with salt and pepper, softened with a few drops of milk, and mixed with chopped toasted almonds. Refrigerate for several hours. Slice very thin before serving.

2. On a toothpick, alternate avocado cubes with rolled anchovy fillets and slivers of canned red pimiento. (Serve at once because avocado darkens.)

3. On a toothpick, arrange in alternate layers small pieces of hot red pepper, mild cheese, and a cube of cooked ham.

COPAS DE FIESTA (*Party Cups*) Makes 12

12 very small round
dinner rolls
1 small jar black caviar
1 small onion, minced
well

2 canned red pimientos,
cut into strips
Fresh parsley as garnish

Cut rolls in half and hollow out both halves very carefully so that they do not break. Fry in deep hot fat (360° on thermometer) and, when they are crisp, remove and drain on absorbent paper. Spread a thin coating of black caviar in the inside of each cup, then a small amount of minced onion and a strip or two of red pimento. Top each one with a sprig of parsley.

ALBONDIGUITAS (*Little Meat Balls*)
Makes 65–70

1 tablespoon butter
1 very small onion,
minced well
1 tablespoon red chili
powder
1 pound lean, ground,
round steak
¾ cup bread crumbs,
extra-fine

1 egg, well beaten
½ cup milk
¼ cup water
Salt and pepper to taste
½ tablespoon freshly
chopped parsley
Oil for frying

Melt the butter and sauté onion in it until transparent; stir in chili powder and set aside. Combine all ingredients with the meat, including the sautéed onions and chili powder, and mix well. In a heavy skillet heat the oil. Form little balls the size of your thumbnail—you should get about 65 or 70 of them—and cook in the shortening. When well browned, keep warm in the oven or in a chafing dish until serving time.

TACOS DE COCTEL (*Cocktail Tacos*)

A taco is a fried or baked tortilla which has been filled with
any number of things from soft ripe cheese to yesterday's roast
beef. Tacos make excellent appetizers or snacks and are especially good for cocktail party service because they can be eaten
with the fingers and passed to guests on a pretty tray.

Some Mexican cooks claim that you must put the filling for
the taco on the face of the tortilla. As charming as this notion
is, we tend to regard it not too seriously. However, for what it's
worth, the face of the tortilla is the slightly raised or bubbled
side. A point which should be taken seriously, even if the one
above is not, is: be sure to heat your tortillas slightly if you
are using canned or other precooked varieties so they won't
break when they are folded over. Folding is more successful
and easier, too, if you dampen the outside of the tortilla slightly
before creasing it. The following tacos are the ones we like with
drinks. Other recipes for tacos can be found in that section of
this book. Before long, you'll probably be inventing your own
way of filling these tasty tidbits.

QUESADILLAS (*Cheese Tacos*) – this is a sort of Mexican
version of the cheese sandwich. You place a slice of mild,
meltable cheese on a tortilla and dust it slightly with chili
powder. Fold the tortilla and fasten it with toothpicks at the
opening. Bake on a greased baking sheet in a 350° oven or
fry in a bit of melted hot shortening in a heavy skillet until
the cheese is melted and the outside is crisp and brown.

TACOS DE CARNE (*Meat*) – using leftover meat, chop the
meat and brown it with a chopped onion and a small amount
of sweet red or green pepper, which has also been chopped.
Add salt and pepper to taste. Fill the tortillas, fold, and proceed as in the above.

TACOS DE PICADILLO (*Hash*) – prepare Picadillo.* Fill tortilla with this Mexican version of mincemeat, and bake or fry.

TACOS DE PESCADO (*Fish*) – use any variety of chopped, cooked fish or sea food. Season with salt and pepper, chopped canned tomatoes, well drained, a dash of chili powder, and a dash of orégano. Fry or bake as in the above.

CHALUPITAS (*Little Boat Tortillas*)

To make Chalupitas, spread each small tostada or tostadita with mashed Frijoles.* Sprinkle with grated mild cheese and broil until cheese melts and browns slightly. Place a slice of avocado or a dab of Guacamole* on top while hot. Serve at once.

TAMALES DE COCTEL (*Cocktail Tamales*)
Makes about 70 tiny tamales

We've noted with interest that the size, filling, and wrapping of a tamale in Mexico can vary as much as the scenery. Way up North, the tamales seem to have more stuffing, be quite tiny, and come wrapped in cornhusks. In the more tropical region, we've had them wrapped in banana leaves and filled with nuts and sweet sauces. We like to serve tiny ones for cocktail gatherings if we are really out to impress our friends. They take time and patience, but always disappear in a moment. Other good tamale recipes can be found in the section of this book which covers tacos, tamales, *etc.*

2 cups shortening (lard is preferred)	¾ cups beef broth (canned may be used)
2¼ pounds masa or nixtamalina (white corn-meal flour available canned in special food stores)	1½ teaspoons baking powder
	2 teaspoons salt
	65–70 cornhusks

Beat lard until light and fluffy; gradually add the masa or the corn meal alternately with the stock. Then add the baking powder and, last of all, the salt. Beat until the mixture is so light and airy that a bit of it will float to the top if placed in a glass of cold water.

Make individual leaves of the cornhusks by separating them; remove the silks and soak for ¼ hour in warm water. Wash thoroughly and drain well. Put a teaspoon of the corn mixture on each husk and spread out with a knife. Top with desired filling (see below). Roll up the husk and fold the ends over like an envelope. Tie with a string or a strip of cornhusk. Carefully place the rolls on a bed of cornhusks, or a rack in a deep pan or steamer. Steam in a small amount of water, covered, for about 30 minutes.

FILLINGS: Use any of the fillings suggested for Tacos de Coctel.* Or use chopped meat mixed with chopped black olives and red pimiento; chopped anchovies with grated cheese and a dash of chili powder; or chopped chicken combined with chopped almonds and chopped pimiento olives.

NOTE: Your guests remove the husks before eating. If you are inclined to be a little lazy, you can make these tamales rather large and cut them into pieces before serving them.

PLATANOS A LA VERACRUZANA
(*Bananas, Veracruz Style*) Serves 4

This recipe comes from Señorita María del Carmen Villa-gómez Fernández of Guadalajara. It calls for *plátanos machos,* which are large meaty bananas, available in most Mexican and Spanish food stores. If you can't find them, use regular bananas but make sure that they are not too ripe.

4 bananas machos, *or*
about 6–7 regular
bananas on the green
side

1 pint cooking oil
1 cup cold water to which
a teaspoon of salt
has been added

Peel and slice the bananas about ¾ inch thick. Fry in a small amount of oil until browned on both sides but not done. Remove from pan. Protect the hands with two sheets of plastic doubled several times; press each banana slice until flat. Soak a few minutes in cold, salted water. Heat the rest of the oil and fry again until deep brown or almost cocoa-colored. Drain on absorbent paper until dry and crisp.

Our good friend, Mrs. Blanca Griffin, of the Mexican National Tourist Council, who helped so much in translating many of the recipes for this book, recommends these chips with beer. She's right!

COSTILLAS DE PUERCO (*Spareribs*) Serves 2–4

1 large lemon
2 pounds pork ribs
1 medium onion, sliced
thin
Salt and freshly ground
pepper to taste
3–4 good-sized tomatoes,
peeled and chopped
(*canned will do*)

1 teaspoon sugar
¼ cup freshly ground
parsley
¼–½ cup water
1–2 teaspoons chili powder
(*more to taste*)

Cut the lemon in half and rub the ribs with it. Then, slice the lemon very thin and place the lemon slices and onion slices on the ribs. Let stand for 15 or 20 minutes. Sprinkle with salt and freshly ground pepper. To the tomatoes add the sugar, parsley, water, and chili powder and pour over the ribs. Bake at 350° for about 1½ hours, basting frequently.

Sopas

❖

(SOUPS)

Dinner, which is always eaten in the middle of the day in Mexico (oh, how we miss those three-hour dinners when we sit at a counter wolfing a ham-on-rye), sometimes includes two *sopas* (soups)—a "wet" soup followed by a "dry" soup.

The "wet" variety of soup is usually Sopa de Fideo* (Thin Noodle Soup). In Mexico, "wet" soup is frequently served with avocado: sometimes the fruit is halved and peeled and placed in the soup dish; other times it is cut into thin slices and floated on top, such as in Sopa Rápida de Tomate y Aguacate* (Quick Soup with Tomatoes and Avocados).

"Dry" soup is usually rice, but occasionally spaghetti or tortilla casseroles are served, such as Macarrones con Chorizos* (Macaroni and Sausages).

This two-soup beginning to a main meal in a Mexican restaurant or home may have been preceded by drinks and appetizers and you may think that one soup will ruin your appetite and that two will make the balance of the meal unnecessary. But, remember the table of Moctezuma and take heart!

SOPA DE FIDEOS I (*Thin Noodle Soup I*)
Serves 4

*4 ounces thin noodles
(vermicelli)
2 tablespoons butter
2 small onions, minced
well
Sprig of parsley
½ 10½-ounce can
condensed tomato soup*

*4 cups water
Salt and freshly ground
pepper to taste
½ cup freshly grated mild
cheese*

Fry noodles in butter until golden brown; turn constantly to prevent burning and sticking together. When brown, place in a casserole and add the onion, parsley, and tomato soup. Stir with a fork for a minute and quickly pour in 4 cups of water. Simmer 5 minutes. Add salt and pepper to taste. Sprinkle with cheese and serve at once.

SOPA DE FIDEOS II *(Thin Noodle Soup II)*
Serves 5–6

1 tablespoon shortening
4 ounces vermicelli (thin noodles)
1 small onion, chopped very fine
1 clove of garlic
¼ cup tomato paste

1 teaspoon crushed orégano
Salt and freshly ground pepper to taste
5 cups clear stock (canned beef broth will do)

Heat fat and sauté the vermicelli until golden, stirring constantly to prevent the noodles from sticking together or burning. Add the onion, garlic, tomato paste, and orégano. Cook, stirring until blended. Discard garlic clove. Add the rest of the ingredients. Cook just long enough for vermicelli to be tender (about 5 minutes).

NOTE: Chopped fresh avocado can be floated on top of the hot soup as it is served. Figure on about 1 tablespoon per bowl of soup. In addition, some people like to add a dash of Tabasco, right at serving time, along with the avocado.

CALDO COLADO *(Clear Soup)* Serves 8

1½ pounds lamb, preferably from the backbone
1 onion

1½ teaspoons salt or more to taste
Freshly ground pepper to taste

Cover lamb bone with 8 cups cold water; add finely chopped onion, salt, and pepper and simmer slowly for 4 hours, skimming the broth whenever necessary.

If you want to add a spicy, exotic tang to the broth, brown the following ingredients together in 2 tablespoons of vegetable shortening and add to the Caldo Colado 1 minute before serving time:

1 chopped onion
1 cup dry Italian-style
  bread crumbs

1 hot chili pulp with a
  few seeds (or about a
  tablespoon of chili
  powder)
½ teaspoon orégano

SOPA DE PAN (*Chiapaneca Bread Soup*)
Serves 6–8   (Recipe from the state of Chiapas)

This was sent to us by Señora Carmen Vda de Gris and we send her our thanks in return.

6 small loaves bolillo
  bread *or 1 large loaf*
  Italian bread
1 pound tomatoes, puréed
1 onion, sliced
1 clove of garlic
1 tablespoon sugar
Salt to taste
4 hard-cooked eggs, sliced
1 large macho *banana*
  (available at Spanish
  and Mexican food
  stores), or 2
  regular-sized bananas,
  sliced and sautéed
  lightly in a small
  amount cooking oil

½ pound white potatoes,
  cooked and sliced
1 jar olives, sliced
3 carrots, cooked and
  sliced
1 cup raisins (3 small
  five-cent packages)
2 cups chicken broth

Slice the bread and sauté in oil. Purée the tomatoes, onion, and clove of garlic in blender; add sugar and salt to taste. Place slices of bread on the bottom of an earthenware crock or Dutch oven. Pour half of the sauce over the bread; cover with a layer of hard-cooked egg slices, fried bananas, boiled potatoes, olives, carrots, and raisins. Cover with the rest of the sauce. Pour over the chicken broth; cover and cook very slowly until all the liquid is absorbed.

CALDO DE CAMARON (*Hot Shrimp Soup*)
Serves 6

This is a favorite in Mexico City. You will find it perfect for an after-theater snack.

½ pound shrimp in their
  shells
1½ quarts (6 cups) water
1 teaspoon allspice
1 clove of garlic

1½ tablespoons oil
1 10½-ounce can
  condensed tomato soup
Pinch chili powder
Salt and pepper to taste

Remove shells of shrimp and boil only shells in 1½ quarts of water with allspice. While shells are boiling, in another pot brown clove of garlic in oil until golden. Discard garlic. Add tomato soup and shrimp. Strain water in which shells have boiled and add to shrimp-tomato soup mixture. Boil 20 minutes. Add chili powder and salt and pepper to taste.

SOPA DE MAIZ (*Sweet Corn Soup*) Serves 8

12 ears sweet corn
3 cups milk
2 tablespoons butter
6 tablespoons tomato
  purée

1 medium-sized onion,
  sliced
Salt and pepper to taste
½ cup heavy cream
Freshly chopped parsley
  as directed

Cut kernels from cobs and mix half of them with milk; sauté other half in butter with tomato purée, sliced onion, salt, and pepper. Add to milk-and-corn mixture. Cook until heated through but do not boil. Cool. Chill until serving time. Whip cream and, when ready to serve, place a dollop of cream on each portion. Float small amount of chopped parsley on each serving.

SOPA DE AGUACATE (*Avocado Soup*)   Serves 8

1 tablespoon flour	*Salt and pepper*
1 tablespoon butter	*3 avocados*
½ teaspoon onion juice	*5 tablespoons cream*
½ cup tomatoes, peeled and drained	*3 Tortillas* or 3 slices of bread, as directed*
4 cups meat stock (canned beef broth may be used)	

Sauté flour in butter. Add onion juice, tomatoes, stock, and salt and pepper, and simmer till slightly thickened. Mash avocados with cream and place in soup tureen. Pour thickened stock over avocados. Serve with fried tortilla squares or bread squares.

SOPA MEXICANA (*Mexican Soup*)   Serves 8–10

1 chicken breast	*½ tablespoon onion juice*
2 quarts (8 cups) water	*1 cup corn kernels*
1 medium-sized onion	*2 cups zucchini, chopped*
Salt and freshly ground pepper to taste	*1 tablespoon shortening*
⅓ cup tomato purée	*2 ounces cream cheese*
	2 avocados

Cook the chicken breast in 2 quarts of water with onion, salt, and pepper. Cook till tender, drain off stock, and reserve. Dice chicken. Sauté tomato purée, onion juice, corn kernels, and zucchini in shortening. Add reserved chicken broth and simmer, covered, for 20 minutes. Just before serving add diced chicken, cream cheese cut into small squares, and slices of avocado.

SOPA DE CALABACITAS (*Squash Soup*) Serves 6

4 medium-sized zucchini	*2 tablespoons flour*
4 cups meat stock	*Salt and freshly ground*
(canned beef broth may	*pepper to taste*
be used)	*½ cup cream*
¼ cup butter	*3 ounces crushed crackers*
1 onion, minced	

Wash zucchini and cut off ends. Cook, covered, in stock for about 5 minutes. Remove zucchini from stock and chop thoroughly. Heat butter in a pan and fry chopped onion until yellow. Blend 1 cup of stock with flour until smooth and add to onion. Add chopped zucchini, flour-and-onion mixture, and salt and pepper to stock. Simmer 10 minutes. Before serving add cream and crackers.

SOPA DE FRIJOLES (*Bean Soup*) Serves 8

2 cups Mexican beans	*1 clove of garlic*
(pinto or kidney will	*1 teaspoon orégano*
do)	*1½ teaspoons chili*
8 cups water	*powder*
2 medium onions, sliced	*Salt and pepper to taste*
½ cup cooked tomatoes	*Bread cubes*
(canned will do)	*Garlic-flavored oil*

Wash beans well and soak overnight. The following day, drain and cook in 8 cups cold water to cover. Boil at least 5 hours—all day if possible. When beans are half-cooked, add onion, tomatoes, garlic, orégano, chili powder, salt, and pepper, and boil. When beans are tender, rub through a colander and reheat. Add boiling water as needed to give soup the consistency of a purée. Garnish with cubes of bread fried in garlic-flavored oil.

SOPA DE LENTEJAS (*Lentil Soup*) Serves 6

Truly a he-man's soup! Try it on the men in your family on a cold night. Keeps well in the freezer.

1 cup lentils	*1 carrot, diced*
1 quart (4 cups) water	*½ bay leaf*
Salt and pepper to taste	*5 slices bacon*
1 medium-sized onion,	*½ cup tomato purée*
* chopped*	

Soak lentils overnight in water to cover. The following day, drain lentils and cook in 1 quart cold water with salt and pepper, onion, carrot, bay leaf, bacon, and tomato purée. Simmer 1 hour.

SOPA DE TORTILLAS (*Tortilla Soup*) Serves 4

1 can tortillas	*1 teaspoon chili powder*
2 tablespoons olive oil	*1 bay leaf*
1 clove of garlic	*2 cups water*
1 cup tomato purée	*1½ tablespoons grated*
1 onion, chopped	* cheese*
1 tablespoon freshly	
* chopped parsley*	

Cut tortillas in narrow strips with scissors and set aside to dry. Heat oil in casserole. Cook garlic clove in oil until burned black and remove. Brown tortilla strips in oil and add tomato purée, onion, parsley, chili powder, bay leaf, and 2 cups water.

Simmer for about 15 minutes or until tortilla strips are soft and soup is almost dry. Sprinkle grated cheese on top.

COCIDO (*Mexican Boiled Dinner*) Serves 5–6

A full meal in itself, this popular Mexican dish makes a wonderful buffet feast. Serve it with tortillas or hot rolls and lots of that marvelous Mexican beer (available in gourmet food shops).

¼ cup dried chick-peas	6 peppercorns
2 quarts (8 cups) water	4 tablespoons tomato purée
1 pound beef, cut into cubes	4 carrots, sliced
	½ pound potatoes, sliced
1 pound lamb, cut into cubes	3 zucchini, sliced
1 marrow bone	4 turnips, sliced
1 onion, sliced	3 ears sweet corn (fresh or frozen), cut into
Salt to taste	pieces

Soak chick-peas in water to cover overnight. Drain. Remove skins of chick-peas and boil the chick-peas in 2 quarts water together with meat, marrow bone, onion, salt, and peppercorns. When meat is partially done (about 2½ hours), add purée and vegetables, except for corn, and simmer another ½ hour or more until both meat and vegetables are tender. Add corn during the last 8–10 minutes of cooking time.

MACARRONES CON CHORIZOS
(*Macaroni with Sausages*)   Serves 5–6

If you think Italian macaroni is good, wait until you taste this dish!

½ pound macaroni
½ teaspoon onion juice
6 peppercorns
1 bay leaf
Sprig of thyme
Salt to taste
3 pork sausages (use
  chorizos, *if available,*
  or make Chorizos*)
1 8-ounce can cooked
  tomatoes

½ medium onion, finely
  chopped
½ teaspoon chopped
  parsley
Salt and pepper to taste
2 tablespoons olive oil
8 tablespoons grated
  Parmesan cheese

Cook macaroni along with onion juice, peppercorns, bay leaf, thyme, and salt according to directions on package. When tender, rinse in cold water and drain. Fry sausage (use fat if necessary) until brown and remove from pan. In the same pan, sauté tomatoes and chopped onion. Add parsley, salt, and pepper and simmer until thickened. Grease baking dish with olive oil and arrange layers of macaroni, sausage, sauce, and grated cheese. Bake in oven about 20 minutes.

GAZPACHO (*Cold Tomato Soup*)   Serves 8–10

We always associated this dish with Spain until we tasted it Mexican style and liked it very much. Sometimes the Mexicans serve it as a soup course and sometimes they reduce the amount of tomato juice, using just enough to form a dressing, and it is eaten as a salad.

5 almonds, blanched
1 clove of garlic
¼ cup olive oil
3 pounds ripe tomatoes
⅓ cup green pepper,
  finely chopped
⅓ onion, finely chopped

1 large cucumber, peeled
  and diced well
2 cups tomato juice
¼ cup red wine vinegar
Salt and freshly ground
  pepper to taste
Dash of cayenne pepper

Mash the almonds with the garlic and a few drops of oil until it becomes a paste. Put them in the bottom of an earthenware or pottery bowl. Singe the tomatoes over an open flame; peel them, and chop into rather large chunks. Do not crush the tomatoes. Put the tomatoes in the bowl; add the rest of the ingredients. Stir well. Chill several hours before serving. When serving, place a tablespoon of crushed ice in each soup bowl.

NOTE: Croutons, sautéed in a small amount of sweet butter, are sometimes served as a garnish with this soup.

SOPA SECA CON SETAS (*Dry Mushroom Soup*)
Serves 6–8

½ pound package
  vermicelli (uncooked)
6 tablespoons olive oil
1 small onion, minced well
1 cup (8-ounce can)
  tomatoes
¾ pound fresh
  mushrooms, sautéed in a
  small amount of butter
  to which a dash of
  garlic powder has been
  added

1 pint chicken stock (2
  cups canned stock can
  be used)
Salt and freshly ground
  pepper to taste
1 tablespoon freshly
  chopped parsley
8 ounces freshly grated
  Parmesan cheese

Sauté the uncooked vermicelli in hot oil, stirring to separate. When golden, place it in a deep earthenware or pottery casserole and remove excess oil, leaving just enough to coat the vermicelli. In the oil drained off the vermicelli, sauté the onion until tender. Add the rest of the ingredients except the cheese. Bring to a boil once. Pour over vermicelli. Dust with cheese and bake, uncovered, for ¼ hour in a 300° oven.

SOPA RAPIDA DE TOMATE Y AGUACATE
(Quick Tomato Soup with Avocado)   Serves 4–5

This soup is only quick the way we make it. In Mexico, fresh tomatoes are cooked to prepare the juice; the beef stock is homemade, too.

1¼ cups tomato juice
4 green onions, chopped,
  including tops
½ dozen whole
  peppercorns
1½ teaspoons salt (or
  more to taste)
1 whole clove
Pinch of basil
1 bay leaf
1 clove of garlic

Dash of Tabasco
1 teaspoon sugar
Juice of ½ lemon
3 cups canned beef broth
1 avocado, chopped
  coarsely
4–5 tablespoons sour
  cream
¼ cup salted almonds,
  chopped

To the tomato juice, add the onions, all the seasonings, the sugar, and lemon juice. Cook for 10 minutes over low flame to blend seasonings. Cool slightly; strain, pushing at the pulp in the strainer to make sure the flavor of the seasonings is squeezed into broth. Add tomato juice to beef stock. Heat to boiling point. Stir well. Chill until very cold. Add avocado. Serve in individual bowls, garnished with sour cream and almonds.

Huevos y Queso

❖

(EGGS AND CHEESE)

Lots of Mexicans in the larger cities, just as lots of Americans in larger cities, have similar eating habits when it comes to breakfast at least five or six days out of the week. They quickly down some fruit, toast, and coffee. On ranches or in the country breakfast is more substantial. On Sundays and holidays, eggs are served and prepared with loving care and great imagination—everywhere.

Our favorites are Huevos Rancheros* (Eggs, Ranch Style), Huevos Revueltos a la Mexicana* (Mexican Scrambled Eggs), and Huevos con Salsa de Aguacates* (Egg with Avocado Sauce). All of these, plus the others we've included in the recipe section that follows, can also be served for supper or light snacks as well as brunch treats.

As to our one cheese dish, Queso Relleno* (Stuffed Cheese), it is a specialty from Chiapas, a state rich in the production of coffee and sugar cane. We think this dish should be listed high among the other good products from that part of the country too.

HUEVOS REVUELTOS A LA MEXICANA
(Scrambled Eggs, Mexican Style) Serves 2

4 eggs
1 tablespoon cream
1 small tomato
Small amount butter
1 tablespoon sweet red or green pepper, minced
1 tablespoon chili powder (or more to taste)

1 small onion, chopped fine (or 2 green onions, chopped fine, including tops)
1 tablespoon fresh parsley, minced
Salt and pepper to taste

Beat eggs with cream and let stand. Over an open flame, lightly scorch tomato skin; peel and chop tomato into small cubes. In butter sauté the green or sweet red pepper, chili powder, tomato, and onion until onion, pepper, and tomato are slightly softened. Add eggs and scramble on very low flame, stirring constantly. Add parsley, salt, and pepper a few minutes before they are done.

We first tasted eggs made this way at La Copa de Leche, a fantastic tri-level restaurant in Guadalajara. It was very late at night and there was no one around to give us the recipe so we made it up as we went along by the taste system. We like these eggs with hot tortillas.

HUEVOS RANCHEROS (*Eggs, Ranch Style*)
Serves 2–4

4 Tortillas*
2 tablespoons oil (or butter)
1½ tablespoons minced onion
1 small clove garlic, crushed
½ teaspoon marjoram
1 teaspoon red chili powder

1 cup (or 1 8-ounce can) tomato sauce
Freshly ground pepper
Salt to taste
1 tablespoon minced parsley
4 eggs
Avocado or Chorizo* (optional)

Make tortillas or use ready-made. Fry them in hot oil before eating and drain on absorbent paper.

In the shortening, sauté the onion, add the garlic, marjoram, chili powder, tomato sauce, pepper, salt, and parsley. Simmer for a few minutes until flavors are blended. You can poach the eggs right in the sauce and then turn them out on the tortillas; or you can fry the eggs, pour the sauce over them, and serve the tortillas on the side. These eggs are sometimes topped with an avocado slice or *chorizo* or other pork sausage.

HUEVOS DOMINGOS (*Sunday's Eggs*)   Serves 3–5

3 tablespoons butter	6 eggs, well beaten
4 tablespoons onion, minced	Salt and freshly ground pepper to taste
2 medium-sized tomatoes, peeled and cubed	¼ cup freshly grated Parmesan or Romano cheese
12 Tortillas,* cut into 8 to 10 pieces each	Freshly chopped parsley

Melt the butter in a heavy skillet. Add the onion and tomato cubes and sauté until onion is very soft. Add the tortillas and brown them slightly. Add the eggs and cook, stirring as you would scrambled eggs. When eggs are done to taste, salt and pepper them and top them with the grated cheese and small amount of freshly chopped parsley. Serve piping hot.

HUEVOS CON QUESO Y JAMON
(*Eggs with Cheese and Ham*) Figure 1 or 2 eggs per person

Talk about originality when it comes to eggs, and you'll have to mention this dish.

4 tablespoons butter (more or less)	½ cup catchup
8 slices mild cheese (American will do)	2 tablespoons chili sauce
3 slices boiled ham, diced	1 tablespoon chili powder (more or less)
¼ cup chopped sweet pickles	Salt to taste
8 eggs	Freshly ground pepper
	8 pitted ripe olives

In a baking dish, which has been buttered, place the slices of cheese. Top them with the ham and chopped pickles. Place eggs carefully on top of these ingredients. Combine the catchup, chili sauce, and chili powder. (Taste the sauce as you add the powder so it doesn't become too hot.) Top each egg with a generous dab of this sauce; dot with a bit of butter. Salt the eggs and bake in a 300° oven until whites are set and yolks are still soft. Sprinkle on freshly ground pepper, top with olives, and serve.

HUEVOS CON SALSA DE AGUACATES
(*Eggs with Avocado Sauce*)   Serves 4

Avocados are rarely cooked in Mexico, but there are nice exceptions to every rule.

¼ cup heavy cream   *8 hot hard-cooked eggs*
1 tablespoon cornstarch   *Paprika*
Salt and pepper to taste   *Chopped chives*
3 large, very ripe
* avocados, peeled,*
* mashed, and passed*
* through a food strainer*

Heat the cream slightly and add the cornstarch, salt, and pepper. Simmer but do not boil, stirring constantly, until the cream is thickened—about 5 or 6 minutes. Add the mashed avocados and, stirring, simmer a while longer until sauce is thick and creamy. Slice the eggs and placed them on serving dishes. Top with the sauce. Garnish with paprika and chives.

HUEVOS DE LOS CHARROS (*Cowboy's Eggs*)
Serves 6

2 Serrano *chilies, or*
 1–1½ tablespoons chili
 powder
1 pound ground beef
½ cup shortening
1 onion, minced well and
 divided into 2 portions
¼ teaspoon thyme
Salt and pepper to taste

¼ teaspoon marjoram
½ cup cream or top
 milk
2 tomatoes
3 avocados
Pinch of coriander
6 Tortillas,* toasted
12 eggs
¼ cup grated mild cheese

Toast the *Serrano* chilies in a skillet, turning to avoid burning. Soak them in hot water until softened, remove seeds and stems, grind, and set aside. (Skip this step if chili powder is used.)

Brown the beef in a small amount of hot shortening; add one-half of the onion and the thyme. Add the salt, pepper, marjoram, and cream when meat is done and onion is softened. Toast the tomatoes over an open flame, peel them, and chop them well. Mix the tomatoes with the avocados, coriander, and the other half of the onion to form a paste similar to *guacamole* (it shouldn't be too smooth). Add additional salt and pepper to avocado mixture.

Toast the tortillas in a small amount of shortening until crisp and brown. Fry eggs. Place some of the meat mixture on each tortilla; put a mound of the avocado mixture in the center. Place 2 fried eggs on each tortilla, one on either side of the avocado sauce. Top with cheese and serve at once.

HUEVOS RELLENOS POTOSI
(*Stuffed Eggs from San Luis Potosí*)　Serves 3–4

We've had great prickly pears from this Mexican state and also this egg dish, which makes a hit with all of our friends.

3½ tablespoons butter
6 hard-cooked eggs
½ cup freshly grated
  Parmesan cheese
Dash of cinnamon
Salt and freshly ground
  pepper
¾ cup chopped spinach
  (cooked)

1 tablespoon milk
1 teaspoon ground ginger
1 cup white sauce of
  medium thickness
  (make according to
  favorite recipe)
Paprika

With one-half of the butter, grease a glass baking dish or pottery casserole. Cut the eggs as you would for deviled eggs. Remove the yolks and mash them with half of the cheese, the cinnamon, and a small amount of salt and pepper. Fill whites with yolk mixture. To the chopped cooked spinach add the milk, the other half of the butter, some salt and pepper, and the ginger. Put the spinach mixture in the bottom of the buttered baking dish, add the stuffed eggs, and top with white sauce. Sprinkle with the rest of the cheese. Bake for about 12 –15 minutes at 300°. Garnish with a light coat of paprika before serving.

HUEVOS CON CHORIZO
(*Mexican Sausage and Eggs*)

Make Chorizo* (Mexican Sausage) or buy it at a good Mexican food store.

2 eggs per person
1 teaspoon oil for sautéing
  each ¼ cup sausage
Chorizo* (about ¼ cup
  for each person)

¼ cup chopped chives
Salt and pepper to taste

Beat eggs lightly and set aside. Heat oil in a skillet. Crumble sausage into the hot oil. Fry until almost done. Add the beaten eggs to the sausage and cook as you would scrambled eggs. Top with chives when done. Let everyone salt and pepper his own—the Chorizo is quite spicy.

NOTE: If you buy *chorizo,* it may come prepared in sausage casing. If so, remove casing, crumble *chorizo,* measure it, and proceed.

TORTILLA MEXICANA (*Mexican Omelet*)

Make individual omelets according to favorite method, figuring 2 eggs per person. Serve with this sauce.

2 tablespoons oil
2 small green onions, chopped, including tops
1 green pepper, chopped well
2 cups (*or* 2 8-ounce cans) tomato sauce

Salt, pepper, and chili powder to taste (*go light on the salt because of the capers*)
1 teaspoon orégano
1 tablespoon capers

Heat the oil and cook the onion and green pepper in it until they are softened. Add the tomato sauce, salt, pepper, chili powder, orégano, and capers and simmer about 15–20 minutes. Pour over omelets.

TORTILLA DE HUEVOS SENCILLA
(*Simple Omelet*)   Serves 2

3 eggs
2 tablespoons milk or cream
1 small onion, chopped
½ green pepper, minced
1½ teaspoons chopped parsley

1 tablespoon butter
Salt and freshly ground pepper to taste
Paprika

Beat the eggs with the milk or cream, and beat in the chopped onion, green pepper, and parsley. Melt butter in omelet pan and pour in egg mixture. Continue as you would for any omelet, roll quickly, and dust with salt, pepper, and paprika. Take care that the inside of the omelet remains soft.

QUESO RELLENO (*Stuffed Cheese*)   Serves 6

This specialty from Chiapas calls for a Chiapas cheese ball, but Holland's Edam cheese will do just as well.

1 large Edam cheese
2 tablespoons shortening
½ pound ground pork
¼ pound ground beef
(all pork or all beef
may be used)
½ green pepper, seeded
and chopped
Salt and pepper to taste
2 teaspoons tomato-onion
purée (2 teaspoons
tomato purée blended
with a dash of onion
juice)
¼ cup capers

¼ cup black olives,
pitted and chopped
¼ cup raisins
¼ cup almonds, blanched
and chopped coarsely
1 tablespoon ground
cinnamon
¼ cup chopped parsley
2 tablespoons white wine
5 hard-cooked eggs,
chopped
¼ cup flour and some
water to make a paste
1 sheet heavy parchment
paper, lightly oiled

Place the cheese in lukewarm water for a few minutes to facilitate the removal of the red covering. Remove the covering. Cut a circle in the top of the cheese and remove it, but save. Scrape out cheese until it resembles a bowl with ½-inch thickness around the outside.

Heat the shortening and brown the meat in it along with the green pepper and some salt and pepper. Add the tomato-onion purée, the capers, olives, raisins, almonds, more salt and pepper, if necessary, and the ground cinnamon. Stir in the parsley. Add the wine and cook until well blended and thick. Remove from stove. Add the hard-cooked eggs and mix well. Stuff cheese with this mixture. Top with the cheese circle. Seal with flour paste and cover the cheese with heavy parchment, which has been oiled, to make an airtight package. Place in the top of a double boiler and cook for about 20 or 30 minutes until cheese is soft. While cheese is steaming, make this sauce.

SAUCE FOR QUESO RELLENO

1 small onion, minced
1 green pepper, minced
3 tablespoons lard (or
    other shortening)
2 tomatoes, peeled and
    chopped

2 cups broth (canned
    may be used)
½ cup flour
Salt and pepper to taste

Brown the onions and green pepper in the hot fat. Add the tomatoes and then the broth. Cook for about 5 minutes or until blended. Strain the broth. Wipe out skillet and, in the same pan, add a little more fat and stir in the flour. When flour starts to get brown, stir in the broth slowly. Add salt and pepper to taste. Cook over a very low flame until thickened, stirring constantly. Pour over the cheese.

NOTE: Cheese left from the inside of the cheese ball can be used grated for other recipes in this book.

Pescados

❖

(FISH)

Possibly the best way to introduce this chapter would be to reproduce a map of Mexico and let you gaze at the magnificent coastline to just imagine the wonderful sea food you can eat in that country. But, we'll venture some sort of written description anyway.

In Puerta Vallarta, a small resort on the West Coast, we've eaten succulent lobster roasted over hot coals at the beach Los Muertos. There have been nights when we've dined late in Veracruz on giant shrimps washed down with cold beer. Stewed Turtle* and turtle eggs are delicacies we've enjoyed eating on hot tropical days as the palms rustled above our heads at beaches or in pink and white plazas. We've done crossword puzzles or attempted to keep our minds on a game of chess while impatiently waiting for fish stuffed with sea food (such as Fish Stuffed with Shrimps*) in La Paz or Mazatlán. All and more of these *pescados de mar* have graced our plates in some of Mexico City's many fine restaurants.

The inland lakes in Mexico produce excellent fresh-water fish, and people have been known to travel for miles to taste whitefish from Lake Chapala (Fish and Parsley*). The Spaniards noted many things in their diaries about marvelous, magnificent Mexico, among them the wonderful dishes made out of sea food and fish. They are, as you will see on the following pages, worthy of their high reputation.

TORTUGA ESTOFADA (*Stewed Turtle*)   Serves 6

A specialty from Baja California, known for its sea food, pearl fishing, and excellent tropical fruits.

1 pound canned or
cooked turtle meat
6 capers
2 anchovies, chopped
10 large green olives,
pitted
1 tablespoon white raisins
¼ cup almonds, blanched
and chopped
2 tablespoons olive oil
1 large tomato, peeled and
chopped
1 pimiento

1 green pepper, seeded
and chopped
Pinch of saffron
Pinch of ginger
Pinch of allspice
1 teaspoon ground
cinnamon
½ teaspoon ground cloves
Salt and pepper
Pinch of epazote (if
available; if not, use
parsley)
½ cup rum

If fresh turtle meat is used, wash well and cook thoroughly in salted water until almost done before going on with recipe.

Cook turtle meat for 10 minutes in liquid from can or a bit of its own liquid if fresh turtle is used. Add the capers, anchovies, olives, raisins, and almonds and set aside. In 1 tablespoon of oil, sauté the chopped tomato, pimiento, and pepper; add the spices, except for the salt, pepper, and *epazote*. Add the turtle meat mixture. Season with salt, pepper, and *epazote* and heat to boiling point. Add the rum and cook another few minutes, stirring to blend the rum. Serve right away.

BACALAO ESPANOL (*Spanish Cod*) Serves 4

Inherited from Spain, this codfish dish is a favorite of the Mexicans.

1 pound salted codfish
1 large onion, minced well
8 tablespoons olive oil
2 large tomatoes, peeled
and chopped
1 clove of garlic, minced
1 small (4-ounce) can
pimientos, shredded

2½ tablespoons parsley,
chopped
2 teaspoons dry sherry
4 teaspoons green olives,
chopped
Salt and pepper to taste
¼ teaspoon orégano

Soak codfish 8 hours in enough cold water to cover it. Drain and shred the fish. Sauté the onion in the oil until it is softened. Add codfish and sauté a few more minutes. Add the remaining ingredients. Simmer slowly until codfish is tender, about ½ hour or more.

OSTIONES EN ESCABECHE (*Soused Oysters*)
Serves 3–4

Sinaloa, a Northwest state, is noted for its tomatoes and this highly seasoned oyster dish. It's pretty hot, so we suggest serving it with lots of ice-cold beer.

24 large fresh oysters in their shells
½ cup water
Juice of 1 lemon
Juice of 1 lime
1 tablespoon orange juice
Salt to taste
Small amount oil
3 peppercorns
1 clove of garlic
¼ cup white wine
6 canned small hot red or green chilies, chopped very fine
1 onion, chopped well
Crushed ice
Freshly chopped parsley as garnish

Steam oysters in a tightly covered pot in ½ cup water in pressure cooker (1 quart in a six-quart saucepan if pressure cooker is not used) for a few minutes. Remove the oysters from their shells. Save the shells and rinse them. Marinate oysters in a mixture of the lemon, lime, and orange juice, and salt for about 15 minutes. Bring mixture to a boil. Remove from stove. Drain well, but save marinade. Sauté oysters in the oil until lightly browned.

Grind together the peppercorns and garlic and add to the wine. Mix the chopped chilies and onions in the wine mixture. Add the oysters to the marinade and mix well. Cover and refrigerate for about 3 hours. Return oysters to their shells and serve them on a bed of crushed ice. Dust with parsley.

NOTE: These oysters make excellent appetizers as well as a light main dish. Figure on 2 or 3 to a person.

OSTIONES EN CAZUELA *(Oyster Casserole)*
Serves 6

36 oysters	*2 cups canned tomatoes*
Salt to taste	*(no. 303 can),*
Juice of 3 limes	*chopped*
Freshly ground pepper to	*Dash of Tabasco*
taste	*1 tablespoon minced*
½ teaspoon cumin powder	*parsley*
½ cup cracker crumbs	*4 eggs, separated*
1½ tablespoons chopped	*Cayenne pepper*
onion	*Butter*
2 tablespoons lard	

Marinate the oysters in salt and lime juice. Mix pepper with cumin powder and three-quarters of the cracker crumbs. Sauté onion in hot lard and, when onion is transparent, add tomatoes, Tabasco, and parsley. Beat egg whites until stiff but not dry and fold in yolks one at a time. In a deep buttered dish, put in a layer of oysters, a layer of the tomato mixture, the eggs, and the cracker crumbs, repeating until all of the ingredients are used up. Top with a layer of crumbs. Dust with small amount of cayenne pepper. Dot with butter and bake in a moderate, or 350°, oven for about 20 minutes or until brown.

PESCADO MAZATLECO *(Fish, Mazatlán Style)*
Serves 3–4

This West Coast resort is a fisherman's paradise . . . the blue waters there abound with sailfish and dolphin and sea food is the *plat du jour* in the many good restaurants.

4 cups water
3–4 slices fresh haddock
  or red snapper (or
  favorite fish fillets)
1 lime, sliced thin
½ teaspoon tarragon
½ teaspoon salt
1 green onion, chopped,
  including top
5 whole black peppers
3 whole cloves
Pinch of rosemary
Pinch of cinnamon
½ bay leaf
¼ cup olive oil
1 small onion, chopped
  fine

1 clove of garlic, crushed
1 8-ounce can (or 1 cup)
  tomatoes, chopped and
  drained
¾ teaspoon parsley,
  chopped
3 tablespoons white wine
Pinch of coriander,
  crushed
Salt and pepper to taste
1 small red or green hot
  pepper, chopped fine
1 tablespoon dry cracker
  crumbs

In the water, simmer the fish, sliced lime, tarragon, salt, green onion, black peppers, cloves, rosemary, cinnamon, and bay leaf for about 10 minutes. Remove from fire. Heat the oil in a heavy skillet; sauté the onion and garlic in it until the onion is transparent. Add tomatoes and parsley and cook for 2 or 3 minutes just to blend the flavors. Add the wine and coriander to this mixture. Remove from heat. Place fish in a greased baking dish and top with the tomato mixture, salt and pepper, chopped pepper, and cracker crumbs. Bake in a 425° oven for about 15 minutes or until fish flakes easily when pierced with a fork.

PESCADO A LA VERACRUZANA
(Fish, Veracruz Style)   Serves 6

In the colonial city of Veracruz this is a popular dish.

6 tablespoons oil
1 no. 2½ can tomatoes,
  chopped
1 teaspoon sugar
3 teaspoons chili powder
½ teaspoon allspice
1 clove of garlic, crushed
½ teaspoon grated orange
  rind
Salt and pepper to taste
1 onion, chopped well

6–8 red snapper fillets
1 small can pimientos,
  chopped coarsely
2 tablespoons capers
1 3-ounce jar green olives,
  pitted and chopped
  coarsely
Parsley, fresh, chopped
  as a garnish
3 boiled potatoes
  (optional)

Heat 3 tablespoons oil in heavy skillet. Combine the tomatoes with the sugar, chili powder, allspice, garlic, orange rind, salt, pepper, and onion. Blend well and simmer in oil for about 10 minutes, covered. Coat baking dish with remaining oil. Put the fish in baking dish; add the pimientos, capers, and olives to the tomato mixture and pour over the fish. Bake in a moderate (350°) oven for about 30–35 minutes or until fish flakes easily when pierced with a fork. Sprinkle with just enough fresh parsley to add a little color.

NOTE: Many people add cubed, hot, boiled potatoes to the fish during the last 5–7 minutes of cooking. We prefer to serve the potatoes on the side.

PESCADO EN JUGO DE NARANJA
(*Fish in Orange Juice*)   Serves 6–8

A dish from Tamaulipas.

8 fish fillets
Salt and pepper to taste
Juice of 2 limes
4 tablespoons olive oil
1½ tablespoons green
  onion, minced
2 tomatoes, peeled and
  chopped
1½ tablespoons green
  pepper, chopped

½ cup orange juice—
  fresh, frozen, or canned
4 tablespoons capers (or
  less, according to taste)
2 oranges, sliced thin, rind
  and all
½ cup toasted, blanched,
  chopped almonds
  (optional)

Season fish with salt and pepper and let it stand in the lime juice for about 20 minutes. Grease baking pan with one-half of the olive oil and place fish in pan. Top the fish with minced onion, tomatoes, and green pepper and drizzle over this the rest of the oil. Place in a 350° oven and, when the fish begins to brown (about 15 minutes after it is placed in the oven), add the orange juice. Cook another 15 or 20 minutes, or until fish flakes easily when pierced with a fork. Garnish with capers, orange slices, and almonds.

PESCADO FRIO CON GUACAMOLE
(*Cold Fish with Avocado Sauce*)   Serves 6–8

6–8 slices fresh fish fillets
Salt and pepper to taste
1 tablespoon tarragon
  leaves, crumbled
¼ cup lime juice
Butter (enough for baking
  dish)
2 fresh tomatoes, peeled
  and chopped
3 very ripe avocados,
  mashed

2 tablespoons onions,
  minced
4 teaspoons chili powder
  (more or less)
2½ tablespoons parsley,
  minced
1 clove of garlic, crushed
1 tablespoon olive oil
13 black olives, pitted
1 can sweet red peppers,
  cut into strips

Season fish with salt, pepper, and tarragon leaves and soak in lime juice for a few minutes. Set the oven at 375° and bake fish in buttered baking dish until it flakes easily when pierced with a fork, about 25 minutes. While fish is baking, combine:

tomatoes
avocado
minced onion
chili powder

parsley
clove of garlic
oil
salt and pepper to taste

(We suggest tasting the *guacamole* as the chili powder is added, so that you can get just the degree of heat you desire.) Spread the above mixture over the cool fish. Garnish with black olive rings and strips of sweet red pepper.

PESCADO Y PEREJIL (*Fish and Parsley*)
Serves 4–6

That famous Lake Chapala whitefish is good for this one
. . . or any whitefish you can get your hands on.

1 large whitefish, filleted and cut into 4 good-sized pieces
2 tablespoons lemon juice
Salt and pepper to taste
1 teaspoon tarragon leaves, crumbled
1 tablespoon onion, minced
1 bunch parsley, chopped
1 clove of garlic, crushed
1 stick butter
1¼ cups dry white wine
½ teaspoon cumin powder

Rub the fish fillets with lemon juice, sprinkle with salt, pepper, and tarragon, and let stand for about ½ hour. Mix together the onion, parsley, and garlic. Sauté the parsley mixture
in the butter until wilted and add the wine; season with salt
and pepper and cumin. Place fish in buttered dish, pour sauce
over it, cover, and bake in a 350° oven for about 30 minutes
or until the fish flakes easily when pierced with a fork. Add
more wine if liquid in the pan appears scant.

PESCADO DE LUJO (*Fish De luxe*) Serves 6

In Mérida this fish is baked in banana leaves, but heavy oiled parchment paper can be used to get very good results.

*½ cup cooked, chopped
shrimp (or ¼ cup
chopped shrimp and ¼
cup chopped crab; or
all crab)
¼ cup white dry wine
2 tablespoons salt
1 teaspoon pepper
1 clove of garlic, mashed
1 small green pepper,
seeded and chopped well
1 very small onion,
minced well
2 medium-sized tomatoes,
peeled and chopped*

*2–3 pounds fish
(mackerel, bass,
whitefish, pompano, etc.)
Juice of 1 lime and 1
lemon
Juice of 2 oranges
¾ teaspoon red chili
powder
3 tablespoons butter,
melted
Olive oil
Small amount butter
Parchment paper
½ dozen large mushrooms,
sautéed and chopped
coarsely*

Combine the shrimp (or crab and shrimp) with the wine, 1 teaspoon of salt, pepper, garlic, green pepper, onion, and tomatoes. Let stand 1 hour or more. Meanwhile, soak the cleaned, boned whole fish in water to cover, lime and lemon juice, and salt for about 15 minutes. Remove and dry. Coat the inside of the fish with orange juice. Mix together the chili powder and salt and rub well on inside of the fish. Brush the inside of the fish with melted butter. Drain off excess liquid from the shrimp or crab. Stuff fish with this mixture. Skewer the fish and tie closed. Pour a small amount of oil over the fish. Butter a sheet of parchment cooking paper and cover the bottom of a lightly buttered glass baking pan with it. Place fish on paper; sprinkle mushrooms on fish. Top fish with another piece of buttered parchment paper cut slightly larger than the first sheet. Make an airtight package of the fish by tucking in the paper all around. Bake at 375° for 25–40 minutes or until fish flakes easily when pierced with a fork.

NOTE: You can also wrap fish in one piece of buttered parchment paper. If so, wrap well and secure with toothpicks if necessary.

PESCADO EN SALSA DE NUEZ
(Fish in Nut Sauce) Serves 6

Salt and pepper to taste	*¼ cup milk*
6 teaspoons lemon juice	*¼ cup sweet cream*
2 pounds haddock, cod,	*4 tablespoons rum*
or mackerel, filleted	*8 ounces grated mild cheese*
¼ cup melted butter	*Pinch of cinnamon*
4 cups ground almonds	*¼ cup bread crumbs*

Combine the salt and pepper and lemon juice. Brush this mixture over the fish slices and let stand for ¾ hour. Place the fish in a greased baking dish and brush with butter. Mix the nuts, milk, cream, rum, and grated cheese and pour this sauce over the fish slices, covering them very well. Sprinkle with additional salt and pepper, the cinnamon, and the bread crumbs. Bake in a hot oven, 450°, for about 30 minutes.

TORTAS DE CAMARONES *(Shrimp Fritters)*
Serves 4–6

1⅓ cups flour	*⅔ cup milk*
Dash of cayenne pepper	*1 egg, well beaten*
¼ teaspoon ginger	*1½ cups cooked shrimp*
Dash of cinnamon	*(canned, well drained*
1½ teaspoons baking	*may be used), chopped*
powder	*coarsely*
¼ teaspoon salt	

Sift together the dry ingredients; blend milk and egg and add slowly to the dry ingredients, a little at a time. Stir in shrimp. Drop mixture from a tablespoon into deep hot fat (365°–375°) and fry for 2–5 minutes or until the fritters are golden brown. Drain on absorbent paper.

PESCADO RELLENO CON CAMARONES
(Fish Stuffed with Shrimps)   Serves 4

2 *large whitefish or striped*
   bass fillets
1 *medium-sized onion*
1 *clove of garlic*

1 *bay leaf*
1 *teaspoon orégano*
¼–½ *teaspoon basil*
Salt and pepper to taste

Simmer fish in water to cover with the onion, garlic, bay leaf, orégano, basil, salt, and pepper until fish separates easily when tested with a fork. Drain and allow to cool. Set aside. For the stuffing:

½ *cup butter*
1 *medium-sized onion,*
   chopped fine
⅓ *cup sifted flour*
1½ *cups milk*
½ *cup cream*

½ *pound small cooked*
   shrimps, chopped
   coarsely
¼ *teaspoon tarragon*
Salt and pepper to taste

GARNISHES

Lettuce
Mayonnaise
1 *pimiento, cut into strips*
1 *hard-cooked egg*

6–7 *large black olives,*
   sliced
Parsley

Melt the butter, add the onion, blend in the flour, add the milk and the cream slowly, a small amount at a time, and cook, stirring constantly, until smooth and thick. Add shrimps, tarragon, salt, and pepper; stir well and cool. To serve: place 1 fish fillet on a serving platter, on a bed of lettuce. Spread filling over it, then cover with another fillet. Chill in the refrigerator for about 2 hours. Before serving, cover with mayonnaise. Garnish with strips of pimiento, slices of hard-cooked egg, sliced black olives, and parsley.

VARIATIONS

1. Crab meat can be used instead of shrimp. Be sure, if canned crab meat is used, to pick it over well and discard bony parts. Defrost frozen crab meat according to directions on package.

2. Crepes can also be filled with the creamed sea food stuffing. Do not garnish with mayonnaise or other items.

LANGOSTA CON ARROZ (*Lobster and Rice*)
Serves 4–6

3 cloves of garlic
4 tablespoons olive oil
2 small onions, chopped well
1 green pepper, seeded and chopped
1 pound uncooked lobster, cut into large chunks
¾ cup dry white wine
3 cups chicken broth (*canned may be used*)

½ cup tomato sauce
½ teaspoon freshly ground black pepper
½ teaspoon orégano
Salt
Pinch of basil
2 cups uncooked rice
Grated mild cheese as a topping

Sauté garlic in oil for a few seconds. Discard garlic. Add the onions to the oil and sauté for a few seconds. Add the green pepper and the lobster cubes and cook until lobster loses its raw look and takes on a reddish color. Add the wine, chicken broth, tomato sauce, black pepper, orégano, salt, and basil. When mixture comes to a boil, add the rice; stir well. Cover and simmer until liquid is absorbed, about 30 minutes or more. Don't let rice get too mushy. Just before serving, sprinkle with cheese and pop under the broiler for a few minutes.

JAIBAS RELLENAS A LA VERACRUZANA
(Stuffed Crabs, Veracruz Style) Serves 6

2 tablespoons chopped
fresh parsley
¼ cup walnuts, ground
1 onion, chopped fine
1 tomato, peeled and
chopped
1 clove of garlic, chopped
fine
8 pimiento-stuffed olives,
chopped

1 anchovy, chopped well
½ cup pine nuts
½ tablespoon red chili
powder
12 crabs
¾ cup cracker crumbs
¼ cup butter

Make a sauce by combining the following:

parsley
walnuts
onion
tomato
clove of garlic

olives
anchovy
pine nuts
chili powder

Take meat out of crab shells. Wash both well. Chop crab meat and add it to the sauce. Fill shells with crab mixture. Cover with cracker crumbs. Dot with butter. Bake at 350° for 30–40 minutes or until well browned.

OSTIONES GUISADOS (*Stewed Oysters*)   Serves 6

3 dozen raw oysters in
their own juices
½ cup green pepper,
chopped
2 tomatoes, peeled and
chopped
2 onions, minced
2 cloves of garlic, crushed
2 tablespoons cooking oil
Salt and pepper to taste
2 tablespoons dry white
wine

½ cup black olives, pitted
and chopped
1 anchovy fillet, chopped
12–15 raisins, chopped
2 teaspoons parsley,
chopped
2 tablespoons bread
crumbs
¼ teaspoon cinnamon
Dash of paprika
¾ tablespoon butter

Drain oysters, but save 1½ cups of the liquid. Sauté pepper, tomatoes, onions, and garlic in the oil for about 5 minutes. Add the salt, pepper, wine, olives, anchovy, raisins, parsley, oysters, and oyster liquor. Cook over moderate heat, uncovered, for about 15 minutes, or until the liquid has nearly evaporated. Brown the bread crumbs, cinnamon, and paprika in the butter. Sprinkle this mixture on oysters.

PULPOS EN SU TINTA (*Octopus in its Own Ink*)
Serves 6

3 cloves of garlic
2 small bay leaves,
crumbled
1 onion
6 tablespoons green pepper,
coarsely chopped
3 tablespoons butter
2 cups (1 16-ounce can)
canned tomatoes,
chopped

2½ tablespoons chopped
fresh parsley
Salt and pepper to taste
½ teaspoon cinnamon
¼ teaspoon paprika
2 cups canned octopus or
squid in its own juice
1 tablespoon dry white
wine
Hot boiled rice (1 14-
ounce package)

Chop the garlic with the bay leaves and onion and add the coarsely chopped green pepper. Cook for about 10 minutes in the butter on a low flame. Add the chopped tomatoes, parsley, salt, pepper, cinnamon, and paprika, and cook until mixture reaches the boiling point. Add the octopus and its ink, to which the wine has been added. Simmer very slowly for about ½ hour. Serve over steaming rice.

Carnes

❖

(MEATS)

Many's the time in Mexico when we've pored over menus in restaurants wishing that there were only two meat dishes from which to choose. It would be so much easier to make up our minds that way, instead of puzzling over a dozen or more succulent *carne* selections which are usually offered in dining spots there.

You can find *biftec* or *bistec* (beefsteak) prepared in exciting new ways—for example, Biftec Suizo* (Swiss Steak), or Biftec con Setas* (Steak with Mushrooms). Veal, lamb, and pork dishes are all familiar, but not at all like those at home because they are prepared with that fine Mexican touch, such as Ternera con Cebollas* (Veal with Onions) or Lomo de Puerco con Cerveza* (Pork Loin in Beer).

Mexican housewives are artists when it comes to blending several different ingredients together with meat to produce extra-flavorful and highly economical dishes. For budget-stretching meals, try Albóndigas en Salsa de Almendra* (Meat Balls in Almond Sauce), Guiso de Tres Carnes* (Three Meat Stew), Albondigón con Ciruelas y Albaricoques* (Meat Loaf with Prunes and Apricots), and Picadillo* (Mexican Hash), which contains not only meat, but citron, bananas, and olives—mincemeat, Mexican style.

Barbacoa, or barbecue, is such a special occasion in Mexico that we've put together a special section to cover it.

But, for now, bring on the *carnes!*

BIFTEC ESTILO MAZATLAN
(*Steak, Mazatlán Style*)   Serves 6

2 pounds lean sirloin, cut into 6 equal strips
Pepper
Salt
6 slices toast

Sprinkle both sides of steak with pepper liberally and let stand for ½ hour. Put a light layer of salt in the bottom of a heavy skillet. Turn the heat to high and, when salt begins to brown, add the steak strips. Cook until well browned on one side and flip over. To produce a rare steak strip, cook about 30 seconds at a high heat and turn. Lower to a moderate flame and cook about 1 more minute.

SAUCE

2 tablespoons butter
1 tablespoon olive oil
1 clove of garlic, crushed
2 tablespoons flour
3 cups tomato purée
1¼ teaspoons chili powder
1 green pepper, chopped
2 teaspoons parsley,
   chopped
¼ cup chives

Heat 1 tablespoon of butter and the olive oil in a skillet. Add garlic. Add the flour and stir until flour is golden brown. Add the tomato purée, chili powder, green pepper, and parsley and let simmer for 30 minutes. Just before serving, stir in the chives and remaining tablespoon of butter. Pour over steaks. Serve on toast slice.

NOTE: Sauce can be made early in the day, except for the last two steps—adding the chives and butter.

ALDILLA RELLENA CON CHORIZO
(Flank Steak Filled with Sausage)   Serves 6–8

¾ pound Chorizo* sausage
1 bunch green onions,
 chopped, including the
 tops
½ cup chopped walnuts
6 tablespoons parsley,
 chopped
1 tablespoon red chili
 powder (*or more to
 taste*)
1 egg, well beaten
½ cup cracker crumbs
Salt and pepper to taste

1 2½–3-pound flank
 steak, pounded lightly
 with a scored wooden
 mallet
1 clove of garlic, crushed
Flour, as directed
2 tablespoons oil
1 cup tomato purée
½ cup broth (canned
 may be used)
½ bay leaf
1 pinch ginger
¼ cup dry red wine

Mix the sausage with the onions, nuts, parsley, chili powder, egg, and crumbs. Season with salt and pepper. Let stand while you rub the flank steak well on both sides with garlic. Spread the filling on the steak and roll into a long strip. Fasten with string or skewers. Dredge with flour, sprinkle with salt, and brown on all sides in oil. Combine the tomato purée, broth, bay leaf, ginger, wine, and salt and pepper to taste. Mix well and simmer. Pour over meat. Bake in a 350° oven for about 1–1½ hours or more.

CHILI CON CARNE Serves 8–10

3 pounds ground lean beef
6 tablespoons olive oil
1¼ cups onion, chopped
1 green pepper, chopped
1 clove of garlic, minced well
4 tablespoons red chili powder
1 teaspoon cumin powder
1 teaspoon paprika
2 whole cloves
1 bay leaf
¼ teaspoon epazote (*if available*)
Salt to taste
8 cups water
1 no. 2½ can tomatoes (or 3½ cups fresh tomatoes that have been peeled and chopped)
2¼ tablespoons flour
2 tablespoons yellow corn meal

Brown beef in oil with onion, green pepper, and garlic. Add the chili powder, cumin, paprika, cloves, bay leaf, *epazote*, salt, and water. Cover and cook at a low heat for 45 minutes, stirring occasionally. Add the tomatoes and cook another ½ hour, stirring occasionally. Add flour and corn meal and cook until thickened.

VARIATION

This dish makes a good casserole too. Turn the thickened chili into a baking dish and cover it with grated mild cheese. Bake in the oven until cheese melts and browns slightly. Dust with paprika before serving.

VARIATION

Beans can be added to this dish. Use 2 cups of canned kidney beans. Add about 15 minutes before cooking time is up. If dried (but not canned) beans are used, soak them overnight and cook well before adding to chili. About 1¾ cups beans will do it.

CARNE EN SALSA ROJA
(*Meat in Red Chili Sauce*)   Serves 4–6

This is what Texans call chili con carne, but it actually comes straight from their neighbor South of the Border.

*2 pounds beef or pork,
cut into cubes as for
stew
2 cups water, lightly salted
8 small red chilies (or 4
tablespoons, more or
less, red chili powder)
2 cloves of garlic*

*1¼ teaspoons orégano
¼ cup dry sherry
2 tablespoons flour
2 tablespoons oil
¼ teaspoon cumin
1 tablespoon parsley
Salt to taste*

Add meat to 2 cups salted water and cook for about ½ hour. Save broth. While meat is stewing, remove the stems and seeds from the chilies and toast in a heavy ungreased pan for 2 or 3 minutes. Do not burn them. Soak chilies in ½ cup warm water to cover until soft—about ½ hour. Drain but save water. Grind the chilies, garlic, and orégano to a paste in a food grinder or blender. (If blender is used, add broth, water, and wine at this time.) Add the broth, water, and wine and strain. Brown the flour in the oil; slowly stir in the broth, cumin, parsley, and salt. Combine with meat and simmer for about 1½ hours or until tender.

VARIATIONS

You can add 2 cups of canned kidney beans or a can of hominy to the above, right before cooking time is up.

NOTE: Save excess stock for making sauces and gravies.

BIFTEC CON SETAS (*Steak with Mushrooms*)
Serves 6

Mexico abounds with strange, interesting, delightful mushrooms. In making this, you'll have to be content with the kind
at your local market.

6 steaks, ½-inch thick
1 teaspoon salt
1 teaspoon freshly ground
    black pepper
8 tablespoons flour, sifted
½ cup sweet butter
½ pound fresh
    mushrooms, sliced
6 tablespoons brandy,
    warm

¼ cup boiling water
8 tablespoons dry red wine
¼ teaspoon cinnamon
1 whole clove
2 tablespoons tomato-onion
    purée (2 tablespoons
    tomato purée and ⅛
    teaspoon onion juice)
½ teaspoon sugar
1 cup sweet cream

Sprinkle steaks with salt and pepper, and dredge with flour.
Sauté quickly in butter until brown on both sides. Remove. In
the same butter, sauté the mushrooms until tender. Return
steaks to the pan with the mushrooms; pour over warm brandy
and ignite. When brandy has burned out, add boiling water.
Then add the wine, cinnamon, and clove. Cover and simmer
8–10 minutes. Add tomato-onion purée which has been mixed
with sugar. Remove clove. Cook 5 more minutes and add
cream during last 2 minutes of cooking. Do not boil.

CECINA MEXICANA (*Corned Beef, Mexican Style*)
Serves 8–10

4–5 pounds corned beef
  in 1 piece
1 medium-sized onion, left
  whole
1 large bay leaf
1 orange, cut into quarters
½ lemon
2 cloves
4 whole black peppercorns

2 cloves of garlic, crushed
2¼ tablespoons chili
  powder (*or more if
  desired*)
Pinch of cumin powder
1 pound summer squash,
  cut into large slices
1 12-ounce can whole-
  kernel corn, drained

Place the corned beef in a large, heavy pot. Add cold water
to cover, the onion, bay leaf, orange, lemon, cloves, and peppercorns. Cover and simmer about 2 or 3 hours, until tender.
Combine the garlic, chili powder, and cumin, and dissolve these
ingredients in about ¼ cup of stock from the corned beef.
Add this mixture to the corned beef. Add the squash slices
and cook 15 or 20 minutes, or until tender but not overdone.
During the last 5–7 minutes or so of cooking, stir in the corn.
Let stand about 20 minutes before serving.

CHILES RELLENOS (*Stuffed Green Peppers*)
Serves 6

6 large sweet green
  peppers
6 tablespoons olive oil
1 pound ground beef
1 small onion, minced
2 cloves of garlic, crushed
2¼ teaspoons red chili
  powder
1 teaspoon salt
3 tablespoons ground
  almonds

3 tablespoons raisins
¼ cup tomato paste
4 tablespoons flour, sifted
¼ cup freshly grated mild
  cheese (Parmesan or
  Romano)
1 cup bread crumbs
2 eggs, lightly beaten
Shortening for deep-fat
  frying

Remove the stems and scoop out the seeds from the peppers, leaving the peppers whole. Parboil by placing them in a saucepan with water to cover and bring the water to a boil. As soon as water has boiled, turn off flame, drain the peppers, and allow them to cool until comfortable to the touch.

While peppers are cooling, heat the oil in a skillet and brown the beef and onion; add the garlic, chili powder, salt, ground nuts, and raisins; stir in the tomato paste. Cook for about 5 minutes. Remove from the heat and add more salt, pepper, and chili powder, if so desired. Stuff peppers with meat mixture. Sprinkle flour on the tops of the peppers at the openings. Mix together the cheese and bread crumbs; beat the eggs lightly in a separate bowl. Dip each pepper in the eggs, then in the crumbs and cheese, once again in the eggs, and again in the crumbs and cheese. Heat the shortening in a heavy, deep pan to 375° on fat thermometer. Carefully put 1 or 2 peppers at a time in fat and sauté until golden brown. Drain on absorbent paper. Serve hot.

BIFTEC SUIZO (*Swiss Steak, Mexican Style*) Serves 6

½ cup flour
1 teaspoon salt
½ teaspoon pepper
¼ teaspoon red chili
    powder
1½ pounds top round
    steak (about ½-inch
    thick), with excess fat
    removed
3 tablespoons cooking oil
1 clove of garlic, minced

1 large onion, chopped
½ green pepper, seeded
    and chopped
1 no. 2 can tomatoes
6 red sweet peppers,
    canned, drained well
3 tablespoons ripe olives,
    sliced
1 small can pinto or
    kidney beans
2 tablespoons sherry

Sift together the flour, salt, pepper, and chili powder. With the edge of a saucer or a wooden mallet, pound one-half of the seasoned flour into one side of the meat and the other half into the other side. In a heavy skillet, heat the cooking oil and brown the meat quickly. Remove meat. Sauté, in same skillet, garlic, onion, and green pepper until vegetables are softened. Return meat to pan. Add ¼ cup water and tomatoes. Cover and simmer (or place in 350° oven) for 1–1½ hours until meat is tender. Add the sliced red peppers, olives, and kidney beans the last 10–15 minutes of cooking. Sprinkle sherry over all and cook for a few more minutes.

ASADO DE LUJO (*De luxe Roast*) Serves 8–10

5–6-pound chuck roast
Salt and pepper to taste
2 cloves of garlic, crushed
¼ cup shortening
1 slice raw ham, cut into
  strips
1 medium-sized onion,
  chopped

1 no. 2½ can tomatoes,
  chopped
2 bay leaves
¾ cup red wine
6 potatoes, halved
5 carrots, diced

Rub roast well with salt, pepper, and crushed garlic and let stand. Heat shortening and brown ham in it. Remove. Brown roast in same shortening. Add onion, tomatoes, bay leaves, wine, and ham to the roast. Add more salt and pepper if so desired. Cover and simmer until meat is tender, about 2 hours, adding more wine or a little water if necessary. Add potatoes 45 minutes before cooking time is up. Add carrots the last 15–20 minutes.

PIERNA DE CARNERO (*Leg of Lamb*) Serves 6–8

¾ tablespoon chili powder
1 tablespoon orégano
¼ teaspoon cumin powder
½ teaspoon ginger
½ teaspoon ground
  rosemary
1 teaspoon powdered
  mustard

2 cloves of garlic, crushed
1 leg of lamb, 5–6
  pounds
¼ cup lemon juice
Salt and freshly ground
  pepper to taste

Stir together the chili powder, orégano, cumin, ginger, rosemary, mustard, and garlic to form a thick paste. Add a drop or so of water or wine if necessary. Score the leg of lamb in a number of places with a sharp pointed knife and insert some paste in each incision. Rub lemon juice over the lamb and refrigerate for 8 hours or overnight. Remove about 1 hour before cooking so that lamb reaches room temperature. Sprinkle with salt and pepper. Roast, uncovered, on a rack at 300°–350°, allowing 18–20 minutes per pound for well-done lamb (175° on meat thermometer) or 12–15 minutes per pound for rare meat (140° on thermometer).

COSTILLAS EN CAMISAS (*Cutlets in Shirts*)
Serves 6

¾–1 cup fine bread crumbs
1 clove of garlic, crushed
1½ tablespoons parsley, minced
½ tablespoon rosemary, crushed
Pinch of ginger

Pinch of dry mustard
Dash of Tabasco
Salt and pepper to taste
Oil (about ¼ cup plus a few drops more)
6 lamb chops
1 egg, lightly beaten
1 tablespoon paprika

Combine the crumbs (reserve ¼ cup), garlic, parsley, rosemary, ginger, dry mustard, Tabasco, salt and pepper, and enough oil to form a paste. (It is suggested that oil be dropped in a little at a time so that paste does not become too loose.) Coat each chop with a "shirt," or paste; roll in remaining crumbs. Dip in beaten egg and roll again in crumbs. Fry slowly in shallow hot oil until very brown and well done. Sprinkle lightly with paprika before serving.

VARIATION

Pork chops can be used.

TERNERA CON CREMA
(*Braised Veal with Cream*) Serves 5–6

This excellent dish came to us from Señora María Ricarda Luz Lara de Morales.

2½ pounds tender veal,
  cut as for stew
Flour to dredge veal
Salt and pepper to taste
Small amount shortening
  for browning the meat
1 large onion

1 cup cold water
2 pounds small potatoes,
  boiled in beef stock
  (canned stock may be
  used)
½ pint sweet cream

Season veal with flour, salt, and pepper. Brown meat on all sides. Slice the onion and add to veal. When onion is transparent, add 1 cup cold water and continue cooking until veal starts to get tender. Add the potatoes and remainder of the beef stock in which the potatoes were boiled. When veal is almost done, add cream and let simmer a few minutes longer but do not boil. If more sauce is desired, add a bit of milk to the cream.

TERNERA CON CEBOLLAS
(*Veal with Onions*) Serves 6

2 pounds veal, cut into
  cubes
6 small white onions,
  peeled and left whole
1 16-ounce (or no. 303)
  can tomatoes (or about
  3 large fresh tomatoes,
  peeled and chopped)
1 bay leaf

1 stick cinnamon
¾ cup olive oil
1 large strip orange peel
  in which 1 whole clove
  has been inserted
2 tablespoons dry white
  wine
Salt and pepper to taste

Put all the ingredients in a saucepan and add water to cover. Cook for 1–1½ hours or until meat is tender. Remove cinnamon stick, orange peel, and clove before serving but do not strain sauce.

TERNERA EN SALSA DE CACAHUATE
(Veal in Peanut Sauce) Serves 5–6

1½ cups peanuts, blanched and ground
4 sprigs of parsley
2 pounds veal, cut into 1-inch squares
¼ cup shortening
1 clove of garlic
1 small onion, chopped fine
3 tomatoes, peeled and chopped

1 tablespoon sugar
Pinch of nutmeg
Pinch of thyme
Pinch of orégano
1½ cups stock (canned broth may used)
½ cup dry white wine
1 teaspoon salt
½ teaspoon freshly ground black pepper

Grind the nuts and parsley and set aside. Sauté the veal squares in shortening until browned on both sides. Add garlic, onion, tomatoes, and sugar. Cook until liquid has evaporated from tomatoes. Discard garlic. Add nuts and parsley which have been ground together. Add nutmeg, thyme, and orégano. Brown. Add stock, wine, salt, and pepper. Cook very slowly; add a little more wine or water if liquid appears scant. Cook until meat is very tender, about 20 or 30 minutes. Sauce should be very thick.

PUCHERO DE SONORA
(Boiled Dinner from Sonora) Serves 10–12

A northern state, Sonora is noted for its chick-peas and excellent tomatoes, both of which play a part in this hearty dish. Puchero is a boiled dish that is popular in other parts of the world as well as Mexico, mainly in South and Central American countries.

1 stewing chicken, cut into serving pieces	*2 pounds lamb, cut into cubes*
Water as directed	*6 potatoes, peeled and quartered*
Salt and pepper to taste	*6 medium-sized carrots, cut into strips*
1 onion	
1 stalk celery	*1 pound fresh string beans, cut into 1-inch pieces*
1½ pounds ground beef	
2 eggs, beaten lightly	
¼ cup grated bread crumbs	*1 bunch broccoli, separated (optional)*
2 tablespoons flour	*12 artichoke hearts*
2 cups chick-peas (which have been soaked overnight in water)	
6 Chorizo* sausages (substitute pork sausage, if necessary)	

Wash chicken and cover with cold water, add salt, pepper, onion, and celery, and simmer for about 35 minutes, skimming when necessary. While chicken is stewing, mix together the ground meat, eggs, bread crumbs, flour, salt, and pepper, and shape into good-sized balls. Set aside. After chicken has cooked for 35 minutes, add the drained chick-peas, sausages, and lamb cubes. Place ground beef balls on top of these ingredients and cook until chick-peas are done—about 1–1½ hours longer. Add the vegetables during last ½ hour of the cooking time; the artichoke hearts 15 minutes before end of cooking time.

GUISO DE TRES CARNES (*Stewed Meats*)
Serves 6–8

½ cup olive oil
½ pound ham
2 Chorizo* sausages
3 chicken breasts
2 cloves of garlic
1 8-ounce can tomatoes,
chopped
2 pounds veal, cut into
cubes

Dash of cinnamon
1 teaspoon sugar
Salt and pepper to taste
½ pound peas (fresh)
6 artichoke hearts (canned
may be used)
2 tablespoons chopped
parsley

Heat oil in skillet and cook cubed ham and sliced sausages until almost done. Remove. In the same oil, sauté the chicken breasts, garlic, and chopped tomatoes and remove when lightly browned. Discard garlic. Add the veal and water to cover; season with cinnamon, sugar, salt, and pepper. Simmer veal for about 1 hour or until tender, adding the chicken breasts about 35 minutes before veal is done. Add the ham-and-sausage mixture, peas, and artichoke hearts about 15 minutes before stew is done and heat through so that vegetables are steaming hot along with the meats. Season with additional salt and pepper and float chopped parsley over all.

ALBONDIGAS EN SALSA DE ALMENDRA
(*Meat Balls in Almond Sauce*)   Serves 6–8

SAUCE

½ cup blanched almonds
1 dry hard French roll,
cubed
1 clove of garlic
3 tablespoons oil
1½ cups chicken broth
(canned may be used)

2 tablespoons onion, finely
chopped
5 tablespoons tomato sauce
Salt and pepper to taste
¼ teaspoon coriander or
parsley

MEAT BALLS

2 slices day-old bread   1 egg
½ cup hot water   1¾ teaspoons salt and
¾ pound ground beef   pepper
¾ pound ground pork (all   Pinch of orégano
   beef may be used)   ¼ teaspoon paprika

Sauté almonds, roll cubes, and garlic in hot oil until lightly browned. Remove from oil, cool, and grind or blend to the consistency of a paste. Dilute with ¼ cup of broth. Set aside. Cook onion until soft in same oil. Add the tomato sauce and remaining broth. Season with salt and pepper and coriander or parsley. Simmer for 5 or 10 minutes.

For the meat balls–soak the bread in the water, drain, and mix with meats. Add the egg, salt, pepper, orégano, and paprika and mix well. Form into small balls and add gently to the simmering sauce. Cook, covered, 25–30 minutes. The almond mixture is added during the last 10–12 minutes of cooking.

ALBONDIGON CON CIRUELAS Y ALBARICOQUES
(Meat Loaf with Prunes and Apricots)   Serves 8–10

2 pounds ground veal (a   1 egg
   combination of beef and   Salt, pepper, and orégano
   pork, 1 pound each, can   to taste
   be used)   Flour and butter in which
1 egg yolk   to brown meat loaf

SAUCE

¼ pound dried, pitted   ½ cup canned beef
   prunes   consommé (or other
¼ pound dried apricots   stock)
1½ cups dry red wine   Salt, pepper, and parsley
1½ teaspoons cornstarch

Combine the ground meat and the eggs and season to taste with salt, pepper, and orégano. Shape into a long roll. Sprinkle with flour and sauté in butter. Soak the prunes and the apricots in the wine for a few minutes; mash them well to a pulp with the wine. Pour fruit-and-wine pulp over the meat in the pan. Dissolve cornstarch in the stock and add to meat. Sprinkle with salt, pepper, and about ½ teaspoon of chopped parsley. Simmer until meat is done, about 1 hour or more. Add a little stock if liquid grows scant in pan.

PICADILLO (*Mexican Hash*)   Serves 6–7

1 pound ground pork
1 pound ground veal (or
  2 pounds ground beef; or
  1 pound ground pork and
  1 pound ground beef)
3 tablespoons oil (omit
  when using pork)
1 onion, chopped
1 cup tomato purée
¼ cup almonds, blanched
  and chopped coarsely
¼ cup raisins (soaked in
  a small amount of
  water)
2 candied citrons, chopped
2 small bananas, sliced
  (optional)

¼ cup black olives, pitted
  and diced
3 teaspoons chili powder,
  more or less (depending
  on taste for hot food)
  or 6 small hot green
  chilies, peeled and
  chopped
1 tablespoon chopped
  parsley
1 stick cinnamon
2 cloves
Dash of cumin powder
1 tablespoon sugar
Salt and pepper to taste

Brown the ground meat and chopped onion in the oil. Add the tomato purée. Mix well. When thickened, add the almonds, raisins, citrons, banana slices, olives, chili powder, and parsley. Season with cinnamon, cloves, cumin, sugar, salt, and pepper. Bring to a boil. Reduce to a simmer and cook for 30–45 minutes or until mixture is thick. Stir occasionally to prevent sticking. Remove cinnamon stick before serving.

Picadillo is the Mexican version of mincemeat. In addition to being served alone, it is sometimes served in pie form or as a filling for Tacos* or Empanadas.*

PUERCO CON CHILES PASADO
(Pork with Chilies) Serves 4–5

We are indebted to Señora Elvira G. de Bañuelos for this one. Do not use chili powder as a substitute in this recipe.

2 pounds pork loin
Shortening, as directed
4 ounces chiles pasado (or any dried red hot pepper)
3 tomatoes, chopped well
1 onion, chopped well
1 clove of garlic, minced
Salt to taste

Cut pork into pieces and sauté in a small amount of shortening, draining off fat if necessary. Wash the chilies, toast them in a heavy skillet for a few minutes, and place them in hot water to soften. Clean out seeds and stems and break the chilies into small pieces.

Mix together the tomatoes, onion, and garlic, all of which have been chopped well. Mix with the peppers. Sauté together with the pork, sprinkle with salt to taste, and cook for about 30–40 minutes or until well done.

LOMO DE PUERCO ESTILO VERACRUZANO *(Pork Loin, Veracruz Style)*
Serves 3–4

We've had this pork loin dish served in banana leaf wrappings, but you can make it in a roaster with great success.

2 *pounds pork loin*
1 *slice cooked ham, cut*
   into strips
2 *slices bacon, fried lightly*
   and cut into strips
2 *pickled* Jalapeño *chilies*
   (*available in cans*)
8–9 *whole cloves*
Salt and pepper to taste

2 *small onions, minced*
1 *clove of garlic, crushed*
3 *teaspoons red chili*
   powder
1 *tablespoon sugar*
Few drops of lime juice
½ *cup beef broth* (*canned*
   may be used)

Make small incisions in the pork loin and stuff each incision with strips of ham, bacon, and the pickled chilies. Place 1 whole clove in some of the incisions. Salt and pepper the meat and let stand for about 20 minutes or while you proceed with next step. Combine the onion with the garlic, chili powder, sugar, and enough drops of lime juice to make a moist paste. Rub this paste on the meat. Roast on a rack, fat side up, uncovered, in a 350° oven, allowing 30–35 minutes per pound or until the meat thermometer reaches 185°. When meat is done, remove it from pan; keep warm. Skim off excess fat from pan. Add broth; simmer gently while stirring. Serve with the meat.

TINGA (*Shredded Pork*)   Serves 6

2 *pounds pork loin*
1 *tablespoon salt*
1 *Spanish onion,*
   cut into rings
2½ *tablespoons shortening*
1 *onion, diced*
1 *slice raw ham, cut into*
   thin strips

3 *tomatoes, chopped*
1 *small red dry* chile
   chipotle, *chopped* (*or 1*
   tablespoon red chili
   powder)
1 *avocado*

Put meat in salted water to cover, and boil gently until tender—about 1 hour or slightly more. While meat is boiling, soak the Spanish onion, cut into rings, in cold salted water. When meat is done, cool it and shred it; save the stock. Melt shortening in heavy skillet and add the diced onion, cooking slowly until onion is transparent. Add ham and, when it begins to get crisp, add chopped tomatoes; simmer 8–10 minutes. Add the shredded meat and one-half cup of the stock. Simmer until mixture begins to thicken. Add the chili pepper or powder and simmer for another 5 minutes. Right before serving, garnish with drained Spanish onion rings and avocado slices. Serve very hot.

NOTE: Good as a filling for Tacos* too.

LOMO DE PUERCO CON CERVEZA
(Pork Loin in Beer)   Serves 6

2 pounds pork loin	1 tablespoon sugar
1 teaspoon salt	1 cup beer
¼ teaspoon freshly ground	¾ cup water
pepper	3 fresh pears, pared and
1 large onion, sliced thin	cut in quarters
1 tablespoon shortening	(optional)

Sprinkle meat with salt and pepper and let stand while onion cooks in shortening, until transparent, but not brown. Remove onion. Brown pork well in shortening. Put onions back in pan with pork. Dissolve the sugar in the beer and add to the pork. Simmer until beer takes on a golden-brown color and then add ¾ cup water; simmer 20 minutes and add more water if needed. Simmer a few more minutes until meat is tender; the whole cooking process should take about 1¼ hours. About 20–25 minutes before meat is done, place pears carefully on top of meat and allow them to steam through. Slice meat before serving and arrange it attractively on a platter with the pears.

CHORIZOS *(Mexican Sausage)*   Yield: 10 patties

As we said in the guide section, Chorizos are used in the preparation of many different Mexican dishes. They can be made rather easily, if you can't find them at a local specialty food store.

1 teaspoon salt
2 tablespoons chili powder
¼ teaspoon cloves
½ teaspoon cinnamon
1 tablespoon paprika
1 clove of garlic, crushed well

1 teaspoon orégano, crumbled well between the palms of the hands
1¾ tablespoons vinegar
¼ teaspoon water
1 pound lean pork, ground

Add all ingredients to the ground pork and mix well. Let stand for several hours and mix again. Shape into patties and fry without any shortening for about 30 minutes.

Chorizos, uncooked, can also be packed in a crock or glass refrigerator jar and kept under refrigeration for several weeks.

When recipes in this book call for one *chorizo*, use about 3 or 4 tablespoons unless otherwise indicated.

GUISO DE GUADALAJARA (*Pork Stew*)
Serves 6–8

We don't know if this dish originated in the second city of Mexico, but it is very popular there and in other places too. We also don't know if this recipe is traditional, but it is our favorite method of preparation for this dish.

1 pig's head, about 2 pounds, cut into pieces
1 pound pork loin, cut into 1-inch squares
1 fricasseed chicken, disjointed
3 pig's feet
1 medium-sized onion, with 4 whole cloves stuck into it
2 whole black peppercorns

2 cloves of garlic
3 quarts water, lightly salted
3 or more tablespoons chili powder (dissolved in small amount of warm water)
1 no. 2½ can hominy
Pinch of epazote, if available
Salt to taste

FOR GARNISHES

chopped green onions
shredded lettuce
chopped radishes

Cook pig's head, pork loin, chicken, pig's feet, clove-studded onion, peppercorns, and garlic in 3 quarts lightly salted water for about 1 hour, covered. Dissolve the chili powder in a little warm water and mix it with the hominy. Add both to above broth. Add *epazote*. Continue cooking another 45 minutes until meats are tender. Discard the onion and garlic. Add more salt, if necessary. Serve in soup bowls and let everyone garnish their own plate with slightly chilled onions, shredded lettuce, and radishes, which are dropped right on top of the hot *pozole* (stew).

CARNE DE PUERCO EN SALSA DE RAJAS
(Pork with Pepper Sauce)   Serves 4–6

Do not substitute chili powder in this recipe.

2 pounds lean pork, cut into cubes
½ cup beef stock (canned may be used)
1 clove of garlic
Salt and pepper
1 large onion, chopped well
1 cup (1 8-ounce can) tomatoes, chopped

1 teaspoon coriander seeds, crushed and soaked in 1 tablespoon water
½ teaspoon rosemary, crushed
1 can peeled green chilies, chopped or cut into strips

Simmer meat with stock, garlic, salt, and pepper until all the stock is absorbed. Discard garlic. Sauté meat in an ungreased pan until it is lightly browned. Add onion. Cook a few more minutes until onion is softened. Add tomatoes, the water drained from coriander seeds, rosemary, chilies, and additional salt, if needed. Cook, covered, for 30 minutes or longer, or until pork is tender.

MONDONGO MEXICANA (*Mexican-style Tripe*)
Serves 8

3 pounds tripe
1 quart (4 cups) water
1 large onion, chopped
¼ cup olive oil
2 cloves of garlic, mashed or pressed
3 8-ounce cans tomato sauce
1 bay leaf
2 teaspoons marjoram
Pinch of ground cloves
2 teaspoons salt
½ teaspoon pepper
4 potatoes, cut into quarters (optional)
1 small jar (or about 20) stuffed green olives, cut into
  slices

Wash the tripe and cut into long strips. Simmer, covered, in 1 quart lightly salted water for about 1 hour. While tripe is simmering, make the sauce as follows:

Sauté onion in oil until soft. Add the garlic, tomato sauce, and seasonings and simmer, covered, for about 15 or 20 minutes. Drain tripe and add to the sauce; cook, covered, until tender. Potatoes may be added during the last ½ hour of cooking. Spread olive rings over tripe right before serving and bring to the table very hot.

LENGUA RELLENA (*Stuffed Tongue*) Serves 6–8

This dish is served cold. It makes a wonderful late supper when served with a salad and a bottle of well-chilled wine.

1 beef tongue (*about 2 pounds*)
Juice of 2 or 3 lemons, depending on size
¾ pound ground pork
4 truffles, chopped
1 slice boiled ham, chopped
3 hard-cooked eggs, chopped

2 uncooked eggs
3 teaspoons salt
2 cups water
½ cup white wine
2¼ teaspoons parsley, chopped
¼ teaspoon marjoram
Pinch of orégano
2 bay leaves, crushed
1½ teaspoons pepper

Clean a raw tongue well and rub with lemon juice. Let stand in juice for about 5 minutes. Drain off lemon juice. Make slit in tongue almost to the tip to create a pocket for stuffing. Mix the ground pork, truffles, boiled ham, eggs, hard-cooked and raw, and 1 teaspoon salt. Stuff tongue. Sew the opening. Simmer tongue in 2 cups water, the wine, remaining salt, and herbs in covered pot until tender, about 3 hours or more (figure about 40–50 minutes per pound). Skin tongue and press into a regular mold. Slice when cold and serve with tartar or horse-radish sauce.

To skin tongue – after tongue is cool, remove it from broth and cut off bones and gristle at the thick end of tongue. Slit the skin from the thick end to the tip on the underside. Use a paring knife to loosen the skin at the thick end, and pull and peel off the skin from thick end to tip.

LENGUA A LA VINAGRETA
(*Tongue Vinaigrette*) Serves 6–8

1 beef tongue (about 2
    pounds)
1 carrot
1 onion
1 stalk celery
1 bay leaf
½ teaspoon marjoram
¼ teaspoon thyme

Pinch of cloves
¼ teaspoon chopped fresh
    parsley
8–10 whole black
    peppercorns
Pinch of epazote (if
    available)
1 teaspoon salt

Cook tongue in boiling water to cover with the rest of the ingredients about 3 hours or until tender. Allow tongue to cool in broth. Remove skin (directions are given in recipe for Stuffed Tongue*) and cut in slices. Serve with the following sauce, which is made by combining all of the ingredients and mixing well.

1 cup olive oil
½ cup red wine vinegar
¾ tablespoon chopped
    parsley
1 teaspoon paprika
1 teaspoon prepared
    mustard

1 tablespoon chopped
    sweet pepper
¾ cup chives
3 hard-cooked eggs,
    chopped
Salt and pepper to taste

Tongue is also delicious with this almond sauce:

¼ cup chopped parsley
4 hard-cooked eggs,
    separated
1 clove of garlic, crushed
4 large tomatoes, peeled
    and chopped

1 cup blanched almonds,
    chopped
4 tablespoons olive oil
1½ tablespoons white wine
Salt and pepper to taste

Chop the parsley. Mix parsley together with mashed egg yolks, garlic, tomatoes, and almonds. Simmer 10 minutes or until liquid from tomatoes has evaporated. Add chopped egg whites, oil, wine, and salt and pepper to taste.

HIGADO ENVINADO *(Liver in Wine)*   Serves 6

6 slices calves' liver, about	*1 bunch green onions,*
½-inch thick	*including tops, chopped*
Flour	*¼ cup butter*
Salt	*½ cup of mushrooms*
Pepper	*⅓ cup sherry*

Dredge liver in flour which has been seasoned with salt and pepper. Set aside. Sauté onions lightly in melted butter, until somewhat softened. Add liver and brown on both sides quickly. Reduce heat. Add mushrooms (if canned are used, add liquid) and sherry. Simmer to the desired degree of doneness—about 3–4 minutes will produce rare liver; 6–8, well done.

Aves

❖

(POULTRY)

Moctezuma, the early journals say, was the kind of fussy host who frequently inspected each pot before it was served. He'd pass among the steaming dishes with his officers and they would explain just what was in them and which concoction was considered to be the best. Very often on the top of the list was fowl, both wild and domestic. Who knows? Moctezuma may have been the first person ever to sample the delicious Mole de Guajolate* (Turkey Mole), which was known in the days of the Aztecs and is popular today.

Leading the list of best-loved dishes in Mexico today are those prepared with chicken. In the Yucatán, Pollo Estilo Yucatán* (Chicken in Banana Leaves) is a favorite. Nearly everyone makes a version of Mancha Manteles* (literally, tablecloth stainers).

Duck, a favorite in the pre-Hispanic days, is still a popular dish.

There are a host of poultry dishes in Mexico which originated in France, Austria, and Italy. They were popularized in the nineteenth century during the reign of Maximilian of Hapsburg and his wife Carlotta. These European dishes also bear that delicious native touch these days.

MOLE DE GUAJOLOTE I (*Turkey Mole*)
Serves 10–12

It is believed that the nuns at the Santa Rosa convent in Puebla embellished the original recipe for Mole de Guajolote to please a visiting viceroy. They added bread to thicken the gravy, and almonds in addition to the peanuts. The kitchen at Santa Rosa—with its red brick-and-ceramic tiled walls which are covered with *cazuelas* (casseroles), *ollas* (pots), and *jarros* (pitchers)—is now a museum. *Mole,* a major masterpiece, remains for all the world to enjoy.

We've included below what some believe to be the original Santa Rosa recipe for Turkey Mole. It is complicated and reads almost like a good short story. Many cooks will not want to tackle it. Therefore, we've supplied a simplified version of the recipe too. Easiest of all is to make use of the canned or powdered *mole* sauce which is available at many fine food stores all over the country.

No matter which method you may choose, when you make Turkey Mole, you'll have a dish fit for a state occasion.

1 turkey, 10–12 pounds, cut into pieces
2 bay leaves
1 whole onion
3 medium-sized tomatoes, peeled and chopped
15 chiles mulatos (*can be found at Mexican food stores*)
15 chiles anchos (*can be found at Mexican food stores*)
6 chiles pasillas (*can be found at Mexican food stores*)
¾ cup almonds
½ cup peanuts
½ cup shelled pumpkin seeds
4 cloves
6 whole black peppercorns
3 cloves of garlic, peeled

½ cup raisins (classic, but optional)
3 onions, chopped
1 Tortilla,* fried crisp
2 slices white bread, toasted lightly
7 tablespoons sesame seeds
1 teaspoon anise seeds
2 ounces grated unsweetened Mexican chocolate (use Dutch chocolate as substitute)
Pinch of epazote (if available)
Grated rind of 1 orange
Pinch of nutmeg
1 2-inch stick cinnamon
½ cup lard
1 teaspoon sugar
Salt to taste
Canned stock, if necessary
½ cup rum or brandy

Place the turkey in a large kettle, cover with lightly salted water, and add bay leaves, the whole onion, and tomatoes. Cook until turkey is almost done, about 2 hours. Cool. Remove turkey, strain broth, and reserve stock. Cut turkey into serving pieces.

Rinse chilies and dry them on absorbent paper. Toast chilies lightly in an ungreased skillet. Remove the seeds and soak them in warm water or milk to cover until tender. Combine the seeds from the chilies, almonds, peanuts, and pumpkin seeds and roast lightly in the oven at 300°. Grind together the chili seeds, almonds, peanuts, pumpkin seeds, cloves, peppercorns, garlic, raisins, chopped onion, tortilla, white bread, 5 table-spoons of sesame seeds, anise seeds, chocolate, *epazote*, orange rind, nutmeg, and cinnamon. Add 1 quart of stock from the turkey and strain.

Heat lard in a large skillet and brown turkey lightly. Remove. Add the strained sauce, sugar, and salt to the lard. Cook, stir-ring often, until sauce is thick. Add the remaining broth, using canned stock to make 2½ quarts if necessary. Put turkey in mixture and cook another 30–45 minutes on a slow flame until sauce is thick and turkey is done and heated through. Put tur-key on platter and sprinkle it with remaining sesame seeds. Heat rum or brandy and douse turkey; ignite when serving.

VARIATION

To make this dish Oaxaca style, add 2 pounds of cut up spare-ribs to broth when turkey is being cooked. When spices are added, include 1 tablespoon of orégano. When turkey is returned to the skillet, so are the ribs.

NOTE: You can also make this dish with chicken.

MOLE DE GUAJOLOTE II (*Turkey Mole*)
Serves 8

1 turkey, 6–8 pounds	*½ cup almonds*
1 onion, whole	*¼ cup salted peanuts,*
2 teaspoons salt	*shelled*
½ cup olive oil	*8 tomatoes*
3 green peppers	*½ teaspoon cinnamon*
2 tablespoons sesame seeds	*½ teaspoon pepper*
½ teaspoon anise seeds	*Chili powder to taste*
6 cloves of garlic	*2 ounces unsweetened*
1 slice dry white toast	*chocolate, grated*

Cut turkey into serving pieces. Cook the turkey pieces in water to cover, together with the onion and 1 teaspoon of the salt. Simmer until almost tender, about 1½ hours. Drain, reserving 2 cups of stock. Dry the turkey. Heat ¼ cup of olive oil in frying pan. Add turkey and brown on all sides. Remove turkey and place in a heavy pot.

Grind together the green peppers, sesame seeds, anise seeds, garlic, toast, almonds, peanuts, and tomatoes. Add the cinnamon, remaining salt, pepper, chili powder, and chocolate, and blend well. Heat the remaining oil and add the mixture to it. Cook over low heat for 5 minutes, stirring constantly. Place the pot over a low heat and pour the 2 cups of stock over the turkey. Spread the chocolate mixture over the turkey. Cover and cook for 2 hours. Baste occasionally.

CUNETE DE PAVO (*Spiced Cold Turkey*)
Serves 4–6

1 6–8-pound turkey, cut
into serving pieces
¼ cup shortening
3 onions
5½ cups vinegar
4 cups olive oil
8 black peppercorns
3 whole cloves
1 bay leaf

¼ teaspoon thyme
½ teaspoon ground
cinnamon
2 teaspoons salt (or more
to taste)
Flour with enough water to
make a heavy paste
3 sweet red peppers
½ cup pitted green olives

Brown turkey in shortening with the onions. Place in an enameled deep soup pan with the vinegar, oil, herbs, and seasonings. Cover tightly and seal the cover well with a paste made of flour and water so that it is completely airtight. Cook very gently for about 3 hours, shaking the pan from time to time to prevent scorching. Do not uncover. Cool and uncover. Pour off stock and refrigerate to form an aspic. Refrigerate turkey. When serving, arrange turkey in the center of the platter; decorate aspic with sweet red peppers and olives.

VARIATION

This dish can be made by refrigerating the turkey overnight in the stock, right in the pot. When thoroughly chilled, garnish and serve right out of the kettle, icy cold. The dish will keep for several days in the refrigerator.

ALBONDIGAS DE GUAJOLOTE
(*Ground Turkey*) Serves 4–5

This is a superb South of the Border solution to the leftover turkey problem. It could be very handy the day after Thanksgiving up North. It's good as a main dish and splendid when made into small balls for hot hors d'oeuvres.

3 slices bread (*more may be necessary*)

8¾ cups boiling salted broth (*turkey or chicken*)

3 cups chopped, cooked turkey (*chicken may be used*)

3 eggs

1½ teaspoons minced parsley

1 teaspoon salt

¾ teaspoon ground coriander

¼ teaspoon ground cloves

Pinch of nutmeg

¼ cup dry sherry

2 tablespoons butter

¾ cup almonds, blanched and ground well

1 green pepper, seeded and chopped

1 avocado, cut into small cubes (*optional*)

Soak bread in ¾ cup of the hot broth; drain well. Grind the turkey and the bread; add the eggs and mix well. Add the seasonings and mix again until well blended. Form into balls the size of a walnut, adding more ground bread, if necessary, to get balls to hold together. Bring the 8 cups broth to a boil. Stir in the sherry. Add the butter to the broth and sherry. Reduce to a gentle boil. Drop turkey balls carefully into sherry-broth mixture. Reduce flame and simmer for about 20 minutes. Remove balls and keep them warm. Allow broth to boil down about half way, add ground almonds, and let cook in broth until the liquid thickens somewhat. Put turkey balls in broth. Cook for another 7–8 minutes, along with chopped green pepper, until balls are heated through and pepper is slightly softened but still crisp. Right before serving, drop cold avocado cubes into hot broth and turkey balls and serve.

NOTE: Do not use avocado if balls are made for cocktail use. The avocado will turn brown as the hors d'oeuvres stand.

PAVO RELLENO (*Stuffed Turkey*)   Serves 10–12

1 turkey, 12–15 pounds
Salt and pepper to taste
Juice of 1 lemon

STUFFING

4 slices bacon
1 large onion, chopped
¼ cup lard
3 pounds ground pork
½ cup tomato purée
½ cup black olives,
  coarsely chopped
¾ cup pine nuts
3 bananas, diced
3 apples, cored, peeled,
  and diced
6 Jalapeño chilies (*or any
  variety of small red or
  green hot peppers; or 5–
  6 tablespoons chili
  powder*)

3 carrots, diced
½ cup raisins
¼ cup oil
¼ cup vinegar
2¼ teaspoons sugar
Salt, pepper, and powdered
  cinnamon to taste
3 cups meat stock (*use
  canned beef broth*)
1 bottle dry white wine
1 onion, sliced

Clean the turkey well and let stand in the refrigerator for 24 hours (or ask butcher to do this step for you). Rub turkey inside and out with salt, pepper, and lemon juice. For stuffing: dice and fry the bacon. Reserve fat. Sauté the chopped onion in the lard. Add the ground pork, tomato purée, chopped olives, pine nuts, bananas, apples, chilies, carrots, raisins, oil, vinegar, and sugar. Season with salt, pepper, and cinnamon. Simmer until thickened.

Stuff turkey with this mixture. Truss. Brown the bird in the bacon fat. Place, breast up, in a moderate oven (300°). Cover breast with double thickness of cheesecloth. Baste with meat stock and wine and surround the turkey with the sliced onion. Let roast until bird is tender, basting frequently. (Figure about 15–20 minutes to the pound.) Gravy should be thick when bird is done. If bird does not look brown enough, remove cheesecloth for last 30 minutes of cooking process.

NOTE: If there is any stuffing left over, form into very small meat balls and cook in gravy right along with turkey.

CREPAS DE POLLO (*Pancakes with Chicken, Mexican Style*) Makes about 16 pancakes

PANCAKES

3 eggs (4, if eggs are
small)
1½ cups milk
1¾ cups sifted flour

1½ teaspoons salt
2½ tablespoons butter,
melted

FILLING

2 cups chicken, cooked
and chopped (turkey
may be used)
1 small onion, minced
2 tablespoons pecans,
chopped

2 tablespoons raisins,
chopped
2 tablespoons blanched
almonds, chopped

SAUCE

Oil
1 small onion, minced fine
1 teaspoon chili powder
3 tablespoons green
pepper, chopped

1 can (no. 2½) tomatoes
Salt and pepper to taste

GARNISH

½ cup grated mild cheese

For pancakes: Beat eggs and add milk; mix in flour and salt. Add butter and stir well. Pour about ¼ cup of the batter into a 7-inch skillet which has been buttered. Tip the skillet so that the batter makes a thin layer over the bottom of the pan. When lightly brown on one side, turn and brown on the other. Repeat until all the batter is gone.

For filling: Mix together all the filling ingredients. Stir well.

Place a tablespoon of filling in each pancake and roll the pancake. Place seam side down in a buttered baking dish.

To make sauce: Heat oil in skillet; cook onion in oil until transparent and soft. Mix in chili powder, green pepper, tomatoes, salt, and pepper and simmer about 5–6 minutes to blend. Pour sauce over all the pancakes. Top with grated mild cheese. Bake at 325° for 20 minutes or until cheese is bubbly.

POLLO TABASQUENA (*Chicken, Tabasco Style*)
Serves 6

From the tropical gulf coast state of Tabasco comes this unusual chicken dish.

*1 roasting chicken, 4½–
5 pounds, cut up into
serving pieces*
*Juice of 1 lime or ½
lemon*
1 tablespoon salt
¼ cup shortening
*3 medium-sized onions,
chopped*
*5 medium-sized tomatoes,
peeled, chopped, and
drained*
*2 tablespoons ripe olives,
chopped*
1 anchovy, chopped
*2 tablespoons seedless
raisins*
*2 tablespoons prunes,
pitted and chopped*

*¼ pound ham, cut into
slivers*
*6 cloves of garlic, minced
well*
*3 tablespoons dry white
wine*
2 tablespoons olive oil
Freshly ground pepper
*½ teaspoon ground
cinnamon*
*1½ cups chicken broth
(canned may be used)*
*½ cup almonds, cut into
slivers*
*2 ounces canned pimientos,
cut into strips*

Rub chicken in lime juice and sprinkle with salt. Sauté in shortening until golden brown. Add all other ingredients except broth, almonds, and pimientos. Sauté for about 10 minutes, turning frequently. Add the chicken broth. Cover. Simmer until chicken is tender, 1 hour or longer. Add a small amount of chicken broth or warm water if liquid appears scant. Serve on platter, pour sauce over chicken and decorate with almonds and pimientos.

MANCHA MANTELES (*Tablecloth Stainers*)
Serves 7–8

1 pound lean pork loin, cubed
1 tablespoon oil
1 tablespoon butter
1 4–5-pound roasting chicken, cut into serving pieces
1 tablespoon blanched almonds
3 teaspoons sesame seeds
1 medium-sized onion, chopped well
1 medium green pepper, chopped well
1 cup (8-ounce can) tomato sauce
4 cups chicken broth (canned broth may be used)

1 tablespoon chili powder
4 tablespoons sugar
3 tablespoons white wine
¼ teaspoon cinnamon
3 whole cloves
1 bay leaf
Salt to taste
1 medium-sized sweet potato, cut into cubes
1 apple, peeled, cored, and cubed
1 cup pineapple, cubed (canned, well drained may be used)
2 bananas, sliced (optional)

Brown pork in skillet in a mixture of oil and butter. Remove. Brown chicken in same drippings. Remove. Lightly sauté almonds and 1 teaspoon sesame seeds in the same fat. Stir in onion and green pepper. Sauté a few minutes more. Add tomato sauce. Mix in an electric blender or put through food grinder until smooth. Combine the ground mixture with the broth, chili powder, sugar, white wine, cinnamon, cloves, bay leaf, and salt. Cook for about 15 minutes. Strain. Pour sauce over the chicken and pork. Simmer for ¾ hour. Add sweet potato. Cook gently for 15 minutes. Drop in the apple and pineapple. Simmer for another 10–15 minutes. Serve hot in deep soup plates, slicing the bananas right into the hot stew and sprinkling with remaining sesame seeds before serving.

VARIATION

This recipe can also be made with Chorizo* or pork sausages instead of pork loin. Use 3 sausages, cut into small pieces. Brown them in lard; add enough water to cover bottom of skillet. Cover and steam for about 15–20 minutes. Then, proceed as above with chicken.

POLLO CON POBLANOS
(Chicken and Peppers) Serves 6

¼ cup cooking oil
4 onions, chopped
4 green bell peppers,
  parboiled and cut into
  large pieces
3 cups cooked chicken (or
  turkey), cut into cubes
½ pint sour cream

Salt and freshly ground
  pepper to taste
Dash of marjoram
Dash of thyme
1 cup grated mild Cheddar
  cheese
Parsley
Paprika

In a heavy skillet, heat the cooking oil and sauté the chopped onions and pepper pieces. Add cubed chicken, sour cream, salt, pepper, marjoram, and thyme. Simmer but do not allow the mixture to boil. When hot, top with cheese, parsley, and paprika.

VARIATION

Want some more zest? Use hot peppers rather than sweet.

NOTE: This dish is very good with Arroz Clasico.*

PECHUGAS RELLENAS
(*Stuffed Chicken Breasts*) Serves 6–8

1 medium onion, chopped
  fine
1 clove of garlic, minced
⅔ stick butter
½ pound raw ham (do
  not trim away all the
  fat)
¼ pound mushrooms,
  chopped
1 crusty roll, cut into small
  cubes

Salt and pepper to taste
Dash of cinnamon
Dash of cloves
White wine to moisten
  dressing
6–8 large chicken breasts,
  boned (but not split in
  half)

Cook onion and garlic in butter until wilted; stir in ham and mushrooms. Cook until mushrooms are tender. Add roll cubes. Season to taste with salt, pepper, cinnamon, and cloves. Add white wine to moisten the dressing so it is slightly wet. It should not be too loose. Fill chicken breasts, skewer tightly, and tie with string. Dot butter on chicken breasts and roast at 325° until tender, about ¾ hour or more.

NOTE: Most butchers will bone chicken breasts, but here's how, in case you have to do your own. Place chicken breast on a flat surface, skin side up. Cut in half or leave whole. Pull off the skin with the fingers. It will come off easily. Turn breast over and flatten it by gently pressing down on it, if breast is whole. With a paring knife, make a small incision between the meat and the breast bone at the thinnest part of the outer edge of the breast, where bone appears to attach. Using fingers and knife, carefully pull and scrape away the meat from the bones, taking care not to tear the meat. If the tendon that runs about two-thirds of the way down the center of the breast has not been removed by the butcher, slip a knife under it gently and remove. Trim away any jagged edges. Flatten again with heavy knife. Use immediately or store in the refrigerator and use in a few hours. Breasts can be frozen if wrapped well.

POLLO ESTILO YUCATAN
(*Chicken, Yucatán Style*) Serves 4

In the Yucatán, chicken is frequently steamed or baked in a bed of banana leaves. However, short of robbing an exotic florist shop or finding one or two of the rare banana trees which grow in private gardens north of the border, the best thing is to steam the chicken in a tightly covered pan.

2 broiling chickens, 1½
  pounds each, halved
3 tablespoons butter
Salt and freshly ground
  pepper to taste
2 cloves of garlic
¼ teaspoon ground
  cinnamon
¼ teaspoon ground cloves
Pinch of epazote (if
  available)

½ teaspoon chili powder
1 toasted white roll
1 cup tomato-and-onion
  purée (1 cup tomato
  purée mixed with ½
  teaspoon onion juice)
1 teaspoon lemon juice
Pinch of saffron
½ cup sweet dessert wine

Brush the chickens with half of the butter which has been melted. Season with salt and pepper and broil until browned on both sides. Melt the rest of the butter in a saucepan, brown the garlic in it, and discard them. Grind together the spices and the roll and add to butter in pan. Add the tomato-onion purée and lemon juice, and cook 5 minutes. Add the broiled chicken, saffron, and wine. Cook until chicken is done and sauce is thick, 30–40 minutes. Serve hot.

CHICKEN LA BODEGA Serves 4

3 pounds chicken legs and
   breasts
1 teaspoon salt
1 teaspoon paprika
½ cup olive oil
1 tablespoon butter
3 tablespoons powered
   saffron
1 cup uncooked rice

1 can (12 ounces)
   chicken broth
3–4 bay leaves
1 small jar (2 ounces)
   pimientos, chopped
1 cup ripe olives, pitted
   and chopped
1 cup peas

Season chicken with salt and paprika. Sauté in olive oil slowly until lightly browned. Melt the butter. Mix in the saffron and add the rice. Cook the rice for 10 minutes, turning once or twice with a spatula. Add broth. Cover. Simmer for 15 minutes. Place bay leaves on the bottom of a casserole and add the rice, chicken, pimientos, and olives. Cover. Bake at 350° for about 1 hour or until the chicken and rice are tender. Add warm water if liquid appears too scant. Around 15 minutes before the chicken is done, add the peas.

POLLO EN JUGO DE NARANJA
(Chicken in Orange Juice) Serves 3–4

1 cup orange juice (fresh,
   frozen, or canned)
½ cup raisins
½ cup crushed pineapple,
   drained
2 tablespoons sugar
1 teaspoon cinnamon
½ teaspoon ground cloves
1 cup dry white wine
1 fryer, cut into serving
   pieces

Seasoned flour for
   dredging (⅔ cup flour,
   3 teaspoons salt, ½
   teaspoon pepper)
Small amount of
   shortening
¼ cup chopped nuts,
   toasted

Combine all ingredients except the chicken, flour, shortening, and nuts. Dredge the chicken in the seasoned flour and sauté in the shortening until well browned, turning now and then. Transfer the chicken to casserole or glass baking dish. Pour over sauce and bake at 325° for 15 minutes; raise heat to 350° and finish baking, about another 20 minutes. Top with nuts and add more salt and pepper if necessary.

POLLO A LA CREMA (*Creamed Chicken*)
Serves 4–5

We thank Angela de León Pérez for this delightful chicken in cream sauce.

1 chicken, cut into serving
*   pieces*
Salt and pepper to taste
Shortening
1 cup white sauce, made
*   according to your*
*   favorite recipe*

2 egg yolks, well beaten
1 8-ounce package noodles
¼ cup grated mild cheese
1 teaspoon meat extract
½ pint sweet cream
Watercress

Disjoint the chicken, season with salt and pepper, and sauté in shortening until golden brown and almost done. Turn once or twice to brown evenly. When almost done, remove chicken from bones and cut into chunks.

Prepare a rich white sauce according to your favorite recipe and add to it 2 well-beaten egg yolks. Cook noodles according to directions on package and add white sauce, salt, pepper, grated cheese, and meat extract, and pour into a buttered ring mold. Heat in a 350° oven over a pan of hot water for about ½ hour or until mold is firm.

Place chicken pieces in cream and heat, but do not allow the cream to boil. Unmold the noodles and fill with creamed chicken in the center. Garnish with watercress.

POLLO EN PANTALONES (*Chicken in Trousers*)
Serves 6–8

8 small drumsticks	Chili powder to taste
2 tablespoons parsley, chopped fine	Garlic salt to taste
	Pepper to taste
1 teaspoon orégano	Juice of 2 limes

Season pieces of chicken with parsley, orégano, chili powder, garlic salt, pepper, and lime juice. Let stand for 1 hour while making the following batter and sauce.

BATTER

1 egg	1 teaspoon orégano
¾ cup water	2 teaspoons parsley, chopped fine
1½ cups sifted flour	
½ teaspoon salt	1 teaspoon ground ginger
1 teaspoon baking soda	Shortening for frying
1 teaspoon chili powder	

SAUCE

2 cups tomato-onion purée (*Mix together 2 cups tomato purée and 1 teaspoon onion juice*)	2 tablespoons dry white wine
	1 small (4-ounce) can pimientos, cut into strips
1 clove garlic, mashed	

To prepare batter: Beat until smooth and fairly thickened the egg, water, flour, salt, soda, chili powder, orégano, parsley, and ginger. Dip the chicken, a drumstick at a time, into the batter, so that each piece is well covered. Drop into hot fat (370°–375°) and cook until chicken is done. The crust should be a deep golden brown. Drain on absorbent paper and serve with the sauce.

To prepare sauce: Simply combine all the sauce ingredients. Simmer gently about 15 minutes or until flavors are blended. Garnish with a light sprinkling of parsley.

POLLO EN NOGADA (*Chicken in Walnut Sauce*)
Serves 4–5

1 broiling chicken, about
2–3 pounds, cut into
serving pieces

1 stalk celery
1 8-ounce can tomatoes

Put chicken in kettle and cover with lightly salted boiling water, add stalk of celery and can of tomatoes, and simmer until almost done—35–40 minutes. When chicken is almost tender, remove from broth, reserving the stock, and make the following sauce:

6 ancho *chilies (can be*
found in Mexican food
stores)
2 tablespoons lard
1 slice white bread, cubed
½ cup chopped walnuts
¼ teaspoon ground
cinnamon
½ bay leaf
2 cloves

Freshly ground pepper and
salt to taste
2 cloves of garlic
2 medium-sized onions,
chopped
2½ cups stock (use stock
from chicken, or canned
broth)
½ cup white wine

If *ancho* chilies are used, toast in oven for a few minutes, clean them of veins and seeds, and soak outer skins in warm water until tender.

In half of the shortening fry the bread and walnuts until lightly browned. Grind together the bread and walnuts with the spices, garlic, onions, and chilies. Mix well. Add these ingredients to the soup stock along with the wine and the rest of the shortening. Cook until mixture reaches the boiling point. Add the chicken pieces and additional salt and freshly ground pepper to taste. Let simmer until sauce is thickened and chicken is completely done, about 15 minutes–½ hour.

POLLO CON CHORIZOS (*Chicken with Sausages*)
Serves 4

2–3 Chorizos* or pork
sausages
1 fryer, 3–4 pounds, cut
into serving pieces
¼ cup white wine
¼ teaspoon ground
cinnamon
Pinch of ground cloves
¼ teaspoon freshly ground
pepper

2 cups boiling water in
which 1 chicken
bouillon cube has been
dissolved
3 tablespoons butter
1 crusty roll, split in half,
toasted, and ground
1 tablespoon sesame seeds,
toasted lightly in oven

Slice sausages. Place in saucepan with chicken, wine, and spices and let stand 2 or 3 hours. Add water with bouillon cube dissolved in it. Add butter and ground roll. Cook until tender, about 1 hour or a little more, adding water if liquid in the pan appears to be scant. Serve garnished with hot toasted sesame seeds.

PASTEL DE POLLO (*Chicken Pie*)   Serves 4

½ pound raw ham
1 tablespoon butter
1 small onion, chopped
1 8-ounce can tomatoes,
chopped
Salt and pepper to taste
1 clove
2 eggs, beaten lightly
1 tablespoon chopped
parsley
2 teaspoons chili powder
(or more to taste)

½ cup cooked peas and
corn, mixed (fresh or
frozen; or Limas can be
used)
1½ cups cooked chicken,
cut into bite-size chunks
Piecrust to fit 9-inch pan,
bottom and top, as
directed

Sauté ham until done and set aside. In butter sauté the onion until soft and transparent. Add tomatoes, salt and pepper, and clove and cook until thickened. Discard clove. Add all other ingredients and mix well. Line 9-inch pie plate with pastry. Pour filling in shell. Cut another strip of pastry about 2½ inches wide and long enough to fit all around the edge of the pie plate. Dampen edge of lower crust with milk or water. Place the strip of dough on top all the way around the pie, sealing it firmly to lower crust with tines of a fork but leaving center of pie open. Bake at 375° for ½ hour or until golden brown.

PASTEL DE TAMALES Y POLLO
(Tamale Chicken Pie)   Serves 4–6

18 canned tamales
1 cup tomato-onion purée
   (mix together 1 cup
   tomato purée and ½
   teaspoon onion juice)
¾ cup chicken consommé
   (canned may be used)
1 cup sour cream
3 tablespoons sherry

2 cups cooked chicken,
   cubed
1 teaspoon chili powder
1 cup grated mild cheese
   (Parmesan or similar
   type)
Salt
Pepper

Butter a shallow casserole well. Slice tamales lengthwise. Line casserole with 1 layer of tamale slices. Mix all other ingredients well. Put a layer of the chicken mixture on top of the first tamale layer; top with a layer of tamale slices. Repeat layers until all ingredients are used up. Top with grated cheese and bake in a moderate oven at 350° until thoroughly heated, about ¾ hour. Serve right away.

PATO A LA VERACRUZANA
(*Duck, Veracruz Style*)   Serves 4

A recipe from the gulf coast state of Mexico.

4–5-pound duck, cut into serving portions	*8 ounces almonds, blanched and ground*
3 cups water to cover duck	*2 cloves of garlic, minced well*
1 tablespoon salt	*½ teaspoon cumin powder*
Pepper to taste	*1 egg yolk, beaten well*
2 tablespoons lard	*2 cloves*

Cover duck with 3 cups of water, add salt and pepper, and cook until tender. Melt lard. Combine almonds, garlic, cumin powder, and egg yolk. Cook this mixture in the lard slowly, stirring constantly, for about 5 minutes. Drain duck. Reserve liquid. Add 1½ cups of the liquid to the egg mixture. Simmer slowly until sauce becomes thick. Stir occasionally. Add the duck and cloves and continue to cook until duck is heated through. Remove cloves.

PATO EN JUGO DE NARANJA
(*Duck in Orange Juice*)   Serves 4–5

1 5-pound duck, cut into serving pieces	*2 tablespoons seedless raisins*
3 cups orange juice	*Sprig of parsley*
½ cup dry red wine	*2 bay leaves*
2 onions, chopped	*Pinch of thyme*
4 tomatoes, chopped	*Pinch of marjoram*
2 cloves garlic, chopped	*Salt to taste*
¼ cup almonds, sliced thin	*Flour*

Wash duck well and dry with absorbent paper towels. Place in a large kettle and add the rest of the ingredients except the flour. Cover the pot. Seal it with a heavy flour-and-water paste to make it airtight. Cook over a low flame for 3 hours. Shake the pot frequently to prevent sticking, but do not uncover it. Serve the duck hot in this gravy.

CONEJO A LA ESPANOLA
(Rabbit, Spanish Style)   Serves 4–6

1 rabbit, cut into serving
   pieces
Flour, salt, and pepper for
   dredging rabbit pieces
   (for 2½-pound rabbit
   use ⅔ cup sifted flour,
   3 teaspoons salt, and
   ½ teaspoon pepper;
   vary for larger rabbit)
3 slices bacon

1 clove of garlic
2 medium-sized onions,
   minced
1 bay leaf
Pinch of thyme
1 cup dry white wine
1 tablespoon lemon juice
2 tomatoes, peeled and
   chopped

Dredge rabbit in seasoned flour. Fry bacon in heavy skillet until crisp. Remove, and in the bacon fat brown the rabbit pieces well with clove of garlic. When rabbit is brown, discard garlic clove. Add the rest of the ingredients and transfer to a kettle with a tight-fitting cover. Simmer, covered, for about 1 hour or until tender.

TORTOLAS BORRACHOS (*Drunken Turtledoves*)
Serves 8

The theory behind this very old Mexican recipe is that the birds get tipsy by sipping on the wine in the pan. Substitute squab or Rock Cornish game hens, if you so desire.

8 turtledoves
½ cup fat
½ cup warm brandy
5 medium-sized tomatoes, peeled
1 slice toasted white bread, cubed
½ cup blanched almonds, in slivers
1 clove of garlic, crushed
2 teaspoons minced parsley

2 cups dry red wine
¼ cup raisins
20 medium-sized ripe olives, sliced into rings
2½ teaspoons grated lemon rind
Salt, pepper, ground cinnamon, and cloves to taste
8 strips bacon (*optional*)

Brown the birds in the ½ cup fat and put them in a casserole. Heat the brandy and pour it over the birds; ignite, let flame for a minute or 2, and extinguish the flame. Remove birds and keep warm in a casserole. In the same browning pan, sauté the tomatoes, bread cubes, almonds, garlic, and parsley. Cook together 5 or 6 minutes. Add the wine, raisins, olives, and lemon rind. Season with salt, pepper, cinnamon, and cloves to taste and simmer for a minute or 2 to blend. Pour liquid over birds and cook, uncovered, breast side up, at 325° for about 45 minutes or an hour until done, basting occasionally with juices in the pan. (A strip of bacon can be placed on each bird's breast for additional flavor before roasting.)

Barbacoa

❖

(BARBECUE)

What a clambake is to a New Englander, the barbecue is to the Mexican. And it's a far cry from the chrome-plated grill-style cooking of the suburbanite.

At an authentic Mexican barbecue the food is cooked in a hole in the ground. Where the Yankees use seaweed, their neighbors South of the Border use maguey leaves to line the pit. It's a rather complicated process. The leaves are used to line a hole about four feet deep and also to enclose the meat. The lamb, kid, mutton, or side of beef cooks about five hours very slowly, wrapped securely in maguey leaves. Very frequently a broth is steeped right alongside the meat in the pit and it is served as an appetizer. When the food is served, mugs of *pulque*, an alcoholic beverage, go with it.

Possibly the best barbecue we've ever eaten was in Mexico City. This type of cooking is a specialty of the region and so we've included an authentic pit-style recipe from a Mexico City barbecue on the following pages. You may not want to dig your yard to try it, but it makes for interesting reading, anyway, as do the recipes for flavored *pulque*, which you probably won't be able to try because the beverage is not readily available in this country.

There are, indeed, lots of Mexicans who barbecue the modern way too. And so we've included some good dishes for your outdoor setup, whatever it might be. They are Asado al Pastor con Salsa Borracha* (Shepherd's Roast with Drunken Sauce), Pollo Adobado* (Spicy Chicken), Costillas con Chile* (Veal Chops with Chili), and Carne Molida con Queso* (Hamburgers with Cheese).

Be sure and serve ice-cold beer, *frijoles,* tortillas, and fresh sweet corn with these dishes. They go with them very well!

CARNE MOLIDA CON QUESO
(*Hamburgers with Cheese*)   Serves 6

2 pounds ground beef
2 teaspoons salt
½ teaspoon freshly ground
   pepper
½ cup dry red wine

1 small onion, minced
6 cubes sharp cheese
   (*Roquefort or its
   equivalent*), about the
   size of walnuts

Mix all ingredients except the cheese. Use all of the meat to form 12 patties. Put cube of cheese on each of 6 patties and top with remaining 6. Seal edges well. Flatten patties slightly. Put on hinged broiler grill and cook over hot coals for about 4 or 5 minutes for burgers on the rare side, longer for more well-done meat.

COSTILLAS CON CHILE (*Veal Chops with Chili*)
Serves 6

¼ teaspoon thyme leaves,
   crumbled
½ teaspoon ground cumin
   seeds
¼ teaspoon orégano,
   crumbled
1 teaspoon red chili
   powder
½ teaspoon cayenne
   pepper
1½ teaspoons salt

1 teaspoon white pepper
1 small onion, chopped
   well
⅓ cup dry red wine
¼ cup olive oil
¼ cup tomato purée
1 clove garlic, mashed
1 teaspoon lime juice
6 veal chops, cut about
   1½ inches thick

Combine all ingredients except veal to form a marinade. Put veal in marinade and allow to stand 3–4 hours. Cook the chops slowly over a charcoal fire until brown on both sides, basting with marinade from time to time when meat appears dry.

POLLO ADOBADO (*Spicy Chicken*)   Serves 2–4

½ cup dry vermouth   *Salt*
2½ teaspoons cinnamon   *1 frying chicken (about*
⅓ cup honey   * 2 pounds), disjointed*
2 tablespoons lime juice
1 small clove of garlic,
* crushed well*

Mix together vermouth, cinnamon, honey, lime juice, garlic, and salt to form marinade. Pour over disjointed chicken, turning pieces so that they are well coated. Let stand in the refrigerator for about 5 or 6 hours in the marinade. Remove and bring to room temperature. Broil chicken over charcoal basting with the marinade. Broil about 40 minutes, not too close to the coals. A little additional vermouth can be added to marinade if it becomes too thick while cooking.

ASADO AL PASTOR CON SALSA BORRACHA (*Shepherd's Roast with Drunken Sauce*) Serves 6

In Hidalgo, halves of mutton are hung over a wood fire and slowly turned until the meat is cooked and the outside is crisp and black. Toward the end of the cooking process, the roast is basted with lightly salted butter. It's served with Salsa Borracha, below.

FOR THE ROAST

Use a 5-pound leg of lamb and roast it on a spit over a charcoal fire until done the way you like it (1½–2 hours). Baste from time to time with lightly salted butter in which a clove of garlic has been crushed and a pinch of dry mustard added.

SAUCE

3–4 dried chili pasillas
(*available in Mexican
food stores*), *or 4
tablespoons chili
powder*
1½ cups tepid water
2 cloves garlic
½ cup olive oil
*1 large onion, cut into
chunks*
2 pickled Serrano *chilies
(available in Mexican
food stores), or any
small red or green hot
pepper*

*2 ounces dry grated cheese
(Parmesan or Romano
will do)*
8 tablespoons tequila
2¼ tablespoons salt
¼ teaspoon ground cloves
1 tablespoon dry red wine
½ tablespoon lime juice

In an ungreased skillet, cook the dried *chili pasillas* for a few minutes, turning occasionally to prevent burning. Skip this step if chili powder is used. Remove stems and seeds and cover them with the water, saving the skins. In about ¾ hour, put the chilies in a blender with the remaining ingredients and 4 tablespoons of the water in which the chili seeds were soaked. Blend all until smooth. Strain the remaining chili water and add to sauce. Serve, either by pouring a little over each portion of meat, or letting guests help themselves.

Add more chili powder or chilies for a hotter sauce.

BARBACOA MEXICANA
(*Barbecue from Mexico City*)

*1 lamb, cut into pieces:
backbone, legs, shoulders,
ribs, and head*

*Maguey leaves
Ingredients for Barbecue
Consommé**

To be very authentic, use a lamb which has been slaughtered the day before the cookout and hung overnight. On the day of the big event, the animal is split into sections: backbone, legs, shoulders, ribs, and head.

METHOD

We assume that no one would tackle this kind of barbecue without a large number of guests—the kind who really like to pitch in. So, the first thing to do is to set one group of your guests to digging a hole about four feet by two feet across. Other members of the party can scout up kindling and others can be set to work cleaning each maguey leaf.

Once the hole is dug, it is plastered with mud to keep the walls firm. Large porous stones should then be placed in the bottom of the pit (beware of little hard rocks; they'll split open). Over the stones put enough dry wood to fill the pit, then set fire to the wood and let it burn to the smokeless coal stage. While the fire is burning down, the maguey leaves should be toasted until limp, for this will enable them to release precious juices needed to season the meat.

When the fire has burned down sufficiently, line the pit with the maguey leaves, making sure that all of the mud is covered so meat will not stick to pit. The leaves should be suspended vertically, the tips overlapping all the way around and held down with stones for the moment. The next step is to lower a grate into the hole and on it place the casserole with soup ingredients. On top of the uncovered casserole ingredients, arrange the lamb pieces, starting with the backbone, then the legs, shoulders, rib sections, and the head. Do not salt meat before it is cooked, for this can toughen it.

After meat is in the pit, fold the tips of the maguey leaves into the hole to cover the meat well. Over this place a metal sheet to keep any earth from seeping into the pit and then seal the pit with a coat of fresh mud and build a large fire over the metal sheet and mud cover. Keep the fire blazing for 5 or 6 hours, depending upon the age of the meat. Open the pit, salt the meat before serving it, and accompany it with Salsa Borracha.* The broth is served in small cups.

CONSOMME DE BARBACOA
(*Barbecue Consommé*)

1 cup rice
1 cup chick-peas
½ pound potatoes, peeled
and sliced thin
2 carrots, sliced
3 chipotle *chilies*
(*available at Mexican
food stores*), *or chili
powder*

Pinch of epazote, *if
available*
1½ teaspoons salt
1 medium onion, chopped
(*optional*)

Soak the rice and chick-peas, drain, and place in a large earthenware *cazuela* (casserole) to be lowered into the pit. Add the potatoes, carrots, chilies or chili powder, *epazote,* salt, and onion. Place in pit, uncovered; the meat is put on top of the casserole. The meat drippings will combine with the broth ingredients to form a rich stock. Serve broth with the barbecued meat and the following pulques.

PULQUE DE NARANJA (*Orange Pulque*)

1 quart pulque
1⅓ cups orange juice
¾ cup sugar

Mix together the ingredients. Stir until sugar is dissolved and let stand for 3 hours in a cool place. Strain through cheesecloth or a fine sieve. Chill and serve.

PULQUE DE PIÑA (*Pineapple Pulque*)

1 pound fresh pineapple
1 cup sugar
1 quart pulque

Peel the pineapple and rinse it. Grind the pineapple and combine it with the sugar and pulque. Let stand for 2 hours in a cool place. Strain and chill before serving.

Salsas

❖

(SAUCES)

Throughout this book you'll find specific sauces indicated for specific dishes. This is important to mastering the art of Mexican cookery, for rich sauces are often an integral part of many of the country's most flavorsome dishes.

There are, however, a host of very good sauces which can be served separately, with a variety of foods, such as Salsa Para Pescado* (Sauce for Fish), Salsa de Perejil* (Parsley Sauce), and Salsa Rápida* (Quick Sauce). They'll complement fish, chicken, meats, and other foods as indicated, as will the other sauces on the following pages.

SALSA RAPIDA (*Quick Sauce*)   Yield: 1 cup

2 tomatoes, peeled and
  chopped
1 onion, peeled and
  chopped
1 clove garlic, crushed
1 small red hot pepper,
  chopped extra fine

3 sprigs fresh parsley
½ teaspoon coriander,
  ground
1 teaspoon salt
Dash of marjoram
Dash of ground cloves
Salt to taste

Mix the chopped vegetables and add the seasonings. Serve with meat or tortillas.

SALSA DE PEREJIL (*Parsley Sauce*)   Yield: ½ cup

1½ cups chopped fresh
  parsley
¼ cup vinegar
6½ tablespoons olive oil

1 teaspoon salt, or more
  to taste
Freshly ground pepper to
  taste

Stew the parsley in 1¼ cups of water on a low flame until tender. Drain. Grind the parsley and add the rest of the ingredients. Serve cold or warm, with chicken, fish, or baked meat.

NOTE: ¼ cup of nuts can be ground with the parsley, if so desired. Almonds should be blanched first, if used in this sauce.

A quick version of this can be made by omitting the water, reducing the amount of parsley to ¾ cup, and using nuts. No need to cook: just chop parsley and nuts well and combine with the rest of the ingredients.

SALSA PARA PESCADO (*Sauce for Fish*)
Yield: 1½ cups

¼ cup cooking oil
2 medium-sized onions, minced
2 tomatoes, peeled and chopped
2 small hot green chilies, peeled, seeded, and chopped
½ cup beef stock (canned may be used)
2 tablespoons orégano

1½ teaspoons salt
Sprig of epazote (*if available*)
½ teaspoon pepper
½ teaspoon basil leaves, or more to taste
¼ teaspoon ground cloves
4 tablespoons white wine at room temperature
12 green olives, pitted and chopped

Heat oil and sauté the onions until transparent. Add the tomatoes and chilies and sauté a few more minutes to blend. Add beef stock and spices. Cover and simmer for 10 minutes. Stir in wine and olives. Heat for another minute. Serve with fish, as a side dish.

SALSA DE CEBOLLA (*Onion Sauce*)
Yield: 3–4 cups

3 large onions
Salt and pepper to taste
1 medium-sized bunch of
  parsley
1 small sweet green
  pepper, seeded and
  chopped

1 slice toasted bread
1 tablespoon lemon juice
1 clove of garlic
2 cups chicken broth
  (canned may be used)
2 tablespoons cooking oil

Cook the onions in water to cover, seasoned with a little salt. When very soft, remove and drain them. Grind with parsley, green pepper, bread, lemon juice, and garlic. Mix with broth and add the salt and pepper. Heat the oil in a skillet. Add the onion mixture and cook on a low flame until slightly thickened. Good with meat or fish.

SALSA DE AJO (*Garlic Sauce*)   Yield: about 1 cup

3 tablespoons olive oil
6 cloves of garlic, peeled
3 tablespoons chopped
  parsley

Juice of 2 oranges
Juice of 1 lemon
½ teaspoon rosemary
Salt and pepper to taste

Heat oil. Add garlic and cook until browned. Discard garlic cloves. Add parsley, orange and lemon juices, rosemary, salt, and pepper. Cook until heated through. Spread over fish fillets before serving.

NOTE: For more of a garlic flavor, crush 3 of the cloves of garlic and leave 3 whole. Discard the whole cloves as indicated.

SALSA DE NUEZ (*Nut Sauce*)
Yield: about 3½–4 cups

¼ cup oil
1 hard roll, chopped into
  cubes
25 hazelnuts (comparable
  amount of walnuts or
  blanched almonds can
  be used)
3 sprigs of fresh parsley
1 clove of garlic
1 bay leaf
1 small onion
Dash of orégano
Dash of thyme
Salt and pepper to taste
1½ cups dry white wine
½ cup stock (canned may
  be used)

Heat oil in skillet and sauté roll cubes until well coated with oil and lightly browned. Remove from pan and grind with the rest of the ingredients except the wine and stock. Add the wine and stock and simmer for 10–15 minutes or until slightly thickened, stirring constantly. Serve with fish; also good with tongue, veal, or rabbit.

SALSA DE ALMENDRA (*Almond Sauce*)
Yield: 3 cups

⅔ cup almonds, blanched
1 tablespoon chopped
  parsley
3 hard-cooked egg yolks
½ teaspoon marjoram
1½ cups beef stock
  (canned may be used)
Salt and freshly ground
  pepper to taste

Toast almonds and grind them with the parsley. Mash the egg yolks. Mix well with the almonds, parsley, and marjoram. Add stock and simmer for 15–20 minutes, stirring frequently. Season with salt and pepper. Serve with meat or chicken.

SALSA VERDE (*Green Sauce*)   Yield: about 6 cups

1 small can (4 ounces)
 hot green chilies
6 tablespoons olive oil
2 onions, chopped coarsely
2 sweet green bell
 peppers, chopped
 coarsely
4 beef or chicken bouillon
 cubes

4 cups of hot water
4 cumin seeds
3 tablespoons chopped
 fresh parsley
½ cup cornstarch mixed
 with 1 cup cold water

Drain the canned chilies, remove any seeds, discard membranes. Place the oil in a skillet; heat and sauté the onions and green peppers until transparent, stirring frequently. Dissolve the bouillon cubes in 4 cups of hot water and add the cumin and the parsley. Combine the vegetables and mix in electric blender until puréed, or push through a food grinder a number of times until smooth. Remove to a saucepan and simmer for about 15 minutes, stirring occasionally. Mix the cornstarch with 1 cup of cold water and add to the sauce. Cook, stirring constantly, until mixture thickens. Use as a sauce when making chicken or beef enchiladas (Enchiladas con Carne*).

SALSA SENCILLA PARA TOSTADAS Y TACOS (*Simple Sauce for Tostadas and Tacos*)
Yield: about 3 cups

2 cups (or 2 8-ounce
 cans) tomato sauce
2 small canned hot green
 chilies, chopped (*remove
 seeds and membranes*)

3 teaspoons olive oil
3 teaspoons vinegar
1 teaspoon orégano
Dash of cumin powder
Salt to taste

Combine the above and mix thoroughly until blended.

SALSA DE SEMILLAS DE CALABAZA
(*Pumpkin Seed Sauce*)   Yield: about 5 cups

*¼ cup toasted pumpkin
seeds
4 small hot chilies, green
or red
1 cup freshly chopped
parsley
4 cups warm chicken or
beef stock (in which 1
chicken or beef bouillon
cube has been dissolved)*

*4 tablespoons olive oil
Salt and freshly ground
pepper to taste*

Grind the first 3 ingredients until almost liquid in consistency (easy in electric blender). Add ½ cup of the stock and strain. Heat the oil in a deep pan and add the remaining stock and the pumpkin seed mixture, salt, and pepper. Heat to the boiling point, reduce heat, and simmer a few seconds to blend the flavors well. Stir constantly while heating. Serve with chicken or fish.

SALSA DE TOMATE (*Tomato Sauce*)
Yield: about 4 cups

For veal or tongue.

*1 onion
2 pounds very ripe
tomatoes
2 tablespoons olive oil
1 clove of garlic
1 cup beef stock (canned
may be used)
1 bay leaf, crumbled
½ tablespoon freshly
chopped parsley*

*1 tablespoon orégano
1 teaspoon sugar
¼ teaspoon thyme
Salt to taste
1 dozen green olives,
pitted and sliced
(optional)*

Chop the onion well. Singe the tomatoes over an open flame and peel and chop them. Heat oil and sauté the onion and clove of garlic until onion is soft and transparent but not brown. Discard garlic. Add tomatoes, stock, bay leaf, parsley, orégano, sugar, thyme, and salt to taste. Cook until slightly thickened. Add the olive rings.

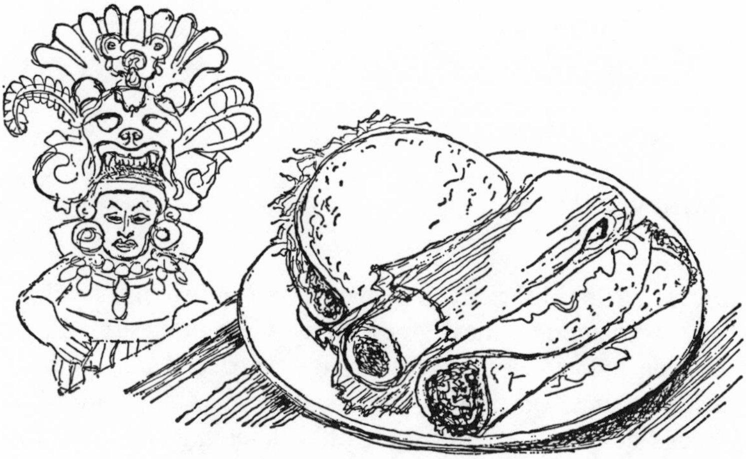

Enchiladas, Tacos, Tamales, Tostadas, Empanadas

Antojitos: all the dishes in this chapter fall under that heading and the word literally means capricious whim or desire. We've never been able to decide whether the Mexicans meant them to satisfy whims, or created them many years ago out of a capricious desire for something a little different. Whatever the case, they've been in the Mexican diet since colonial days, or around the sixteenth century, although the tortilla, which is the base for many of these snacks, has been around a lot longer than that.

Antojitos are popular for that late evening meal of the day and they are featured at fairs, bazaars, and festivals. Indeed, every housewife has her favorite *antojito*. Every village, town, and city has a specialty in this line. We are fond of Gorditas* (fat-stuffed tortillas), Enchiladas* of all kinds, but especially those we've eaten in Taxco, Tacos de Rajas* (tacos with a rich pepper filling), and Empanadas* (Turnovers) with almost any kind of filling, piquant or sweet.

As we've said, many of these dishes are made from tortillas —flat little corncakes. Tortillas are best when made with masa or *nixtamalina* (special corn meal), and they are rather difficult to whip up at home, but we've included a recipe you can try which we've especially adapted for the modern American kitchen. There are very few Mexican women these days who make their own tortillas the old-fashioned way by grinding their own corn meal. They, too, buy them ready made. And, to clear up one more misconception about tortillas, they are not the only breads served in Mexico. Indeed, the rich assortment of breads and pastries in that country are guaranteed to make the most conscientious calorie-counter forget about arithmetic.

NOTE: In the following recipes we have indicated the number of tortillas, tacos, *etc.*, rather than the servings. The number of servings would depend on whether the dish is to be an appetizer, main dish, or snack.

TORTILLAS About 1½ dozen tortillas

This is not an authentic recipe, but it's a good one. Remember that tortillas are always served hot. If you use canned or other ready-made tortillas, be sure and sprinkle them with a little bit of water to freshen them, and pop them in the oven right before serving. We like to heat tortillas in the broiler with the flame turned down low. Be sure and turn them often or you'll end up with imitation tostadas, not tortillas.

2 eggs
½–¾ teaspoon salt
5½ tablespoons white
* corn meal*
¾ cup cornstarch

1 cup milk (at room
* temperature)*
2 tablespoons melted
* cooking oil or butter*

Beat the eggs and salt together, add the corn meal, and mix well. Combine the cornstarch and milk and form a smooth batter. Add the eggs, salt and corn meal and mix again until smooth. Add the melted shortening, stirring constantly. Grease a seven-inch skillet and heat it. Pour a small amount of the batter on the bottom of the skillet, tilting the pan to make sure that the batter covers the bottom evenly. When brown on one side, flip over and brown. Tortillas should be almost paper thin.

TORTILLAS DE HARINA (*Flour Tortillas*)
Makes 12–14 tortillas

There are places in Mexico where tortillas are made as follows:

4 cups flour
1½ teaspoons salt
¼ pound butter, or ½ cup shortening

Sift together the dry ingredients. Cut in the shortening and mix well. Add enough tepid water to form a soft dough. Turn onto a lightly floured board and knead a few times. Divide into 14 balls the size of an egg, cover with a cloth, and let stand for about 20 minutes. Roll out the balls into flat pancakes or tortillas. Cook in an ungreased skillet over a moderate flame; turn once.

NOTE: Tortillas made with flour can be made on the sweet side too—rather like crepes. Eliminate the salt and add about ½ cup sugar instead.

TACOS

Tacos are simply tortillas filled with fish, meat, or other tidbits and rolled up and fried, grilled, or baked. If you bake them, you can so do in advance and reheat them before serving time. The simplest taco requires no cooking at all—it's just a fresh tortilla wrapped around some filling. We've included a number of recipes for tacos on the following pages, but that's not all. You'll find others in the cocktail section of this book. Be sure and try them too.

TACOS CON CARNE MOLIDA
(*Tacos with Ground Meat*) Makes 12

FILLING

2 tablespoons shortening
1 pound ground beef
1 small green pepper,
 chopped
1 medium onion, minced
1 large potato, cooked and
 diced
1 cup tomatoes (8-ounce
 can), chopped

½ teaspoon sugar
1 tablespoon chili powder
1 teaspoon coriander
Salt and pepper to taste
½ cup green
 pimiento-stuffed olives,
 chopped
Fat for frying

GARNISHES

lettuce
tomato wedges
oil-and-vinegar dressing

Heat shortening in a heavy skillet, brown the meat with the green pepper and onion until onion is transparent, pepper is soft, and the meat nearly cooked through. Add the potato, tomatoes, sugar, chili powder, coriander, salt, and pepper and stir to blend, cooking a few minutes more. Mix in the olives. Cook for about 10 more minutes, stirring constantly. Heat the tortillas to soften them, place some of the meat on each tortilla, spread it out, roll the tortilla, and fasten with toothpicks. Fry in hot oil until crisp. Serve with lettuce and tomatoes which have been drenched in your favorite oil-and-vinegar dressing. Mexicans place the lettuce and tomatoes right on top of the taco.

TACOS DE LUJO (*De luxe Tacos*)　Makes 6

6 slices any mild cheese
6 Tortillas*
Small amount flour
Pinch of powdered ginger
Pinch of salt and pinch of
　pepper
1 egg, lightly beaten
¾ cup shortening (*more
　or less*)

1 small onion, chopped
　well
2 tomatoes, peeled and
　chopped
Dash of Tabasco
Salt and pepper to taste
1 beef bouillon cube,
　dissolved in 1 cup
　boiling water

Place a slice of cheese on each tortilla. Fold and fasten with toothpicks. Roll in the flour, to which ginger, salt, and pepper have been added. Dip into beaten egg. Sauté in shortening until golden brown. Melt about 2 teaspoons of shortening in a heavy skillet and sauté the onion until wilted; add the tomatoes, Tabasco, salt, and pepper. Cook about 10 minutes on a very low flame to blend the flavors. Add the bouillon and cook until stock has reduced enough to produce a fairly thick sauce. Dip the tortillas in the sauce and sauté very slowly again for a few minutes.

TACOS DE RAJAS (*Tacos with Peppers*)
Makes 6

½ cup oil or other
　shortening
1 large onion, minced
　very well
3 green peppers, cubed

2 tomatoes, peeled and cut
　in very small cubes
½ cup sour cream
Salt and pepper to taste
6 Tortillas*

Heat one-quarter of the shortening in a heavy skillet and sauté the onion and peppers until softened. Add the tomatoes and cook just long enough for tomatoes to heat through. Remove skillet from fire and add the sour cream, salt, and pepper, stirring constantly. Heat mixture again, but do not boil or you may cause the cream to curdle. Put a tablespoon of the mixture on each tortilla, fold, and fasten with toothpicks. Fry in the rest of the shortening until golden.

SAUCE

1 tablespoon shortening	*Salt and pepper to taste*
1 small onion, minced	*¼ teaspoon orégano*
1 small tomato, peeled and chopped fine	

Melt the shortening in a skillet. Cook the other ingredients in it to blend and serve with the above tacos.

TACOS CON CHORIZO *(Sausage-stuffed Tacos)*
Makes 12

4 Chorizo* sausages, or ½–¾ pound chorizo	*Salt*
¾ cup cooked corn	*12 Tortillas**
¾ cup cooked Lima beans	*Shortening for frying (about ¾ cup)*
1–2 tablespoons red or green hot chili pepper, chopped	*3 hard-cooked eggs, sliced*

After removing the sausage from the casing, crumble it and sauté in heavy skillet, without any fat. When the sausage is crisp, add the corn, Lima beans, peppers, and salt. Heat tortillas in the oven to soften them and put some of the filling on each tortilla. Roll and fasten with toothpicks. Fry in hot fat until golden brown and crispy. Top each taco with hard-cooked egg slices and serve with this sauce:

SAUCE

1 sweet pepper, chopped
¼ cup water
1 small onion, chopped
½ cup tomato purée
Salt and pepper to taste

¼ teaspoon thyme
1½ teaspoons Jalapeño
  sauce, or more to taste
(Jalapeño *sauce is*
  available in cans)

Combine all ingredients and simmer about 10 minutes.

TACOS DE GUAJOLOTE (*Turkey Tacos*)
Makes 12

This is a delightful way to use up leftover turkey.

1 small onion, minced
  well
2 tablespoons butter
1 8-ounce can tomatoes,
  well chopped
2 small hot peppers, red
  or green, chopped well

2 cups cooked turkey,
  cubed
½ cup walnuts, chopped
12 Tortillas*
Shortening for sautéing
Salt to taste

GARNISHES

avocado slices
tomato slices
hard-cooked eggs

Wilt onion in butter, add the tomatoes, and simmer for about 5 minutes. Stir in the peppers, turkey, salt, and nuts. Warm the tortillas to make them pliable. Put some filling on each one, roll, fasten with picks, and fry to desired degree of doneness. Garnish with avocado slices, tomatoes, and sliced hard-cooked eggs.

NOTE: Chicken can be used in this too.

TACOS NACIONALES (*National Tacos*)   Makes 12

These tacos are so named because they resemble the Mexican flag in color scheme.

*1 dozen Tortillas**

FILLING

2 cups chicken or turkey, minced
4 tablespoons cream cheese, softened with a few drops of milk
¼ cup blanched almonds, chopped
Salt and pepper
Oil

SAUCE

1½ tablespoons olive oil
1 green onion, minced well, including the tops
1 small can tomato sauce
¼ cup canned hot green chilies, chopped
1 small clove of garlic, minced

GARNISHES

green pepper strips
sour cream
sauce mentioned above

Combine the chicken or turkey with the cheese and almonds. Mix into a paste and season lightly with salt and pepper. Crisp the tortillas by sautéing them in a small amount of oil and spread some of the chicken or turkey mixture on each one. Roll up and fasten with picks, concealing the picks by placing them underneath the tacos. To make the sauce, combine all the ingredients and mix well. Put a strip of green pepper, a band of sour cream, and the red chili sauce on each taco before serving. Those are the colors of the Mexican flag.

TACOS EN CAZUELA (*Baked Tacos in a Casserole*)
Makes 12

1 pound beef or pork,
  ground
¼ cup cooking oil
1 medium-sized onion,
  chopped
1 sweet red or green
  pepper, chopped
5–6 tomatoes, peeled and
  chopped
1 anchovy, cut up into
  small pieces

1 tablespoon raisins
2 tablespoons red wine
1 tablespoon nuts, chopped
¾ cup stock (canned beef
  broth may be used)
¼ teaspoon orégano
12 Tortillas*
½ cup grated Swiss cheese
Paprika to taste
Salt and pepper to taste

Sauté the meat in the cooking oil. When almost browned through, add one-half of the onion, one-half of the pepper, and 2 of the tomatoes. Mix well and add the anchovy, raisins, wine, and nuts. Cook over low flame for about 5 minutes. Make a sauce of the following: the rest of the onion, the rest of the green pepper, the remaining tomatoes, the broth and the orégano. Cook together for about 15 minutes.

Heat tortillas to soften them. Put a dab of the meat mixture on each tortilla. Roll and fasten with toothpicks. Place in a greased casserole and top with tomato mixture and cheese. If there is any meat left, it can be formed into balls and added to the casserole before the tomato mixture and then topped with the cheese. Bake at 350° for about 15 minutes or until cheese melts and is slightly brown. Dust with paprika, salt, and pepper to taste.

TAMALES

We mentioned in the appetizer section of this book that tamales can vary in size, shape, and filling from one section of

Mexico to another. They also look slightly different if you buy them in the United States—Americans make them somewhat larger and thicker. Tamales are not so difficult to make as they might seem, as you will see when you try them. But, they are time-consuming, and, for this reason, we think they are best for a large group rather than a small family gathering.

As to fillings for tamales, you can use the ones listed in the appetizer section, or you can use those listed following this basic tamale recipe—or make up your own.

2 cups shortening (classic recipe calls for lard)
1½ pounds masa or nixtamalina (special Mexican corn meals; available at specialty stores)

⅓ cup baking powder
1½ teaspoons salt
¾ cup canned or fresh stock
About 35–40 good-sized cornhusks

Whip the shortening by hand until it looks frothy. Combine the masa, baking powder, and salt and mix with the broth. Add this to the shortening and continue to whip until the mixture is light and airy. It is ready to use when a dab about the size of a walnut will float to the top when dropped in some cold water.

For the husks—Soak them in warm water for about an hour; drain and dry them by patting with absorbent paper to remove excess moisture. Flatten out the husks and on each one put a dab (about 1 tablespoonful) of the corn meal mixture. Spread, going clear to the sides but leaving some room at both ends so that if rolled they can be tied without any filling oozing out. Put desired filling on top of the corn mixture and roll or fold the cornhusks so that the corn mixture is covered. Fold down the ends slightly and tie up each end with string or a bit of cornhusk. Cook tamales on a rack in a steamer for about 45 minutes–1 hour. You can freeze them or eat 'em!

RELLENOS PARA TAMALES
(Fillings for Tamales)

1. Combine

1½ cups oil
1¼ cups all-purpose flour
3 cloves of garlic, crushed
3 cups tomato sauce
4 onions, chopped
2½ cups hot chili sauce
(available in cans at
special food or Mexican
stores)
Salt to taste

3 teaspoons orégano, more
or less (add by tasting
to see how you'd like
the flavor)
3 pounds cooked, ground,
or minced beef, pork,
veal, chicken, or turkey
1 teaspoon cayenne pepper
or more to taste

Heat the oil in a large skillet and stir in the flour. When flour is a delicate brown, add the garlic, tomato sauce, onions, chili sauce, salt, orégano, meat, and cayenne pepper. Cook for about ½ hour or until sauce is quite thick. Cool and use in tamales. Makes about 1½ quarts, or a bit more, of sauce.

2. Mix together cooked, minced, cold chicken, turkey, chopped almonds, and capers, and moisten with a small amount of oil to hold the ingredients together. Fill tamales.

3. Use canned beans—either pinto or kidney—and add bits of cooked ham, strips of mild cheese, some Tabasco sauce, plus a small amount of tomato sauce to moisten. Fill tamales.

4. Combine cooked, crisp, crumbled bacon with cheese and a bit of chili powder.

OCHEPOS *(Sweet Tamales)*
Makes 45–50 small tamales

We like these best when the corn dough contains nuts, although lots of people make them without. These tamales should be made small because they are rich and filling. Try them for tea or for dessert after a light meal.

1 cup sugar
1 cup nuts, ground well
½ cup milk (or chicken broth)
1 stick sweet butter
¼ cup lard
4 cups white corn meal (use masa or nixtamalina, *available at Mexican food stores)*

1 teaspoon baking powder
Dash of salt
1½ teaspoons vanilla extract
45–50 small cornhusks
1 teaspoon cinnamon

Combine the sugar and nuts with the milk or broth and stir well to dissolve the sugar. Set aside. Cream the butter and lard until light and airy. Add the sugar, nuts, and milk or broth. Add the sifted dry ingredients and ½ teaspoon vanilla.

Prepare the cornhusks as in the recipe for Tamales* by soaking them in warm water to soften, but add a teaspoon of vanilla and dash of cinnamon to the water for flavor. Drain and dry on absorbent paper. On each husk place a small spoonful of the corn mixture and spread as directed in basic tamale recipe. Make a very light custard filling. Let it cool and spread a spoonful on top of the corn mixture. Roll and tie tamales and steam for about 30 minutes as directed before in tamale recipe. Steam a little longer if tamales are rather large.

OTHER FILLINGS

On top of the corn mixture you can spread:
1. Cherry jam.
2. Fig preserves mixed with a little brandy.
3. Chopped fruits mixed with chopped nuts.
4. Puréed prunes seasoned with orange and lemon rind.

PASTEL DE TAMALE (*Tamale Pie*)   Serves 6

You can make a very tasty casserole using canned tamales; here's how.

1 can or jar tamales,
  sliced into 1-inch pieces
1 8-ounce can tomato
  sauce
½ cup cooked corn
½ cup olives, chopped
½ cup raisins
¾ tablespoon chili powder
  (optional)
1½ cups boiled chicken,
  cubed

½ pint sour cream
¼ cup white wine
1 cup stock (canned may
  be used)
Salt and pepper to taste
½ cup grated mild cheese
Paprika and chives as
  garnishes

Grease a glass or pottery baking dish. Slice the tamales and line the baking dish with them. Combine the tomato sauce, corn, olives, raisins, chili powder, chicken, sour cream, wine, broth, salt and pepper. Pour this mixture over the tamales. Top with cheese and bake about 1 hour at 350° or until cheese is melted and casserole is heated through. Sprinkle with paprika and chives before serving.

TAMALES AMERICANOS (*American Tamales*)
Makes 12

Just in case the other recipes for tamales sounded too complicated, or in the event you couldn't find all the ingredients, here is a tamale recipe adapted for small kitchens and harried housewives.

1½ cups yellow corn meal
½ cup sifted all-purpose
  flour
2 teaspoons salt

½ pint beef broth
2 tablespoons shortening
12 parchment papers,
  7×9 inches

Combine the dry ingredients and sift together 4 times. Bring broth to the boiling point, add the shortening to it, and immediately add it to the dry ingredients, stirring constantly to form a thick paste of a consistency to spread on the parchment paper. If the paste looks too solid, add a bit more hot broth. Wet the parchment papers and spread 2 tablespoons of the corn mixture on each one. Spread and fill with any of the fillings described previously for tamales, figuring on about 2 cups of filling. Roll the parchment papers to tamale shape and twist or tie the ends. Place tamales in a saucepan. Pour the following sauce on top of them:

SAUCE

6 *tablespoons shortening*
1 *onion, chopped fine*
1 *clove of garlic*
2 *cans tomato paste*
2 *cups hot water*
2 *cups beef broth*
1 *cup tomato juice*

2 *tablespoons salt*
1 *teaspoon cayenne pepper*
1 *tablespoon chili powder*
¼ *teaspoon freshly ground*
   black pepper
¾ *cup grated cheese*

Combine all ingredients except cheese and cook for 30–40 minutes, covered, until sauce is of medium thickness. Pour over tamales, making sure to cover them fully with sauce. Add a little water if sauce does not cover. Steam 30 minutes, covered. Garnish with grated cheese.

SALSA DE CHILE A LA FONDA
(*Chili Sauce*)   Yield: 1 quart sauce

This sauce is a creation served at New York's chic La Fonda del Sol restaurant. It can be used with chicken, beef, or pork tamales.

1 medium onion, chopped
2 cloves of garlic, chopped
½ cup oil
½ cup flour
1½ quarts chicken stock
½ cup tomato purée

Salt to taste
Monosodium glutamate to
  taste
7 ounces red chili
  powder

Sauté onion and garlic in oil. Add flour to make a thick paste. Add hot chicken stock, tomato purée, salt, and monosodium glutamate, and simmer. Dissolve the chili powder in a small amount of water and pour into the saucepan in which the chicken stock and the rest of the ingredients are simmering. Reduce heat to very low and simmer about 30 minutes. Strain and season to taste.

This sauce can be used with various meat tamale fillings. For chicken tamales, the cooked chicken should be diced and dipped in enough of the sauce to cover. Beef and pork should be cooked in one piece in the sauce, then cooled and diced. The cubed meat is placed on top of the masa mixture, which is the base of the tamale,* and is spread on cornhusks. The husks are folded over and tied, as directions described in the tamale recipes in this chapter.

Place 1 tamale layer on top of the other lattice-fashion in a double boiler and cook 2 hours.

ENCHILADAS

Enchiladas are rather like first cousins to tacos. To make them, the tortilla is dipped in the sauce, then fried or baked and filled with various mixtures. Recipes follow.

ENCHILADAS CON CARNE (*With Meat*)
Makes 12

*2 large tomatoes, peeled
  and chopped (with a
  pinch of sugar)
1 clove of garlic, minced
¼ cup shortening
1½ teaspoons salt
Pepper to taste
12 Tortillas**

*1 large onion, minced
1 pound meat, cooked and
  minced
¼ cup grated mild cheese
Orégano to taste
Lettuce wedges and tomato
  slices*

Mix the chopped tomatoes and the garlic. Sauté for about 5 minutes on a low flame in half of the melted shortening. Add the salt and pepper. In another skillet, or in the oven, sauté the tortillas in the remaining shortening. Be sure and brown on both sides. In the center of each tortilla, place 1½ teaspoons of tomato mixture, some chopped onion, and meat. Roll the tortillas and place on serving dish. Top with grated cheese and orégano to taste. Serve with lettuce wedges and tomato slices.

ENCHILADAS ESTILO TAXCO
(*Enchiladas, Taxco Style*)   Makes 12–15 "crepes"

These are somewhat like French crepes, but puffier; they are not traditional tacos.

2 cups flour, sifted
¼ teaspoon salt
1¼ teaspoons baking
* powder*
2 cups milk
2 large eggs, separated

½ teaspoon vanilla,
* almond, or orange*
* extract (optional)*
¼ cup shortening
¼ cup butter, melted

Sift together the dry ingredients. Stir in the milk and strain the batter. Beat the yolks until thickened and pale yellow. Beat the whites until they stand in peaks. Blend the yolks with the milk and flour and fold in the egg whites and the extract. Heat a bit of shortening about the size of a cherry in a heavy 7-inch skillet and, when very hot, pour in a small amount of batter. Tilt the pan so batter covers the bottom of it. Cook until golden on both sides, turning once. Spread each crepe with melted butter. Serve very hot. Makes a dozen or so, depending on how thin you can get the batter.

NOTE: These are very good filled with your favorite mixture of creamed chicken or sea food. You can add a dash of chili powder to the creamed mixture if you wish.

QUESADILLAS (*Tortillas Stuffed with Cheese*)
Makes 12

In the appetizer section of the book we suggested a very simple way of making these. The following recipe is more elaborate and it hails from San Luis Potosí.

1 red or green sweet chili
* pepper, chopped*
2 tomatoes, peeled and
* chopped*
1 clove of garlic, minced
4 green onions, chopped,
* including tops*
1 tablespoon chili powder
Salt and pepper to taste

1 cup lard or other
* shortening*
12 slices American or
* Cheddar cheese, chopped*
* coarsely*
12 Tortillas*
1 small onion, minced
2 very ripe avocados,
* sliced*

For the filling: Combine all ingredients except the shortening, cheese, tortillas, onion, and avocados, and sauté in about a tablespoon of shortening. Let simmer until thickened. Cook the mixture and add the cheese. Mix well. Heat tortillas to soften them and put a generous dab of the filling on each one. Fold over once, fasten with toothpicks, and fry in deep hot shortening until golden brown. Garnish with minced onion and avocado slices.

NOTE: We also like these covered with Guacamole* sauce. With Guacamole we do not use the avocado slices or minced onion and we eliminate the chili powder in the filling.

ENCHILADAS CON QUESO (*Cheese Enchiladas*)
Makes 12

6 tablespoons shortening
12 Tortillas*
3–4 dried chipotle chilies
 (available in Mexican
 food stores), or 3–4
 tablespoons chili powder
1 small onion, minced
1 clove of garlic
½ cup boiling broth
 (canned may be used)
 in which 1 bouillon
 cube is dissolved

Salt and pepper to taste
1 pound lean pork,
 ground and sautéed
½ cup aged Cheddar
 cheese, chopped well
½ cup milk or cream
1½ tablespoons butter

Melt one-half of the shortening and lightly sauté the tortillas on both sides. Remove; drain on absorbent paper. Keep warm. Soak chilies in tepid water, drain, remove seeds, and chop well. (Skip that step if chili powder is used.) Add onion, garlic, and broth with bouillon cube. In the other half of the shortening cook chilies, onion, garlic, and broth until slightly thickened. Salt and pepper to taste. Moisten each tortilla with this sauce and in the center of each tortilla place about a tablespoonful of the ground meat and a few dabs of cheese. Fold each tortilla and place in the bottom of the buttered baking dish. Cover with another layer of the enchiladas until all of the meat mixture is used up. If there are extra tortillas left over, they can be arranged over the top of the others, flat, without filling. Pour milk or cream over all. Dot with butter. Bake in a 350° oven about 10–15 minutes.

ENCHILADAS CON MOLE
(Enchiladas with Mole)

To make the following 2 recipes, you use a thick *mole* sauce, similar to the one for Turkey Mole.* As we've said, you can buy very good *mole* in powder form in cans, but if not, here's the way to make it for enchiladas.

*12–15 almonds, toasted
and blanched*
*2 teaspoons sesame seeds,
toasted*
1 hard roll, toasted
¼ cup raisins
*1 tablespoon unsweetened
chocolate, grated*
1 teaspoon cinnamon
1 whole clove
*4–5 tablespoons chili
powder (as your taste
dictates)*

¼ cup shortening
1 small onion, chopped
1 clove garlic, minced
2 tablespoons flour
*3 cups (or 3 8-ounce
cans) tomato sauce*
*1½ cups broth (canned
will do), or more if
sauce appears too thick*
Salt and pepper to taste
1 tablespoon sugar

Grind together the almonds, sesame seeds, toasted roll, raisins, and chocolate. Mix well. Grind the cinnamon and clove, mix with the chili powder, and combine with the almond mixture. Heat shortening and sauté onion and garlic until onion is wilted. Add flour and, when flour starts to brown, add all the ground ingredients. Cook a few minutes and add the tomato sauce, broth, salt and pepper, and sugar. Cook until thickened.

Use with the next two enchilada dishes.

ENCHILADAS EXCEPCIONALES
(*Exceptional Enchiladas*) Makes 6–8

2 eggs, separated
2 tablespoons cooking oil
½ pound ground beef
½ pound lean ground pork
½ pound ground veal
½ cup (or one-half of an
8-ounce can) tomatoes,
chopped
¼ cup almonds, blanched,
toasted, and chopped

¼ cup raisins
½ teaspoon orégano
Dash of ground
cinnamon
¼ cup mushrooms, sliced
and sautéed lightly
16–18 Tortillas*
Mole *sauce, as described*
(*Enchiladas with Mole**)

Beat egg whites until they stand in peaks. Fold in lightly beaten egg yolks. Heat the fat and sauté the meats. When nearly cooked through, add the tomatoes and stir well. Cook for about 5 minutes to blend. Add almonds, raisins, orégano, cinnamon, and mushrooms. Continue cooking on a very low flame about 20 minutes, or until thick.

Toast the tortillas lightly in the oven and then dip in the *mole* sauce. Fill with the meat mixture and roll. Fasten with toothpicks. Place a layer of tortillas in a greased casserole; cover this layer with more of the *mole* sauce. Top that with some of the beaten eggs. Repeat until all ingredients are used up and you have layers of tortillas. Brush the top layer with the remainder of the eggs. Bake in a moderate, or 350° oven for about 10–15 minutes until glazed and brown.

ENCHILADAS A LA VERACRUZANA
(*Banana Enchiladas*) Makes 16–18

These enchiladas call for those wonderful bananas *machos* we mentioned in the appetizer section of the book. But, if you can't find them at a specialty food shop, use regular bananas on the green side. The tortillas made with flour are very good for this.

4–5 *big bananas, not too*
   ripe
3–4 *tablespoons melted*
   butter
Ground cinnamon
*16–18 Tortillas**

Mole *sauce, as described*
   (*Enchiladas with*
   *Mole**)
¼ *cup toasted sesame*
   seeds

Cut bananas in half lengthwise and then into quarters until you get 16–18 pieces. Sauté the bananas in butter with a dash of cinnamon for a few minutes. Douse each tortilla liberally with the *mole* sauce. Roll each tortilla around a piece of banana. Place on a warm serving dish and cover with additional *mole* sauce. Top with toasted sesame seeds and a little more cinnamon before serving.

TOSTADAS

We explained way back in the appetizer section how you make Tostadas.* Here we have more ways of dressing up these fried tortillas. Tostadas are best made right before eating. They can lose their crispy quality if they stand too long.

TOSTADAS DE JALISCO (*Jalisco-style Tostadas*)
Makes 12

From the state which contains the beautiful city of Guadalajara, this is the style of tostada.

4–5 pigs' feet
1 onion
1 bay leaf
Orégano
1 can (8-ounce) tomatoes,
  or 3–4 fresh tomatoes
1 onion, minced
3 tablespoons white wine
Salt and pepper to taste
1 clove of garlic, minced
2–3 sprigs of coriander or
  parsley, chopped

12 Tortillas,* made very
  thin; or regular ones
  scraped slightly to
  make them thin
1 cup lard
1 cup Refried Beans*
½ head lettuce, shredded
½ cup mild cheese,
  grated

DRESSING FOR PIGS' FEET

4 cups vinegar
½ cup water
Large onion, sliced

4 black peppercorns
Salt to taste
Dash of orégano

PREPARATION OF PIGS' FEET

You'll save yourself a lot of trouble if you buy them pickled, but if not, clean them well and boil them in salted water to cover to which 1 onion, a bay leaf, and a dash of orégano have been added. When done, remove the meat from the bones and soak overnight in the dressing listed above.

SAUCE

Put tomatoes (fresh ones should be peeled and chopped) through a fine food strainer and add minced onion, white wine, salt, pepper, a dash of orégano, garlic minced, chopped parsley or coriander. Mix well.

TORTILLAS

Brown them in hot fat. Drain them quickly on absorbent paper and, when still hot, spread a layer of beans on them, some shredded lettuce, and bits of pigs' feet. Drizzle over the sauce. Top all with grated cheese.

TOSTADAS DE GALLINA (*Chicken Tostadas*)
Makes 12

2 tablespoons oil
1 green onion, chopped
   well
1 8-ounce can tomatoes,
   chopped well
2 cups chicken, chopped
   (*turkey can be used*)
Salt to taste

12 Tortillas*
4 radishes, peeled and
   sliced very thin
1 avocado, sliced very thin
12 black olives, pitted
½ head lettuce, shredded
   (*optional*)

SAUCE

1 can tomato sauce (8
   ounces)
2 small canned hot chili
   peppers, chopped
   (*optional*)
1 tablespoon oil

½ tablespoon vinegar
Dash of orégano
Dash of coriander
1 small green onion,
   minced

Heat half of the oil in skillet and sauté onion until transparent and soft. Add tomatoes and cook, stirring constantly to blend favors, for about 5 minutes. Add chopped chicken or turkey to the mixture and stir well. Salt to taste. Sauté the tortillas in the other half of oil and, when golden, drain them quickly on absorbent paper. Top with above Sauce, made by combining all ingredients and mixing well. Put radishes and avocado slices on top of this mixture. Garnish with 1 black olive per tostada, plus a small amount of shredded lettuce, if desired.

TOSTADAS CON CHORIZO
(Tostadas with Sausage) Makes 12

Do not substitute chili powder in this recipe.

5 Chorizos (or about ¾
  pound)
1½ cups Refried Beans*
Shortening for deep frying
12 Tortillas,* extra thin
½ head lettuce, shredded
¼–½ cup oil*

*¾ cup wine vinegar
1 red hot chili pepper,
  chopped fine
Salt to taste
¼ cup grated Parmesan
  cheese*

Remove sausage from casing and brown until done. Add Refried Beans and cook together for a few moments. Set aside, but keep warm. Heat shortening to 365° and sauté the tortillas until brown. Spread tortillas with the beans and meat. Mix lettuce with the oil, vinegar, hot chili pepper, and salt. Top the beans and sausage with this. Sprinkle with cheese.

GORDITAS Makes 12–15

The word literally means little fat ones, and so they are— little fat tortillas stuffed with good things to eat. Gorditas are specialties in some places on special feast days.

¼ *cup sifted flour*
1 *teaspoon salt*
3½ *cups masa or* nixtamalina *(Mexican corn meal flour, available at specialty food stores)*
2½ *tablespoons vegetable shortening*

SAUCE

1 *cup tomato sauce*
1 *onion, minced*
1 *clove garlic, minced*
1 *teaspoon orégano*
Salt to taste
1 *ounce white wine vinegar*

3 *tablespoons olive oil*
1½ *teaspoons chili powder (according to taste), or 1 small hot chili pepper, minced*

FILLING

½ *pound ground beef or* Chorizo*
¾ *cup cooked potatoes, diced*
2 *tablespoons oil*
1 *very small onion, minced (omit if you use chorizo)*

¾ *cup grated mild cheese (we like Swiss)*
¼ *cup almonds, blanched and chopped (optional)*
Salt to taste
Shortening for deep frying

Sift the flour with the salt and mix with the Mexican corn meal. Cut in the shortening and keep mixing well until you get a smooth dough. (Add a little more flour if dough appears too soft; it should be fairly firm.) Flour the palms of the hands lightly and roll the dough into 12–15 balls about the size of a small egg. Press the balls into flat cakes. Cook on both sides, on an ungreased cookie sheet for just a few minutes or until they begin to brown. Protect the hands with a sheet of plastic, which has been doubled, and pinch the tortillas while hot to form little tart shells. Let cool.

To make sauce: Combine all sauce ingredients and simmer for about ½ hour, or until slightly thickened. Let cool.

To make filling: Brown the beef and potatoes in oil and add a small amount of the onion, the grated cheese, almonds, and salt to taste. Sauté the little shells in deep fat (365°) for a few minutes; drain on absorbent paper. Fill each shell with meat and top with cheese. Pour some of the sauce over the meat.

SOPES SARDINAS DE JALISCO
(Sardine Cakes, Jalisco Style) Makes 12

2¼ cups masa or nixtamalina (available in Mexican food stores)	¼ cup cream cheese Few drops of warm water Shortening for frying
¼ cup shortening	Salt to taste

Combine all ingredients but the shortening and mix until you have a smooth dough. Form a dozen pancakes from the dough. Pinch up sides to form a raised border all the way around. Fry in deep fat at 365° until golden. Drain on absorbent paper and keep warm. Fill with the following:

1 tablespoon oil	1 tablespoon chili powder
2 green onions, chopped, including tops	½ tablespoon lemon juice
1 tomato, peeled and chopped	1 can boneless sardines, mashed well
1 cup Frijoles* (cooked beans Mexican style)	Salt and pepper to taste

Heat oil and sauté onion until transparent. Add tomato and beans and cook until most of the liquid has been absorbed. Add chili powder, lemon juice, mashed sardines, and salt and pepper. Fill each *sope*, or pancake, with this mixture. Heat in a moderate oven for a few minutes before serving.

EMPANADAS (*Turnovers*)   Makes 12–15

Empanadas are popular in other countries South of the Border as well as Mexico. In the size below, they are used for snacks or late suppers; in miniature, they are good as appetizers or with cocktails.

1 teaspoon sugar	*1 egg, beaten*
1 teaspoon salt	*½ cup ice-cold milk, or*
2½ cups flour	*½ cup ice-cold water*
¼ pound butter	*(about)*

Combine the sugar, salt, and flour and sift together several times. Add the butter, the beaten egg, and the milk or water, using just enough of the liquid to form a dough that holds together. Make about 15 balls and roll them on a lightly floured board to make circles about 4 inches around. Place a little of any of the suggested fillings that follow in the flat cakes and fold over. Moisten the edges with water or milk and seal well with the tines of a fork. You can fry the empanadas in deep fat at 365° until they are golden brown, or you can bake them at 375° for about 15 minutes. If you bake them, brush the tops with a little of the beaten egg and prick the tops with a fork before putting in the oven.

VARIATIONS

You can make little "Tarteletas" (tarts) from the above recipe too. When you roll out the dough, roll it to fit lightly greased muffin tins and fill with any of the mixtures suggested. Top with another round of dough. Seal the edges, pierce the tops with a fork, and bake.

You can make empanada dough with cream cheese. To do

so, use 1½ cups of flour to 1 3-ounce package of cream cheese, ¼ pound of butter, and 1 teaspoon each of salt and sugar. Leave out the egg and milk or water. Refrigerate dough for at least 5 hours before using. Let stand at room temperature for ¼ hour before rolling out on a lightly floured board.

RELLENOS DE EMPANADAS
(*Turnover Fillings*)

Fillings 1, 2, 3, and 4 will stuff 12–15 turnovers. Suggestions 5 and 6 are general, but you can use the previous ones as a guide to quantity.

1.

1 pound fish, cooked: red snapper, for example, or canned tuna (7-ounce can), boned and shredded
1 cup sweet cream
½ cup olive oil

1 tablespoon onion, minced
2 hard-cooked eggs, chopped
Salt and pepper to taste
Dash of chili powder (optional)

Mix all ingredients and stuff the turnovers. Bake or fry.

2.

1 tablespoon butter
1 onion, minced
1 canned tomato, drained and chopped
¾ pound cooked crab meat (frozen can be used)

1 tablespoon minced parsley
¼ cup capers
1 teaspoon vinegar
Salt and pepper to taste
½ teaspoon thyme

Melt the shortening and sauté the onion until transparent. Add the tomato, crab, parsley, capers, vinegar, salt, pepper, and thyme, and cook for a few minutes to blend the flavors. Fill empanadas; fry or bake.

3.

¼ cup olive oil
2 onions, minced well
1 cup grated Cheddar
 cheese
2 canned red pimientos,
 chopped
3 hard-cooked eggs,
 chopped

10 black olives, chopped
 coarsely
1 teaspoon chili powder
 (*or more to taste*)
2 anchovies, chopped
Salt and pepper to taste

Heat the oil and cook the onions very slowly until softened. Do not let them get brown. Remove from the heat and add the rest of the ingredients. If mixture is too dry, add a few drops of water to moisten it. Fill turnovers; bake or fry.

4.

6 tablespoons olive oil
1 small onion, minced
1 pound ground lean
 round steak
2 teaspoons minced parsley
¼ cup raisins, plumped
 in water (*drain raisins
 before adding*)

1 cup (8-ounce can)
 tomato sauce
¼ cup almonds, blanched
 and toasted
Salt and pepper to taste

Heat oil; sauté onion. Brown meat in oil. Stir in other ingredients. Cook until thick. Stuff turnovers. Fry or bake.

5. Picadillo* (Mexican Hash) is also a good filling.

6. Especially recommended for the cheese-dough turnovers are fillings with anchovies and grated mild cheese; minced ham and grated mild cheese; minced turkey or chicken with olives and almonds; and mashed sardines, hard-cooked eggs, and tomatoes that have been chopped and drained well to prevent the turnovers from becoming soggy.

Empanadas are also used for dessert. You alter the dough to bring out the sweet taste as follows: Using the basic empanada recipe, increase the sugar to 2 tablespoons, add 1½ teaspoons baking powder, and just enough cold milk or ice water to hold the dough together. Roll out balls on a floured board and proceed as described with 12–15 turnovers. When they are finished, sprinkle them with a small amount of sugar and cinnamon, if desired, or leave them plain.

SWEET FILLINGS

1. A plain soft custard, or custard with a dash of rum or brandy added for flavor.

2. Cherry jam seasoned with a dash of lemon juice.

3. Cooked apple chunks seasoned with cinnamon, sugar, and a little lime juice.

4. Mashed sweet potatoes mixed with pineapple juice (just enough to moisten them) and chopped candied cherries.

5. Grated canned coconut mixed with preserves and chopped walnuts.

TIPS ON TOSTADAS, TORTILLAS, AND ENCHILADAS

Tostadas– are also very good when topped with any of the *guacamole* sauces suggested in the appetizer section of the book. If you want to decorate them a bit, try thin tomato slices, chopped black olives, and shredded lettuce on top.

Tortillas– in simple tacos style—that is, merely wrapped around some filling—are delicious with creamed chicken, tuna, or sea food. Be sure and heat the tortillas well before putting the creamed mixture in them. We sometimes add a little chili sauce *Jalapeño* (available in cans at most Mexican food stores) to the creamed mixture for flavor, or top the tortillas with strips of canned red sweet potatoes.

Enchiladas—in a hurry, use frozen or canned enchiladas and dress them up with the following sauce, which yields about 2½ cups:

¼ cup oil
1 onion, chopped well
1 clove of garlic, crushed
1 no. 2½ can whole
    tomatoes, chopped

1 4-ounce can hot green
    chilies, chopped very
    well
Salt to taste

Heat the oil, add the onion and garlic, and brown slightly. Add the tomatoes and simmer for a few seconds. Add the chilies and salt and cook uncovered for about ½ hour or until thick. Can be eaten either hot or cold.

Frijoles y Arroz

❖

(BEANS AND RICE)

If you think of beans and tortillas only, when you think of Mexican food, then you are leaving out an important third partner—rice. True, *frijoles* are more traditional, but the Mexican way with rice would be hard to beat, even by the Chinese.

Beans never seemed too mysterious to us until we found out the way they came to Mexico is not known for sure. And, the lowly bean never meant much to us as an important factor in the business of finance and trade between the Old and New Worlds, until we realized that once the Spanish found beans in Mexico, they fed their sailors on them. These seafarers saw to it that the ships fostering trade between the continents crossed safely. So, now you can see how important a bean can be!

Our favorite Mexican bean dishes include good old Frijoles de Olla* (Beans in a Pot) and Frijoles Nastosos* (Creamy Beans).

Rice, of course, is frequently associated with Spanish cookery, and two of our recipes, Arroz con Pollo* (Chicken with Rice) and Paella* (Sea Food and Chicken with Rice) come from Spain, but are now considered a part of the national cuisine in Mexico. We also like Arroz con Guacamole* (Rice with Avocado Sauce) and an exotic-sounding dish called Arroz con Alcachofas* (Rice with Artichoke Hearts).

Beans and rice made the Mexican way can perk up family appetites and make good dishes for buffets and Sunday suppers.

FRIJOLES (*Basic Recipe for Beans*)   Serves 6

2 cups red kidney or pinto beans	½ cup, or a bit more, lard, or comparable
Salt to taste	amount bacon fat

Soak beans overnight with water to cover them. In the morning some of the water will be absorbed, so add more to cover. Add the salt and cook the beans about 1½–2 hours or until very tender. Mash the beans well and add the melted hot lard to them. Simmer until all of the fat is absorbed by the beans, stirring frequently to prevent sticking or burning.

FRIJOLES REFRITOS (*Refried Beans*)

It's easy to prepare this dish: Heat some fat in a frying pan and cook the mashed beans as prepared in the Basic Recipe.* You stir constantly until they are completely dry. A tablespoon of minced onion can be added for flavor. Sauté the onion slightly in the fat, then add the beans.

VARIATIONS

We like refried beans with a bit more flavor, so we sometimes add tomato sauce or cheese or both as follows:

1. *For the Tomato Variation*–Allow the mashed beans in Basic Recipe* to cool. Sauté a small minced onion in some hot oil—again, the Mexicans prefer lard. Add 8 tablespoons of tomato paste and a tablespoon of hot chili powder. When the onion is very soft, add the beans and cook until beans are warmed through and the ingredients are well blended.

2. *For Cheese*–We take the mashed beans straight from the Basic Recipe* and fry them in some oil, as in the Refried Beans* recipe. As they are sautéing slowly in the pan, we add a grated mild cheese, such as Cheddar, to taste.

3. *For Cheese and Tomatoes*—Follow the recipe for tomato variation above and add grated mild cheese when you add the beans, stirring constantly as cheese melts.

NOTE: Save time by using canned kidney beans and beginning your preparation of these dishes at the point after the beans are cooked.

FRIJOLES DE OLLA (*Beans in a Pot*)   Serves 10

This is great if you're having a crowd in for Sunday supper.

2 cups pinto or kidney
  beans
½ pound salt pork, cubed
Favorite hot chili sauce
  (*to taste*)
2 Spanish onions, sliced
  very thin and soaked in
  small amount cold
  salted water

½–¾ cup freshly grated
  Parmesan cheese
1 tablespoon orégano
Salt to taste

Soak beans in water to cover overnight or for 8 hours. Drain and cover with cold water. Add pork and simmer very slowly until done, or about 1–1½ hours or more. If water in the pan appears scant during cooking process, add a little more warm water. When beans are done and all the water is absorbed, put them in a large bowl and mix them gently with hot chili sauce, just enough to moisten them. Top with sliced onion rings, grated cheese, orégano, and salt.

VARIATION

A cup of hot cooked rice can be tossed through at the end too.

NOTE: Very good prepared hot Chili sauce can be found in Mexican food stores.

FRIJOLES CHINITOS (*Crispy Beans*)

Cook beans according to Basic Bean Recipe.* When they are done, melt 2 tablespoons of fat (the Mexicans prefer lard) and cook a small minced onion in the fat until transparent. Add the mashed beans and fry, stirring constantly, until crisp and dry, adding salt to taste. Top with grated cheese and serve with Tostadas.*

FRIJOLES NASTOSOS (*Creamy Beans*)   Serves 5–6

2 tablespoons bacon drippings	*¼ cup water*
1 small onion, minced	*Salt and pepper to taste*
1½ tablespoons flour	*1 tablespoon chili powder or more to taste*
1⅓ cups canned kidney beans	*1 hot sausage, fried and cut into small pieces*

Melt fat, add the onion, and cook until the onion is soft. Add the flour and, when it starts browning, add the beans and the liquid from the can plus ¼ cup of water and salt and pepper to taste. Cook, stirring often, until creamy and soft. Beans should be almost like a heavy custard—in other words, falling apart and very soft. Add more water, if necessary, to achieve this custardy texture. Add the chili powder as beans are cooking and, toward the end of the cooking process, add. the hot sausage which has been fried and cut up.

VARIATION

Can be made with chick-peas which have been cooked until very tender.

FRIJOLES CON PLATANOS
(Beans and Bananas)   Serves 6–7

2 slices bacon
1 small onion, chopped
½ cup tomato purée
1½ cups canned kidney beans
Salt and pepper to taste
2 small (or 1 large) bananas, cut into round slices

Sauté bacon, remove from the pan, and cut into small pieces. In the bacon fat, sauté the onion until transparent, add the tomato purée, and simmer for a few seconds. Add the beans, the bacon, and the salt and pepper to taste. Heat through and toss quickly with the banana slices. Serve right away.

VARIATIONS

1. The above dish can be made with lentils instead of beans. We use apples with the lentils. Peel and core the apple and cut into chunks. Boil until tender before adding to the lentils. Pears, parboiled, are good, too. Just peel and core first, and then cut up.

2. You can make the above dish with Refried Beans.* You form the beans into flat patties. Use very ripe bananas and mash them with a little salt. Spread the bananas on the bean patties and fold over beans to conceal fruit. Sauté for a few minutes in hot oil. Serve hot.

CORONA DE FRIJOL (*Bean Crown*)   Serves 6–7

Do not substitute chili powder in this recipe.

*1½ cups cooked red or
  pink beans
1 small onion, minced
1 can peeled green chilies,
  minced
½ teaspoon orégano
¾ cup grated Monterey
  Jack, mild Cheddar, or
  Wisconsin brick cheese*

*2 eggs, beaten
2 teaspoons salt
3 tablespoons sweet butter,
  melted
3–4 tablespoons bread
  crumbs
2 Chorizo* sausages or 3
  pork sausages, fried
  until well done*

Prepare the beans as for Basic Bean Recipe.* Grind together the mashed beans, onion, chilies, orégano, ¼ of the cheese, eggs, and salt. Pack the bean mixture into a mold which you've greased with one-half of the butter and coated with bread crumbs. Pack the beans down firmly. Drizzle over remaining butter and cheese and bake at 350° for 15 minutes. Dot with hot sausage when serving.

The above recipe, with a few changes, can make 6 croquettes. Here goes:

Use only 1 egg in the beans and the other for coating.
Keep the cheese in chunks.
Reduce the butter to 1 tablespoon.

Combine as you did for crown of beans, but don't put into a mold. Instead, make 12 patties and in the center of 6 of them put a chunk of cheese. Top these 6 patties with the other 6 and form into balls, covering the cheese well. Roll in crumbs; dip in beaten eggs; dip again in crumbs. Fry in hot deep fat at 375° for a few minutes or until nicely browned. Drain. Serve hot with your favorite hot chili sauce.

NOTE: Here again you can use canned kidney beans and save the time of preparing the beans as for basic recipe.

GARBANZOS EN TOMATE
(*Chick-peas in Tomato Sauce*) Serves 4

1 pound chick-peas
Water for soaking, plus 6
  cups water for cooking
1 large clove of garlic
1 large onion
Salt and freshly ground
  pepper to taste
2 cups (or no. 1 can)
  tomatoes, chopped; if
  fresh tomatoes are used,
  peel them first

½ sweet green pepper,
  chopped and seeded
1 4-ounce jar pimientos,
  chopped into large, even
  pieces

Soak the chick-peas in water to cover overnight. Drain them and add 6 cups of water. Put them to boil with the garlic, onion, salt, and pepper and cook for about 1 hour. Add the tomatoes and green pepper and cook until peas are done. During the last 10 minutes of cooking time, mix in the pimientos. Add more salt if necessary.

GARBANZOS MEXICANOS
(*Chick-peas, Mexican Style*) Serves 6–7

¾ pound chick-peas
  (which have been soaked
  overnight)
2 slices bacon
1 small onion, minced
1 clove of garlic, crushed
1 cup tomato sauce
1 teaspoon cumin powder,
  or about 3 cumin seeds,
  crushed to powder stage

¾ tablespoon chili powder
  (or more to taste)
Dash of epazote (if
  available)
3 Chorizo* sausages or
  pork sausages (fried
  well)
Salt to taste

After soaking the peas overnight, drain, cover with water, and cook for about 1 hour or more until almost done. Fry the bacon and remove from the pan. Sauté the onion and garlic in the bacon fat and, when onion is soft, add the tomato sauce, cumin, and chili powder. Cook a few minutes to blend flavors. Add the *epazote* and mix through. Add the chick-peas and the water in which they were cooked, the sausages, which have been fried and cut into pieces, and the bacon, which has been chopped. Add salt and cook until sauce is thickened.

NOTE: Mexican-style chick-peas can be made with canned chick-peas. Just follow directions after those for soaking and cooking the peas, and use liquid from can plus a little water for last step.

ARROZ CLASICO (*Classic Rice*)   Serves 5–6

⅓ cup oil	*1½ tablespoons minced*
1 onion, minced	*parsley*
1 cup raw rice	*Salt and pepper to taste*
2 cups hot broth (canned	*½ cup freshly grated*
may be used)	*Parmesan cheese*

Heat the oil, add the onion, and cook until wilted. Add the rice and stir until each grain is coated with oil and turns yellow in color. Drain excess oil if necessary. Add the broth, parsley, salt, and pepper. Simmer, covered, for 20 minutes, add the cheese, stir well, and cook until all the liquid is absorbed. Rice should not be mushy, but if additional liquid is needed to cook rice, add a little more warm broth or water.

VARIATIONS

1. Cooked mushrooms or fried sausages or sautéed chicken livers can be added during the last few minutes of cooking time with cheese.

2. Sweet red pepper (¼ cup) and sweet green pepper (¼ cup)—both chopped—can be sautéed with onion. Continue as recipe instructs.

ARROZ CON POLLO (*Chicken with Rice*)
Serves 5

A Spanish dish which is a Mexican favorite and made the
Mexican way.

1 cup rice
½ clove of garlic
½ onion
4 black peppers
Salt to taste
Cumin seed to taste
1 frying chicken, 2–3
   pounds, cut into serving
   pieces
Shortening for frying
3 Chorizos* or pork
   sausages (optional)

2 tomatoes, chopped
2 cups chicken broth
   (canned may be used)
¼ teaspoon saffron
   (dissolved in the
   chicken broth)
2 small green peppers,
   sliced
1 can (2 ounces)
   pimientos, chopped

Soak rice in warm water for 15 minutes and drain. Grind
together the garlic, onion, black peppers, salt, and cumin seed
and spread over raw chicken pieces. Melt shortening in large
skillet and brown sausages well. Remove sausages. Brown
chicken in the fat, add rice, and cook until rice gets lightly
browned. Add tomatoes and cook 5 or 6 minutes. Add the
broth, in which saffron has been dissolved, sausages, and green
peppers. Cover and cook slowly until rice, chicken, and sausages are done—about 35–45 minutes. Add a bit more broth if
necessary. A few minutes before rice is done, add the chopped
pimientos and mix them through with the chicken and rice.
All the liquid should be absorbed into rice during cooking
process. Season with additional salt if necessary.

PAELLA *(Sea Food and Chicken with Rice)*
Serves 6–8

This is a Spanish dish which the Mexicans have adopted and changed. Every Mexican has his favorite way of preparing *paella*. This is ours.

1 teaspoon chili powder
2¾ cups chicken broth
(canned may be used)
½ cup olive oil
3 medium-sized onions
2 broiling chickens, about
2 pounds each, cut into
serving pieces
¼ pound ham, cut into
strips
2 cups rice (long-grain
preferably), rinsed in
cold water and drained
2 dozen fresh shrimp (well
washed, but in their
jackets)

2 dozen or more small
clams (well washed, but
in their shells)
12 thin slices Chorizo* or
Italian sausage
3 cloves of garlic
1 teaspoon saffron
Pinch of orégano
¼ cup dry white wine
Salt and pepper to taste
1 small can peas, well
drained
1 small can pimientos, cut
into strips

Dissolve chili powder in chicken broth and bring to the boiling point. Let it simmer on a low flame. Heat oil in deep casserole or heavy pot and sauté onions. Add chicken and sauté until golden brown on all sides. Add the ham and the rice. When the rice absorbs the oil, add 1 cup of hot chicken broth. When this is absorbed, add another cup of broth. Continue to cook on a low flame until chicken and rice are nearly tender. Add the shrimps, clams, and sausage. Cover and cook until shrimps are tender, about 8–10 minutes.

In another bowl mix together the garlic, saffron, orégano, and ¾ cup of hot broth. Using a muddler, blend these ingredients until the broth is colored with the saffron (a bright yellow-orange) and the garlic is mashed well. Strain liquid into the casserole and add the wine and salt and pepper to taste. Mix through peas and heat thoroughly about 5 more minutes. Decorate with pimiento strips.

ARROZ CON ALCACHOFAS
(*Rice with Artichoke Hearts*)   Serves 6–8

½ cup black beans
2 medium-sized onions
Salt and pepper to taste
5 tablespoons cooking oil
Chicken broth as directed
   (canned may be used)
1 cup rice
1 small clove of garlic
¼ cup tomato purée
1 tablespoon fresh chopped
   parsley
1 cup peas, canned or
   frozen (if frozen, cook
   them)

6 artichoke hearts, canned
   or frozen (if frozen,
   cook them)
1 small (2-ounce) jar
   pimientos, cut into strips
¼ cup almonds, blanched
   and toasted
½ cup ham, cut into
   strips

Soak the beans in water to cover for 8 hours or overnight. Drain. Put the beans up to boil with water to cover, 1 onion, left whole, salt, and 2 tablespoons of the cooking oil. Cook until very tender. Cool and put into blender with enough of the bean liquid and chicken broth to make about 2½ cups. Blend until mixture is smooth and watery, not thick.

Soak the rice in warm water to cover for about 10 minutes. Rinse in cold water. Drain. Melt the remaining cooking oil and sauté the rice, stirring in a minced onion and crushed garlic, until rice is nicely brown. Stir in the tomato purée and simmer a few minutes. Add the bean liquid, salt and pepper, to taste, and parsley. Mix. Cover and simmer for 20 minutes, or until rice appears to be done and liquid is almost absorbed. Add a little more broth if liquid appears scant. Add the peas, artichoke hearts, and pimientos. When finished, turn into a hot dish and garnish with the toasted almonds and ham strips.

ARROZ CON HIGADITOS DE POLLO
(*Rice with Chicken Livers*)   Serves 6–8

1½ tablespoons butter
8–10 chicken livers
Salt and pepper to taste
¼ cup cooking oil
1 large onion, minced
1½ cups long-grain rice

4 cups chicken broth
(canned may be used)
1 cup tomato sauce
2 tablespoons hot prepared
mustard
¼ cup grated fresh parsley

Heat the butter in a skillet and sauté the chicken livers with a small amount of salt and pepper until tender. Chop and set aside but keep warm.

In a heavy skillet, heat the oil and add the onion. When wilted, add the rice and sauté, stirring constantly, until the grains are well coated with oil and they begin to turn light yellow. Mix the broth with the tomato sauce and mustard. Add slowly to the rice along with the parsley and salt and pepper. Simmer rice, covered, until the liquid is almost gone. Add cooked chicken livers and mix through. Cover again until liquid has been absorbed and rice is tender. If rice is still tough and needs additional liquid, a small amount of water or broth can be added. Remove cover and cool for a few minutes before serving.

CHILES RELLENOS CON ARROZ
(*Peppers Stuffed with Rice*)   Serves 8–10

8–10 solid sweet bell
peppers, not too large
¼ pound freshly grated
Parmesan cheese
3 cups cooked rice

2 cups sweet cream
1 cup tomato soup or
sauce
Salt and pepper to taste
Paprika

Parboil the peppers. Drain and seed, leaving whole. Let cool so they can be handled. Mix together one-half of the cheese, the rice, the cream, and the tomato soup or sauce. Season well with salt and pepper. Stuff the peppers with rice mixture. Butter a casserole, and if any of the rice mixture is left over, place it in the bottom of the casserole. Then, arrange stuffed peppers on top. Sprinkle the rest of the grated cheese over the peppers. Cook at 350° until heated through or for about 15 or 20 minutes, until cheese is brown and peppers are tender. Garnish with a light coat of paprika.

ARROZ CON CHILES Y QUESO
(Rice with Chilies and Cheese)   Serves 4–6

2⅓ cups rice, cooked
Salt, pepper, and orégano to taste
1 can hot green chilies, peeled and chopped
1 pint sour cream
½ pound grated mild cheese (anything from American to Wisconsin)
Parsley
Paprika

Season rice with enough salt, pepper, and orégano to make it tasty. Mix the chopped chilies and sour cream well. In a buttered casserole, arrange a layer of rice, top with a layer of chilies and sour cream, and add a layer of cheese, saving a small amount of the cheese. Continue in this fashion until you've used up all the ingredients. Your last layer should be rice. Bake at 350° for about 30 minutes. During the last 5 minutes of cooking, sprinkle remainder of the cheese, the parsley, and a dash of paprika over the rice.

ARROZ CON CARNE MOLIDA
(*Rice with Ground Meat*) Serves 5–6

¼ *pound mushrooms,*
  chopped
2 *tablespoons cooking oil*
3 *eggs, separated*
1½ *cups rice* (*cooked*)
1 *pound ground beef* (*or*
  half beef and half pork)

1 *cup* (*8-ounce can*)
  tomatoes, chopped and
  drained
¼ *cup almonds, chopped*
¼ *cup raisins, chopped*
Salt and pepper to taste
Small amount butter
Cinnamon

Sauté the mushrooms in a small amount of the oil until wilted. Set aside, but keep warm. Beat the egg yolks until lemon-colored. Beat the whites until they stand in peaks. Fold the whites in the yolks and mix well. Add the rice and mix well. Heat remaining oil, add the ground meat, and brown it well. Add the tomatoes, nuts, raisins, sautéed mushrooms, and salt and pepper, and cook until most of the liquid is absorbed. In a lightly greased casserole, arrange layers of rice alternately with layers of meat. Finish with a layer of rice. Dot with small amount of butter here and there. Bake at 375° for about 20–30 minutes or until all the ingredients have a chance to heat through well. Sprinkle with cinnamon and serve hot.

ARROZ CON GUACAMOLE
(*Rice with Avocado Sauce*)

Make rice according to your favorite method and pack into a well-buttered ring mold. Place mold in a *baño de Maria,* or another pan of warm water, and cook in a 350° oven for about 30 minutes. When hot, unmold on a pretty platter and cover with the first Guacamole* sauce suggested in the appetizer section of this book.

FRIJOLES ENVINADOS (*Beans in Wine*)   Serves 6

The French aren't the only ones who cook beans in wine, as you will see when you try the following recipe. The Mexicans use *habas,* but Lima beans are just as good. Personally, we like to imitate the French and use small dried pea beans, which aren't exactly classic when it comes to Mexican cookery, but are nonetheless delicious.

4 tablespoons olive oil	1 8-ounce can tomatoes,
Large onion, sliced	chopped
1 clove of garlic, minced	2 cups fresh habas, Limas,
¾ cup cooked tongue, cut	or cooked pea beans
into strips	1 cup dry white wine
2 tablespoons parsley	Salt and pepper to taste

If you use dried pea beans, you'll need:

2½ cups dried pea beans	Pinch of epazote (if
1 carrot	available)
1 onion, left whole	Salt to taste
4 whole cloves	4 whole peppercorns
1 clove garlic, left whole	1 bay leaf
½ stick cinnamon	¼ cup chopped salt pork

If fresh *habas,* Limas, or cooked pea beans are used, heat the oil, add the onion, and cook until softened and transparent. Add minced garlic, tongue, and parsley and cook for about 5 minutes, covered, to blend the flavors. Add the tomatoes, beans, wine, and salt and pepper and bake, covered, at 350° for 35–40 minutes or until beans are tender.

If the dried pea beans are used, soak them overnight or for at least 8 hours. Drain. Add water to cook and simmer them with remaining ingredients. They should cook about 1 hour or slightly more until tender with ingredients as listed. Remove carrot, onion, cloves, clove of garlic, cinnamon, peppercorns, and bay leaf before proceeding. Bake, covered, at 350° for 35–40 minutes or until beans are tender.

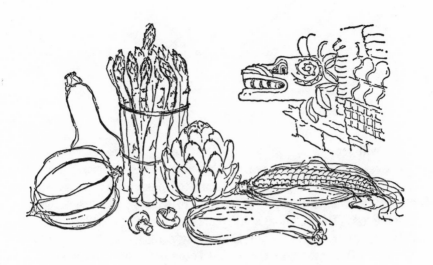

Legumbres

�֎

(VEGETABLES)

For every person in the world who dislikes vegetables, there is a Mexican way of preparing them to make him change his mind. The Mexicans cook vegetables in wine—see Col Morada Envinado* (Red Cabbage in Wine)—as well as with sauces, as in Coliflor Estilo Santa Clara* (Cauliflower, Santa Clara Style) or Tomates con Crema* (Tomatoes with Cream).

Surprisingly enough, although potatoes come from South of the Border, the Mexicans prefer the sweet variety and do not make as much use of the white potato as their neighbors do North of the Border. A notable sweet potato recipe is Camote y Piña* (Sweet Potato and Pineapple).

Some Mexican vegetables are good enough to eat for dessert . . . and sometimes they are served that way, which is the case with Torta de Elote* (Corn Torte). There is one thing for certain: whether you serve these vegetables with meals, as side dishes, as meals in themselves, or as dessert, they are sure to get all the attention that they deserve, for they are colorful as well as tasty.

CALABACITA CON QUESO (*Squash with Cheese*)
Serves 4–6

1 small red or green hot pepper, chopped coarsely
2 cups tomatoes, peeled and chopped, or 1 no. 1 can
1 clove of garlic, crushed
½ cup canned corn
1 small onion, minced

Salt and pepper to taste
¼ cup olive oil
2 cups summer squash, chopped
1 3-ounce package cream cheese, diced into small pieces

Mix together the hot pepper, tomatoes, garlic, corn, onion, and salt and pepper to taste. In a casserole lightly greased with olive oil place a layer of chopped squash, cover with a layer of the tomato mixture, add another layer of squash, and continue until all the ingredients are used up (except the cheese). Bake in a 350° oven for 20–25 minutes or until squash is done. Put diced cheese over the top when casserole is baked through.

EJOTES EN SALSA DE ALMENDRA
(String Beans in Nut Sauce) Serves 6

2 tablespoons butter
¾ cup almonds, blanched
1 small hard roll, chopped
   into cubes
1 cup beef broth (canned
   may be used)

Salt and pepper to taste
1 pound string beans, cut
   "French style" and
   cooked until tender but
   not too soft
½ cup chives

Melt the butter, add the almonds and bread cubes, and brown well. Mash into a paste. Add the stock to the paste and season with salt and pepper. Cook on a low flame, stirring all the while, until thickened. Add the cooked green beans and cook a few minutes more to heat through. Sprinkle with chives.

TORTA DE CALABAZA *(Squash Pudding)*
Serves 8

For this dish, Mexicans use *calabacitas,* little tender green squash which grow in the cornfields. The flowers of these succulent squash are also used in Mexican cookery to make soups and other delicate dishes. At home you can use zucchini and get good results with this pudding.

1 no. 303 can whole tomatoes	⅔ cup freshly grated Parmesan cheese
3 tablespoons butter	1 tablespoon orégano
1 small onion, minced	Salt and pepper to taste
1 clove of garlic, crushed	4 eggs, separated
4 cups boiled zucchini, sliced very thin	Bread crumbs

Chop the canned tomatoes. Melt 2 tablespoons of butter in skillet and add the onion and garlic, cooking until onion is transparent. Add the tomatoes; cook a few minutes to blend, and stir well. Add the boiled sliced zucchini, the cheese, and the orégano. Season with salt and pepper to taste. Beat the egg whites until stiff but not dry. Add yolks a little at a time, beating after each addition. Add the eggs to the zucchini and fold in gently. Pour into a buttered baking dish. Cover with bread crumbs; dot with the remaining tablespoon of butter. Bake at 350° until brown and set, 30–35 minutes.

CHILES CON CREMA (*Creamed Chilies*)   Serves 4

1 tablespoon butter	1 teaspoon orégano
3 green peppers, cut into strips	Salt and pepper to taste
	½ cup sweet cream

Melt butter and sauté pepper strips until slightly softened. Mix the seasonings with the cream and pour over the peppers. Cook until heated through, but do not boil.

ESPARRAGOS CON PIMIENTO
(*Asparagus with Pimientos*)

Select tender young asparagus and clean well. Cook, covered, in a small amount of salted boiling water until just tender but not soft. This should take between 6 and 8 minutes. Drain. For topping, combine ⅓ cup of bread crumbs with salt and pepper to taste. Sauté in a small amount of butter until moistened. Add 2 tablespoons of chopped sweet red pimiento and 1 chopped hard-cooked egg. Stir quickly through crumbs; add salt and pepper to taste. Sprinkle seasoned crumbs over the asparagus. Serve hot.

NOTE: This same topping is good on fresh green beans too.
Frozen asparagus and green beans can be used with the above topping, but take care not to overcook them.

ALCACHOFAS PARA LA REINA
(Artichokes Fit for a Queen) Serves 12

This is the way the Mexicans stuff artichokes, and the title is not misleading. They are fit for a queen—or king, for that matter.

1 dozen medium-sized artichokes	*4 tablespoons very dry bread crumbs*
1 clove of garlic	*¼ teaspoon ground ginger*
Juice of 1 small lemon	*¼ teaspoon chili powder*
Pinch of coriander	*4 tablespoons freshly grated Parmesan or other mild cheese*
½ stick butter (if all beef is used)	
1 small onion, chopped	*Salt and pepper to taste*
¼ pound ground pork ⎫	*½ cup beef broth (canned may be used)*
¼ pound ground veal ⎬	
¼ pound ground beef ⎭	*¼ cup dry white wine*
(all beef may be used)	

For the Artichokes: remove the discolored leaves, pare down the stems, and trim the prickly points off the artichoke leaves. Plunge into boiling salted water to which 1 clove of garlic, the lemon juice, and coriander have been added. Cook until tender, but not ready to fall apart, about 30–40 minutes. Drain.

Cool slightly. *Stuffing:* Heat the butter (if pork is used, decrease the butter to about 2 tablespoons) and sauté the onion until transparent. Add the meats and cook until well browned. Add the crumbs, which have been mixed with the ginger and chili powder, and sauté until crumbs are blended well with meats. Add the cheese and stir until well blended. Add salt and pepper to taste. Remove from the stove and gently stuff the leaves of the artichoke with meat. Place the artichokes in a baking dish, being careful that they do not touch, and pour the broth and wine in the pan. Cook, basting now and then, for about ½ hour at 350°. Add more wine or broth if liquid appears scant. Serve hot. If any of the meat mixture is left over, form into balls and cook beside artichokes.

COLIFLOR ESTILO SANTA CLARA
(Cauliflower, Santa Clara Style)   Serves 6

1 medium-sized cauliflower	*1 whole clove*
¼ cup cooking oil or	*1 tablespoon cinnamon*
butter	*1 bay leaf, crumbled*
¼ cup onion, minced	*Salt and pepper to taste*
¼ cup sweet green	*8 large black olives, sliced*
pepper, chopped	*¼ cup bread crumbs*
1 can (8-ounce size)	*2 tablespoons freshly*
tomatoes, chopped	*grated Cheddar cheese*
1 tablespoon chili powder	*Butter*

Wash cauliflower. Divide into flowerets and boil in salted water until tender, about 8–10 minutes. Do not let vegetable get overdone. Drain. Melt oil in skillet and sauté the onion and pepper until softened. Add the tomatoes and cook until heated through. Add the seasonings. Cook a few minutes to blend. Add the olives. Put flowerets in buttered baking dish and cover with sauce. Mix the crumbs and cheese together and top the sauce with this mixture. Dot a tablespoon of butter here and there over the crumbs. Bake at 375° for about 10 minutes until crumbs and cheese are well browned. Serve hot.

COL MORADA ENVINADA
(Red Cabbage in Wine)   Serves 3–4

1 head red cabbage
½ stick sweet butter
1 cup dry white wine

½ cup raisins
Salt and pepper to taste

Wash the cabbage and shred. Melt butter in a deep saucepan, add the cabbage, and cook on a very low flame for about 15–16 minutes. Add wine, raisins, salt, and pepper and simmer until the cabbage is done, or about 10–12 minutes more if cabbage is young and tender and a little longer if cabbage is not. Add a little more wine if necessary.

COLIFLOR CON GUACAMOLE
(Cauliflower with Avocado Sauce)   Serves 8

1 large cauliflower

DRESSING

2 cups salad oil
¾ cup lemon juice
2 teaspoons salt
1½ teaspoons red chili
powder

½ teaspoon dry mustard
½ teaspoon freshly ground
pepper

TRIMMINGS

Romaine lettuce
2 cups Guacamole*
½–¾ cup shredded
pickled beets

¼ cup almond slivers,
blanched and toasted

Steam cauliflower, covered, in boiling salted water that just covers the bottom of the pot. Cook about 10–12 minutes or until just tender but not too mushy. Drain and cool. Combine all dressing ingredients in a deep bowl and beat with a fork until well blended. Plunge the cauliflower head down in the dressing, cover, and chill for 8 hours.

Wash the lettuce and arrange in leaves on a platter. Put the cauliflower right side up in the center of the lettuce. Pour over it any remaining dressing. Cover the cauliflower with Guacamole. Place beet strips around the base of the cauliflower, saving a few for the top of the vegetable. Put remaining beets on top of the cauliflower. Sprinkle almonds over all. Serve right away.

CHILES CON QUESO (*Chilies and Cheese*)
Serves 5–6

> *6* chiles poblanos, *if available* (*if not, use small sweet green peppers*)
> *¾–1 pound mild chopped cheese* (*Monterey Jack, Wisconsin brick, or Cheddar*)
> *1½ tablespoons* salsa Jalapeño (*the sauce available in cans in Mexican stores*)
> *3 eggs*
> *½ cup sifted flour* (*a little more may be needed*)
> *3 tablespoons bread crumbs*
> *Shortening for deep frying*

Make a small opening in each pepper, leaving them whole, and remove the seeds and veiny parts. Mix cheese with the sauce, adding more sauce if a hotter dish is desired. Roll the cheese into long strips to fit the *poblanos* or roll into balls to fit the bell peppers, figuring on about 2–3 ounces for a pepper. Stuff the pepper and close to conceal all of the cheese. You can use picks to close the opening of the pepper.

Separate eggs and whip the whites until stiff, adding 5 teaspoons of flour, a teaspoon at a time. Beat the yolks until lemon-colored and fold into whites and flour. Roll each pepper in the remaining small amount of flour. Dip into egg mixture, then roll lightly in crumbs. Fry in deep fat at 375° until peppers are browned. Serve hot.

NOTE: Additional *salsa Jalapeño* may be served on the side.

CORONITAS DE ESPINACA
(Little Spinach Crowns) Serves 6

2 pounds spinach, cooked
  and chopped well
2 tablespoons butter
1 tablespoon sweet cream
1 tablespoon milk

2 eggs, beaten lightly
1 small onion, minced well
Salt, pepper, and ground
  cinnamon to taste
2 teaspoons chives

Mix the spinach with the butter, cream, and milk. Add the eggs, onion, salt, pepper, and cinnamon. Grease custard cups and pack each one with spinach mixture, bearing down to make it solid. Place cups in a pan of warm water and cook at 350° for about 20–25 minutes or until set. Unmold and serve with chives sprinkled on top.

HONGOS A LA MEXICANA
(Mexican Mushrooms) Serves 6–8

2 pounds fresh mushrooms
3–4 tablespoons olive oil
2 cloves of garlic, crushed
Sprig of epazote, if
  available (if not, use
  fresh parsley)

5 tablespoons chili powder

Soak mushrooms in cold salted water for a few minutes to clean them. Drain and dry. Heat oil in a skillet and add the garlic. Cook for a few seconds. Add the mushrooms, *epazote* (or parsley), and chili powder and cook for a few minutes until mushrooms are tender but not overdone.

CAMOTE Y PINA (*Sweet Potato and Pineapple*)
Serves 6

5 medium sweet potatoes
  (boiled in jackets,
  peeled, and mashed)
2 tablespoons sugar
2 tablespoons sweet butter
1 teaspoon lemon juice
6 chunks canned
  pineapple, well drained

2 lightly beaten egg whites
2 cups crushed corn flakes
1 teaspoon cinnamon
Pinch of cloves
Shortening for deep frying

Season the mashed potatoes with sugar, butter, and lemon juice. Shape into balls around pineapple chunks. Chill for 1 hour. Dip in egg whites and roll in corn flakes to which seasonings have been added. Fry in deep fat (375°) until golden. Drain on absorbent paper. Serve hot.

NOPALES

Nopales are tender cactus leaves and are sold fresh everywhere in Mexico. You can get them canned or bottled in the United States. If you are able to get your hands on some fresh *nopales*—don't! By that we mean handle with care until you remove all the spiny parts of the cactus leaves. If you use the canned type, wash them before cooking.

To prepare fresh *nopales:* cut them into strips and then crosswise. Cook in water to cover until tender. Pour off water, add salt and pepper, chopped cooked tomatoes, and hot cooked pieces of pork or bits of cooked sausage.

Nopales come in 4-, 5-, 7-, and 10-ounce cans or jars. Seven ounces will serve 2–3 generously. Use 1 tomato with this size can or jar and 1 or 2 small sausages, or more to taste.

TOMATES CON CREMA
(Tomatoes with Cream) Serves 4

4 medium-sized tomatoes
2 tablespoons red chili
  powder
¼ cup chives
¼ cup bread crumbs
Salt and pepper

2 tablespoons sweet butter
1½ tablespoons cornstarch
½ pint heavy cream
1 sweet pimiento, cut into
  strips
Paprika

Cut off tops of tomatoes and scoop out insides. Chop the insides and drain well. Mix with the chili powder, chives, and 2 tablespoons of bread crumbs. Add salt and pepper to taste. Stuff tomatoes. Sauté the rest of the crumbs in the butter lightly. Place tomatoes in a lightly greased baking pan and drizzle the sautéed crumbs over them. Bake at 350° for about 20 minutes or until tender, but not mushy, and completely heated through.

For sauce: Dissolve cornstarch in a small amount of the cream. Add the rest of the cream. Heat mixture in a skillet, stirring until thickened. Do not boil. When thick, pour over the baked tomatoes. Place strips of pimiento on the tops of the tomatoes and dust lightly with paprika.

There are a number of Mexican dishes which we classify as vegetables but which are served in Mexico as separate courses right before dessert or are served as dessert. The following are three of these:

1.

TORTA DE ELOTE *(Corn Torte)* Serves 4–6

2 tablespoons sweet butter
1½ cups canned corn
2 tablespoons sugar

1 teaspoon ground
  cinnamon
2 eggs, separated

Melt the butter and mix with the corn. Add the sugar, cinnamon, and egg yolks. Mix well. Beat the whites until stiff but not dry. Fold into corn mixture. Turn into a buttered baking dish and bake at 350° for 35–40 minutes, or until set. Serve hot with a bit more sugar and cinnamon sprinkled all over.

2.

BUDIN DE MAIZ (*Corn Pudding*)   Serves 8

1 dozen ears of corn with small kernels	*2½ tablespoons ground cinnamon*
4 cups milk, at room temperature	*¾ cup sugar*
3 egg yolks	*½ cup raisins, soaked in a small amount of water*
3 whole cloves	

Scrape the kernels from the ears of corn. Grind the kernels and add to the milk. Mix well for about 5 minutes. Strain to eliminate all kernels, but be sure to force the juice through the strainer. Beat the egg yolks until foamy and add to the corn. Mix in the cloves, cinnamon, and sugar. Cook over a low heat in a double boiler, stirring constantly, until thick. Remove cloves. Drain raisins and add them. Put the pudding in a serving dish and sprinkle with more cinnamon. Serve at once.

3.

CORONA DE TARASCA (*Tarascan Crown*)
Serves 8

This pre-dessert dish was sent to us by Señora Mercedes F. de Gonzalez of Mexico City. It is, however, a favorite in the state of Michoacán.

1 pound masa (special corn meal available at Mexican food stores), moistened with enough water to make a dough	*¼ pound butter*
	⅔ cup sugar
	1 tablespoon baking powder
	Salt and cinnamon to taste

SAUCE

4 large tomatoes	*Sugar*
4 hot chili peppers	*½ cup water*
1 large onion	*Salt and pepper to taste*
2 tablespoons olive oil	

GARNISH

½ cup mild cheese, cut into strips

In a large bowl, place the corn meal dough, butter, sugar, baking powder, salt, and cinnamon. Mix with a wooden spoon until smooth. Grease a crown mold and pour in mixture. Bake at 350° for about 10–15 minutes or until mixture has risen. Reduce heat to 325° and bake for 30 minutes. Place on a platter. Pour over the sauce.

Toast tomatoes over an open flame, peel, and purée. Clean chili peppers of seeds and cut into strips. Cut onion into fine pieces. Sauté the onion in the oil until transparent. Add the chili pepper strips. Add the tomatoes and a pinch of sugar. Cook for about 10 minutes to blend, stirring constantly. Add ½ cup of water and salt and pepper and cook 10 minutes more. Pour over mold. Decorate with cheese strips. Serve as a pre-dessert or dessert course.

PAPAS REALES (*Royal Potatoes*)   Serves 6

4–5 medium-sized white potatoes, boiled (should measure about 2½ cups when mashed)	*Salt and pepper to taste*
	½ cup heavy cream
	½ cup grated fresh Parmesan cheese
¼ cup warm milk, or more if needed	

Mash the potatoes with enough warm milk to make them light and airy. Add salt and pepper to taste. Spoon into lightly greased custard cups. Whip the cream and, when stiff, fold in the cheese; blend. Put cream and cheese mixture on top of each potato cup. Bake at 350° for 15–20 minutes or until golden brown.

CALABACITAS CON CACAHUATES
(*Zucchini with Peanuts*) Serves 6–8

8 good-sized zucchini
Small amount cooking oil
1 pomegranate, peeled and
  seeded
1 avocado, peeled and
  chopped coarsely
1 tablespoon vinegar
2 tablespoons granulated
  sugar

Salt and pepper to taste
¾ cup unsalted peanuts,
  chopped
½ cup bread crumbs
1 tablespoon lemon juice
1 tablespoon orégano

Steam the zucchini, covered in a small amount of salted water, until tender. Drain and cut into pieces. Set aside, but keep warm. Heat a small amount of cooking oil in a skillet and add one-half of the pomegranate seeds, the avocado pieces, vinegar, sugar, salt, and pepper. Cook 3 or 4 minutes until heated through. Mix with the hot zucchini.

Sauce: Heat a bit more oil in a pan, add the nuts, bread crumbs, lemon juice, and salt and pepper to taste. Cook until heated through, stirring to blend. Toss over zucchini. Top with remaining pomegranate seeds and orégano.

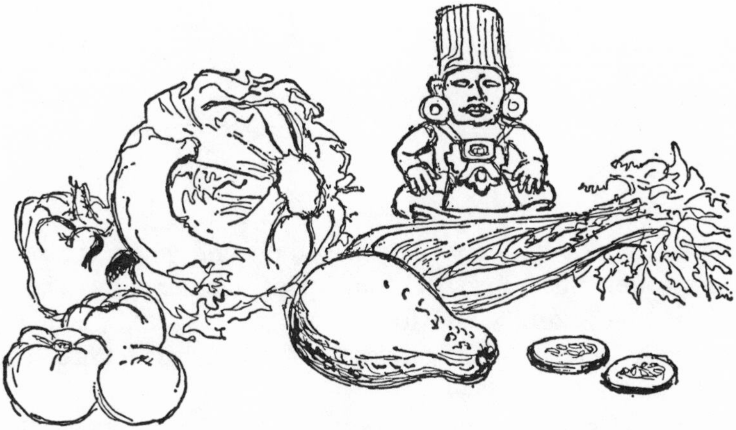

Ensaladas

(SALADS)

Mexico may be the only country in the world where the salad course often rides piggyback on top of another dish. This is true of many tortilla-base foods, such as tostadas, which are frequently served with garnishes of shredded lettuce and tomatoes.

There have been many times when we've been guests at a Mexican table which could fit the true definition of the groaning board, and always, somewhere among the many tempting dishes, we've spotted a platter of radishes, green onions, olives, and a variety of chilies. You'd think these would suffice as a salad, but our hosts have always provided another dish as a salad course.

These salads often made use of avocados, as in Ensalada de Tomate y Aguacate* (Tomato and Avocado Salad) or Aguacates Rellenos* (Stuffed Avocados).

Other salads are good examples of how imaginative you can be with something as simple as squash. See Zucchini Rellenas* (Stuffed Zucchini).

There are fruit salads, too . . . delicious and unusual combinations such as Ensalada de Piña y Manzana* (Pineapple and Apple Salad) or Ensalada de Naranja y Cebolla* (Orange and Onion Salad).

The Mexicans are fond of using sweet red and green peppers in their salads. They add lots of color, flavor, and texture.

AGUACATES RELLENOS I (Stuffed Avocados I)
Serves 8

4 avocados
1 head of lettuce
½ cup cold cooked white
  potatoes, diced

½ cup cold cooked peas
½ cup cold cooked
  carrots, diced

DRESSING

1 teaspoon sugar
1 teaspoon dry mustard
½ teaspoon cayenne
  pepper

2 tablespoons lemon juice
2 tablespoons vinegar
½ cup salad oil

Cut avocados in half lengthwise and remove seed. Shred one-quarter of the head of lettuce. Mix the lettuce with the other ingredients. To make dressing: combine all ingredients in a jar with a tight-fitting lid and shake well. Toss the salad ingredients with the dressing. Stuff the avocados. Serve on a bed of lettuce.

AGUACATES RELLENOS II (*Stuffed Avocados II*)
Serves 6

3 avocados
½ cup celery, diced
¼ cup chopped apples,
  unpeeled
¼ cup blanched almonds
  in slivers

1 banana, diced
¼ cup raisins which have
  been plumped in a small
  amount of water

DRESSING

½ teaspoon salt
Dash of dry mustard
Dash of paprika
Dash of chili powder
2 tablespoons lemon juice
1 tablespoon vinegar

2 tablespoons unsweetened
  pineapple juice
3 tablespoons orange juice
1½ teaspoons sugar
⅓–½ cup salad oil

Peel avocados and cut in half lengthwise. Remove pits. Mix all of the salad ingredients together. For the dressing: combine all the ingredients and beat well. Stuff the avocados with the fruit mixture. Pour dressing over all. Serve extra dressing, if any, on the side.

NOTE: You can dice the avocados and mix with the other ingredients instead of stuffing them, if you prefer.

AGUACATES RELLENOS III
(*Stuffed Avocados III*) Serves 4

2 avocados
1 cup small fresh cooked
  shrimp (crab meat can
  be used)
1 hard-cooked egg,
  chopped
6 ripe olives, chopped

Salt and freshly ground
  pepper to taste
Favorite French dressing,
  or dressing for Stuffed
  Avocados I*
Lettuce leaves

Cut the avocados in half lengthwise; peel and remove seeds. Mix shrimp with the hard-cooked egg and chopped olives. Add salt and pepper to taste. Mix with your favorite French dressing or the dressing for Stuffed Avocados I. Stuff the avocados and serve on lettuce leaves.

NOTE: A few fennel seeds may be added to your dressing for a delightfully different taste.

ENSALADA DE EJOTES (*String Bean Salad*)
Serves 4–6

A very nice lady in Tuxtla, Señora Amalia Bermúdez R., sent us this delicious and different salad.

1 pound cooked string
  beans
Oil and vinegar
Salt and pepper to taste

2 hard-cooked eggs, sliced
1 avocado, peeled and cut
  into wedges
1 onion, sliced

Cut string beans "French" style or diagonally. Add the oil and vinegar. (We prefer a 3–1 ratio . . . that is, three parts oil to 1 part vinegar.) Toss with the beans and salt and pepper. Place in a deep salad bowl and garnish with hard-cooked egg slices, avocado wedges, and slices of onion.

ENSALADA DE CALABACITAS (*Squash Salad*)
Serves 6–8

6 good-sized zucchini
1 clove of garlic
½ teaspoon vinegar
1 small onion, minced
3 stalks celery, chopped
  well

4 tablespoons French
  dressing
Salt and freshly ground
  pepper to taste
Lettuce leaves
Mayonnaise

Cut squash into pieces about ½ inch thick and place in a saucepan with a small amount of salted water, garlic, and vinegar. Cover and cook about 10 minutes until tender but not too soft. Drain; remove garlic. Let stand in a bowl until cold. Add all other ingredients except the lettuce leaves and mayonnaise. Toss. Serve on lettuce leaves with a dab of mayonnaise on top of each salad.

ENSALADA DE CARNES (*Mixed Meat Salad*)
Serves 6–8

1 cup cooked beef, cut
  into narrow strips
½ cup cooked ham, cut
  into narrow strips
¾ cup cooked chicken,
  cut into narrow strips
½ head lettuce, shredded

1 sweet red or green
  pepper, diced coarsely
10 pitted green olives,
  chopped
1 Spanish onion, cut into
  thin rings

DRESSING

⅓ cup cider vinegar
1 cup oil
1 teaspoon marjoram
½ teaspoon thyme

½ teaspoon orégano
Dash of cayenne pepper
Salt and freshly ground
  pepper to taste

Mix the dressing ingredients and beat well until blended. Allow the beef, ham, and chicken to stand in the dressing for 2 hours. Add the lettuce, pepper, olives, and onion rings and toss with the rest of the ingredients.

ENSALADA DE COLIFLOR (*Cauliflower Salad*)
Serves 6–8

*1 head of cauliflower, cut
  into flowerets
2 teaspoons salt
½ tablespoon lemon juice
2½ tablespoons olive oil
1 tablespoon vinegar
1 avocado, sliced*

*1 slice cooked ham, diced
  (tongue may be used)
Freshly ground pepper and
  parsley to taste
Lettuce leaves
Mayonnaise*

Cook cauliflower in 1 teaspoon of the salt, the lemon juice, and a small amount of boiling water in a covered saucepan until tender, or about 8–10 minutes. Drain and let it get completely cold. Mix the remaining ingredients, except the lettuce leaves and mayonnaise, and combine with the cauliflower. Place a lettuce leaf on each salad plate and put a mound of salad in the center of each leaf. Cover completely with mayonnaise.

PIMIENTOS VERDES Y COLORADOS
(*Red and Green Pepper Salad*) Serves 4–6

*1 large sweet green pepper
1 large sweet red pepper
Oil
Vinegar*

*1 clove of garlic
Salt and freshly ground
  pepper to taste*

Toast peppers over an open flame until skin is blistered and charred. Plunge them into cold water. Remove and peel off charred skin. Cut the peppers in half, remove the seeds, and cut the meat into long strips. Combine 4 parts oil to 1 part vinegar and add clove of garlic which has been crushed well.

Cover the pepper strips with the dressing and add salt and freshly ground pepper to taste. Marinate about 1 hour at room temperature before serving.

ENSALADA DE TOMATE Y AGUACATE
(*Tomato and Avocado Salad*)   Serves 6

Bunch of watercress
3 avocados
3 tomatoes, not too ripe
4 green onions, including
  tops

French dressing, or
  dressing suggested with
  Zucchini Rellenas*

Soak watercress in ice water to crisp it. Peel avocados, cut in half lengthwise, and remove pits. Chop the tomatoes but take care not to mash them. Chop the onions, including the tops. Mix onions and tomatoes. Drain watercress. Place some watercress on each plate. Stuff the avocados with the tomato mixture and place on the watercress. Drench with dressing.

NOTE: Avocado can be sliced instead of stuffed and placed on watercress along with tomato slices.

ZUCCHINI RELLENAS (*Stuffed Zucchini*)
Serves 10–12

1 dozen medium-sized
  zucchini
1 can sardines
1 teaspoon lemon juice
Salt and freshly ground
  pepper to taste
Favorite French dressing,
  or, dressing suggested
  below

1 avocado, peeled and
  sliced
2 small tomatoes, peeled
  and chopped
¼ cup freshly grated
  Parmesan cheese
2 tablespoons parsley

Boil the whole zucchini in a small amount of salted water in a covered pot until just tender but not soft. Cut in half, lengthwise, and carefully scoop out the insides. Chop the insides. Drain the sardines and mash them. Mix with the chopped squash and the lemon juice. Add salt and pepper to taste. Stuff the zucchini shells. To your favorite French dressing or the dressing suggested below, add the avocado and tomato pieces. Pour over the stuffed squash. Top with grated cheese and parsley.

DRESSING

1 cup olive oil
½ cup tarragon wine
vinegar

2½ tablespoons sugar
1 clove garlic, crushed
2 teaspoons salt

Mix all ingredients and put in a jar with a tight-fitting lid. Shake well. Let stand for 5 hours before using. Shake again right before pouring over salad. This dressing is also good on more conventional mixed green salads.

CHILES CON TOMATES (*Peppers and Tomatoes*)
Serves 6

3 green peppers
3 ripe tomatoes
Lettuce leaves
French dressing
2 tablespoons chives

2 tablespoons fresh
chopped parsley
Salt and freshly ground
pepper to taste

Seed the peppers and slice into rings. Slice the tomatoes. Arrange tomatoes and peppers on lettuce leaves. Top with French dressing and sprinkle with chives, parsley, and salt and freshly ground pepper to taste.

ENSALADA DE CHAYOTE (*Chayote Salad*)
Serves 4–6

Call it chayote or *christophine,* this vegetable is popular in Mexico as well as the southwestern part of the United States.

2 chayotes
1 medium-sized onion
1 tomato
5 tablespoons oil
2 tablespoons cider vinegar
1 teaspoon fresh chopped
    parsley

Salt and freshly ground
    pepper to taste
Grated mild cheese
    (*optional*)

Simmer chayotes until tender in boiling water, about 15–20 minutes. Peel and slice into thin pieces. Slice onion and tomato and arrange attractively with the chayote slices on salad plates. In a bowl mix the oil, vinegar, and parsley, and add salt and pepper to taste. Beat with a fork. Pour dressing over salad. Top with cheese, if so desired.

COL CON TROZOS DE ORO
(*Cabbage with Gold Nuggets*) Serves 5–6

8 ounces shredded coconut,
    fresh, if possible
8 ounces small cubes fresh
    pineapple

16 ounces red cabbage,
    shredded extra fine
½ cup heavy cream
8 ounces mayonnaise

Combine the first 3 ingredients. Toss several times to distribute evenly. Chill until very cold. Right before serving, whip the cream until stiff and fold in the mayonnaise. Mix quickly through salad. Serve at once.

NOTE: Dried coconut may be used if fresh is not available. Soak it for 15 minutes in cold water and drain well before using.

ENSALADA DE PINA Y MANZANA
(Pineapple and Apple Salad)   Serves 6–7

4 apples, peeled, cored,
  and diced
¾ cup chopped pineapple
2 tablespoons lime juice
¼ cup raisins which have
  been plumped in a small
  amount of water

¼ cup sugar
¼ cup wine vinegar

Combine the apples, pineapple, and lime juice. Drain the raisins and mix with the sugar and vinegar. Mix all the ingredients together.

ENSALADA DE NARANJA Y CEBOLLA
(Orange and Onion Salad)   Serves 4

2 large Spanish onions
2 large navel oranges
1 avocado
Lettuce leaves

French dressing, or
  dressing for Stuffed
  Avocados I*
Tarragon leaves to taste

Peel onions and slice very thin. Place onion rings in ice water to which a small amount of salt has been added. Peel, slice, and seed the oranges. Peel and slice the avocado. Arrange the lettuce leaves in a shallow bowl. Drain onions. Place onion slices alternately with orange and avocado slices on lettuce leaves. Drench with your favorite French dressing, to which some tarragon leaves have been added, or use the dressing in the recipe for Stuffed Avocados I and add tarragon leaves to it.

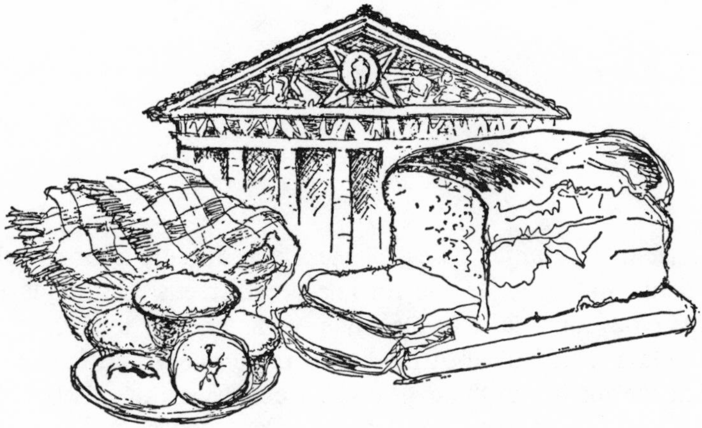

Panes y Repostería

(BREADS, CAKES, COOKIES)

Breakfast in the larger cities in Mexico is usually continental style, consisting of coffee and rolls or sweet breads. On Sundays in large cities, and daily in the small towns and on the ranches and farms, the first meal of the day is more hardy and features some of the recipes in the eggs and cheese section of this book.

It's great fun to shop for freshly baked goods in Mexico. You can stroll for hours in one of the great bakeries and be enchanted by the wide assortment of breads and rolls. *Pan,* or bread, is so much a part of the Mexican way of life that many of the states have developed special *panes.* At village festival time they are baked in fanciful shapes and sold on the streets or in stalls.

An assortment of breads and pastries frequently makes up the light evening meal, along with coffee or chocolate, in this country where luncheon is the main meal of the day. For this light snack, the sweet breads are purchased around five in the afternoon fresh out of the oven. There are Panecillos* (Cookies), Puchas de Canela* (Cinnamon Doughnuts), a specialty of the state of Zacatecas, and Gaznates (Fried Cakes) made with rum. There are also breads and cakes prepared just for fiestas and you'll find them in the fiesta section of this book. Be sure, also, to look into our recipes for Empanadas.* The sweet ones make delicious desserts or are good for afternoon tea service.

It occurs to us that Mexico may well be the only country in the world where a sigh is not only an expression of longing, but, as Suspiros,* which means sighs, the name of a delicious and airy sweet.

BIZCOCHUELOS (*Yeast Bread*) Yield: 2 loaves

1 cake yeast
1½ cups plus 2
tablespoons sugar
2 cups tepid water
6 cups flour
½ cup vegetable
shortening

2 eggs
1 teaspoon salt
1 teaspoon anise seed
2–3 tablespoons melted
butter (for muffins)
Brown sugar (for muffins)

Dissolve the yeast and 2 tablespoons of sugar in 2 cups of tepid water. Sift the flour and stir one-half of it into the yeast and sugar. Let stand in a warm place for 2 hours. Meanwhile, cream the shortening with the remaining sugar. Add this to the flour and yeast after it has stood for 2 hours. Combine the eggs, salt, anise, and remaining flour and beat until well blended. Add this to the other mixture. Knead well and let stand in a large, lightly greased bowl covered with a cloth, in a warm place, until double in bulk. Knead again. Let stand for another ¾ hour. Knead again and shape into 2 loaves. Let stand in loaf tins until double in size. Bake at 425° for 10 minutes; lower temperature to 350° and bake about 45 minutes longer.

You can make *molletes* (muffins) with this same recipe, with a slight variation: after the second rising, mold into small round buns and place on a greased baking tin. Cover and let rise until double in bulk and a slight impression remains when pressed with finger. This should take about 1 hour. Brush lightly with melted butter and put a pat of brown sugar about the size of a walnut on each bun. Bake in a moderate 350° oven for about ½ hour, or until done.

MOLLETES DE CALABAZA (*Pumpkin Muffins*)
Yield: 8–10

*8 ounces cooked, mashed
  pumpkin (canned will
  do)
6 ounces warm milk
1 egg
1½ cups flour*

*1 teaspoon salt
1 tablespoon baking
  powder
½ teaspoon ground cloves
½ cup raisins*

Preheat over to 425°. Mix pumpkin with milk. Stir well and add the egg. Sift dry ingredients including cloves. Add to pumpkin mixture, stir in raisins, and pour into greased muffin tins, filling only halfway. Bake at 425° for ½ hour or until nicely browned.

PANECILLOS (*Cookies*)   Yield: 3 dozen

*2 cups flour
½ teaspoon baking
  powder
¾ cup sugar
Pinch of salt*

*1 cup butter
¼ cup boiling water
½ teaspoon anise seed
½ cup sugar
3 tablespoons cinnamon*

Sift together the flour, baking powder, sugar, and salt. Melt the butter in ¼ cup of boiling water. Combine these ingredients and add a little more flour if necessary to make a soft dough. Roll out on a floured board to a thickness of ¼ inch. Cut with floured cookie cutter, place on a lightly greased cookie tin, brush lightly with additional melted butter, and sprinkle with anise, sugar, and cinnamon. Bake at 375° for 10 minutes.

VARIATIONS

1. Add ¼ cup rum to butter and hot water.

2. Press ½ pecan or candied cherry on cookies before baking.

3. Instead of cinnamon and sugar, sprinkle cookies with powdered sugar after they are baked but while still hot.

PUCHAS (*Baked Doughnuts*) Yield: 2 dozen

6 egg yolks	*2 egg whites*
¼ cup sugar, sifted	*2 tablespoons confectioners'*
1¾ cups flour, sifted	*sugar*
4 tablespoons rum	*1 teaspoon lime juice*

Beat egg yolks until lemon-colored. Add the sugar and beat again. Add the flour and the rum alternately. Mix well. Roll the dough on a lightly floured board and cut into about 2 dozen squares, 3×3 inches. Make rings of the squares. Bake on a greased baking sheet for twenty minutes at 350° or until brown.

Topping—While the Puchas bake, beat the egg whites until they stand in peaks but are not dry. Add the confectioners' sugar and the lime juice. When doughnuts are brown, spread this mixture on them. Turn off oven, return Puchas to oven, and allow to stand for about 3 or 4 minutes. Remove and serve.

PUCHAS DE CANELA (*Cinnamon Doughnuts*)
Yield: 3 dozen

These are Mexican doughnuts as made in Zacatecas, a state where the terrific variation in climate permits everything from the raising of cattle to the growing of sugar cane and tropical fruits.

¼ teaspoon baking powder
½ cup strained orange
  juice, fresh, canned, or
  frozen
12 egg yolks
Flour
1½ cups shortening or
  lard

Pinch of salt
½ teaspoon orange extract
1½ cups sugar
4 tablespoons ground
  cinnamon

Dissolve the baking powder in the orange juice. Beat the egg yolks until lemon-colored. Add enough sifted flour to them to make a dough. Add 1 tablespoon of cold melted shortening, the juice, a pinch of salt, and the extract. Knead dough until workable. Let stand 1 hour. Shape the dough into small rings. Fry them in the remaining shortening at 375°. Drain on absorbent paper. Dip them in the following syrup before dusting with cinnamon.

Syrup: Cook the 1½ cups sugar in ½ cup water until it spins a thread or reaches 230° on a candy thermometer. Let cool for 20–30 minutes before dipping doughnuts. Sprinkle with the ground cinnamon.

SUSPIROS (*Sighs*) Yield: 2½ dozen

½ cup water
4 tablespoons butter
⅓ cup sugar
½ teaspoon salt
Dash of vanilla
¼ teaspoon ground
  cinnamon

1¾ cups all-purpose flour,
  sifted
2 large eggs, lightly beaten
Shortening for deep frying
Confectioners' sugar

Bring ½ cup water to a boil with butter, add sugar, salt, vanilla, and cinnamon, and boil rapidly for 2 minutes. Add all the flour at once. Stir until mixture forms a ball and pulls away from the sides of the pan. Remove from heat. Allow mixture to get tepid. Add eggs and stir until blended. Beat rapidly until you have a thick paste. Chill for several hours so dough will be easy to handle. Roll out dough on a well-floured board until very thin. Cut dough into 2-inch squares. Lift with a spatula and fry in deep fat at 350° on the thermometer until golden brown. (This takes about 2 minutes.) Turn and cook on the other side. Remove from the fat. Drain on absorbent paper. Dust with confectioners' sugar.

GAZNATES (*Fried Cakes*)   Yield: 2 dozen

2 cups all-purpose flour,
   sifted
6 egg yolks, beaten
½ cup rum
2 cups shortening for deep
   frying

2 tablespoons ground
   cinnamon
1 cup confectioners' sugar

Add the flour slowly to the egg yolks, beating constantly. Knead well while sprinkling the dough with the rum until it is blended well. Roll out very thin and cut into small squares; fold by making the lower right corner touch the upper left corner. Fry in hot shortening at 350°. Remove and drain on absorbent paper. Combine the cinnamon and sugar and sprinkle on the hot cookies.

PASTEL DE COGNAC (*Brandy Cake*)   Serves 8–9

4 eggs
½ cup sugar
1 cup flour, sifted
1 teaspoon baking powder
¼ teaspoon cinnamon

Pinch of salt
5 tablespoons melted butter
½ cup almonds, blanched
   and chopped well

SAUCE

1¾ cups sugar
2 cups water
1 tablespoon light corn
syrup, or ¼ teaspoon
cream of tartar
¾ cup brandy

Grease a 2-quart baking dish and set aside. Preheat oven to 375°. Separate the eggs. Beat whites with one-half of the sugar until stiff and standing in peaks. Beat yolks lightly and add to the other half of the sugar. Add yolks to egg whites. Combine all dry ingredients and fold into the eggs. Add the melted butter. Stir in nuts. Pour batter into the casserole and bake about ½ hour. *For the sauce:* Boil 2 cups of water, sugar and syrup or cream of tartar, until it forms a ball (236°). Add the brandy. When cake is done, make little holes all over it with a thin skewer; pour sauce over.

PANECILLOS BORRACHITOS (*Drunken Cookies*)
Yield: 3–4 dozen

1 cup shortening   *3 cups flour, sifted*
⅔ cup sugar   *Dry red wine*
2 eggs yolks   *Cinnamon*
¼ teaspoon salt   *Sugar*

Cream the shortening with the sugar; add the egg yolks and salt. Add the flour alternately with enough wine to make a soft cookie dough. Roll out on a lightly floured board. Cut into desired shapes. Bake at 375° for 10 minutes. Dust with cinnamon and a little sugar while hot.

MERENGUES (*Meringues*) Yield: 2 dozen

⅛ teaspoon salt
¼ teaspoon vanilla

7 eggs whites
1 pound granulated sugar

Add salt and vanilla to the egg whites and beat until mixture stands in peaks. Add sugar gradually and continue beating until very stiff. Drop mixture by teaspoonful onto a well-buttered cookie sheet. Bake at 250° for 30 minutes or until lightly browned.

GALLETAS DE NUEZ (*Nut Cookies*) Yield: 36

1 cup butter
4 tablespoons confectioners'
  sugar
2 teaspoons vanilla extract
2 cups flour

1 cup chopped nuts
  (pecans or walnuts)
Additional confectioners'
  sugar

Cream butter and sugar; add vanilla and 1 tablespoon cold water. Stir in flour. Add the nuts. Stir well. Form small rolled strips about 2 inches long. Bake on an ungreased cookie tray at 300° for 20 minutes or until brown. Roll in additional confectioners' sugar while hot.

POLVORONES (*Melt-aways*) Yield: 2½ dozen

2½ cups flour
½ pound butter
½ cup confectioners' sugar

½ teaspoon vanilla extract
Additional confectioners'
  sugar

Sift the flour. Cream the butter and the ½ cup sugar. Add the flour and vanilla and mix well. Chill for 5 hours. Roll out on floured board. Cut rounds about 1 inch in diameter. Bake on a greased tin for 15 minutes at 400°. Dust them while hot in confectioners' sugar. Cool on a rack and dust again with sugar.

CHURROS (*Crullers*)   Yield: 1–1½ dozen

These crullers derive their highly unusual flavor from a slice of white bread and one-half of a lemon added to the oil.

Oil for deep frying *1 cup boiling water*
1 slice white bread *1 egg*
½ lemon *Confectioners' or*
1 cup flour *granulated sugar*
1 teaspoon salt

Prepare oil for frying by heating it with the bread and lemon. Sift flour 4 times. Add the salt to 1 cup boiling water and add to the flour all at one time, beating vigorously to produce a fluffy batter. Add egg and beat until batter gets shiny. Remove bread from fat as soon as it is dark brown; remove lemon. Put batter into a pastry tube and drop 2- or 3-inch pieces in the fat. Cook until golden. Drain on absorbent paper. Roll in sugar.

BESOS (*Kisses*)   Yield: 2 dozen

1 cup shortening *1½ teaspoons ground*
2 cups sugar *cinnamon*
¼ teaspoon baking soda *Favorite jam*
2 cups flour

Cream shortening and sugar. Sift dry ingredients and combine with shortening. Roll out quite thin on a lightly floured board. Cut into squares, rounds, or "teardrops." Bake for 12 minutes at 400°. Make cookies "kiss" by putting them together while hot with a layer of your favorite jam.

TORTA DE GARBANZO *(Chick-pea Torte)*
Serves 8–10

*3 cups cooked chick-peas
(canned will do)
½ cup milk (room
temperature)
1 cup sugar
4 egg yolks, beaten until
they are thick and
lemon-colored*

*½ teaspoon ground cloves
¼ cup rum, sherry, or
brandy
4 egg whites, stiffly beaten*

Purée the peas and blend with the milk. Add the sugar to the beaten egg yolks and stir in cloves and rum, sherry, or brandy. Combine with peas and milk. Fold in the stiffly beaten egg whites. Bake in a buttered casserole for about 1 hour at 350°. (Should be served quite cold.)

NOTE: If canned peas are used, drain them well.

PAN DE VINO *(Wine Cake)* Yield: 2 loaves

*½ pound butter
1½ cups sugar
½ dozen eggs
1 teaspoon grated orange
rind
3 teaspoons lemon juice*

*2 cups cake flour
2 teaspoons baking powder
¼ teaspoon salt
1 cup cornstarch
¼ cup sherry*

Cream butter, add sugar, and blend well until sugar is dissolved and mixture is very creamy. Add eggs, one at a time, beating after each addition. Add rind and juice. Sift dry ingredients together. Add alternately with sherry, making 4 additions of dry ingredients and 3 of the wine. Mix well. Grease

2 loaf pans (9×5 inches, 3 inches deep) and pour in batter. Bake about 90 minutes at 325°. Wait 15 minutes before removing to racks. Cool well before cutting.

PAN DE AJONJOLI (*Sesame Seed Cake*)　Serves 8

CAKE

1½ cups flour
2 teaspoons baking powder
¼ teaspoon salt
½ cup sugar
4 ounces milk

1 egg
3 tablespoons melted
　butter
¼ teaspoon vanilla

TOPPING

½ cup flour, sifted
½ cup brown sugar
1 tablespoon ground
　cinnamon
Pinch of salt

2 tablespoons melted butter
½ cup chopped nuts
2½ tablespoons sesame
　seed

Sift together the dry ingredients. Add the milk, egg, and butter. Add vanilla. Stir until blended. Pour batter into a well-greased 9-inch baking pan; cover with topping made by blending all ingredients except the sesame seed. Sprinkle sesame seed over the topping. Bake in a 350° oven for 30 minutes.

Postres y Dulces

❖

(DESSERTS AND CONFECTIONS)

"El que se levanta tarde ni oye Misa ni come carne."

"A late riser misses Mass and meat as well," says a wise old proverb. To which we can only add that an early riser—one who leaves the table before the end of a Mexican dinner—will miss his just desserts.

In Mexico, every housewife prides herself on her collection of recipes for sweets and candies, which are usually handed down as treasures from one generation to another. Many of these confections originated among the early Spanish nuns who perfected them in convents and sent them as gifts to viceroys. An example of this is Viceroy's Pudding.*

Other sweet dishes were inspired by native fruits, the coconut being the most popular, with old-time cooks claiming to know one hundred or more recipes with coconut as a base. Cocada* is a famous coconut sweet. The climate was probably responsible for the invention of the many different *atés* found in the more tropical regions of Mexico. These are jams used to preserve fruits in the warm, moist climate, as is the case with Até de Guayaba.* Be sure, also, to look into "sweet tamales," or Ochépos,* as they are called, when thinking about desserts.

Flan,* a light custard, is considered a national dessert. It is almost as much of a staple menu item as tortillas and it can be purchased from street vendors as well as found in Mexican homes and restaurants.

Mexican children are frequently given sugar cane to soothe them in infancy, and thus they acquire a taste for sweets early in life. It's no wonder that there are shops in the country which sell over three hundred different kinds of sweets, and there are devotees of each of them.

DULCE DE COCO A LA HOTEL MAYALAND (*Coconut Dessert a la Hotel Mayaland*)
Serves 20

Almost in the shadows of the fabulous Maya ruins of Chichén Itzá in the Yucatán stands one of the most beautiful hotels in the world—the Mayaland. After a day of inspecting the ancient ruins, guests return to this luxurious lodge to sip cool drinks on the patio, swim in a pool which is brimful of flowers, and dine on excellent food. A dessert feature of the Mayaland is a favorite of ours.

2 pounds sweet potatoes
1 pound ground coconut (fresh is preferred)
2 pounds sugar

Cook the sweet potatoes in their jackets in water to cover. When tender, cool them and peel. Mash the potatoes and force them through a food strainer. Mix the potatoes with the coconut and sugar. Cook on a low flame, stirring constantly, until the bottom of the pan can be seen in the wake of the spoon. Cool and serve in individual compote dishes.

CREMA DE NANTES (*Nantes Cream*)   Serves 6–8

Our appreciation to Margarita B. de Rodríguez Meléndez for this custard with its unusual sauce.

1 quart milk, less ½ cup   *4 egg yolks, beaten with*
1 cup sugar   *½ cup milk*
1½ teaspoons orange rind   *2 tablespoons gelatin*

In a double boiler bring the milk to the boiling point. Add the sugar and orange rind. Boil once and set aside to cool a bit. When tepid, add the egg yolks slowly, stirring constantly. Place over water in double boiler again, heat it well, and add the gelatin; do not allow to boil. Stir to dissolve completely. Strain into a mold and let cool until firm.

SAUCE

> *1 pound cooked prunes, pitted*
> *1 cup sugar*
> *½ cup orange juice*
> *1 teaspoon vanilla extract*

Purée the prunes by putting them through a fine sieve. Boil them with the sugar, orange juice, and vanilla, stirring constantly until you can see the bottom of the pan in the wake of the spoon. Set aside to cool. Serve over the Nantes Cream.

ARROZ CON LECHE (*Rice Pudding*)   Serves 6–7

> *½ cup rice*
> *½ stick cinnamon*
> *1 cup water*
> *1 cup sugar*
> *¾ cup milk*
> *2 egg yolks, beaten lightly*
>
> *Rind of ½ lemon, grated*
> *2 tablespoons chopped nuts*
> *2½ tablespoons black raisins*

Cook rice with the cinnamon stick in 1 cup of water, or according to favorite method, until liquid is absorbed. Discard the cinnamon stick. Add the sugar and milk and cook about 10–15 minutes, so milk has a chance to penetrate the rice. Remove from flame and add the egg yolks, stirring constantly as they are added and until mixture attains the consistency of a smooth custard. Return to the heat and add lemon rind; cook slowly, stirring constantly, for about 5 minutes. Pour into serving dishes and serve with nuts and raisins sprinkled over the top.

BUDIN DE FRIJOLES (*Bean Pudding*) Serves 6

1 cup pinto beans, which have been soaked in water overnight (or 1 cup canned pinto or kidney beans, well drained)

2 cups water
2 cups milk, scalded
1 thick cinnamon stick
2 whole cloves
Pinch of salt
1 cup sugar

If dried beans are used, simmer them in 2 cups of water for about 1–1½ hours or until they are tender, after soaking them for 8 hours or overnight. (Skip that step if canned beans are used.) Drain the beans and mash them into a paste. Mix the beans with the scalded milk and push through a fine food strainer. Add the cinnamon, cloves, salt, and sugar. Cook, stirring constantly, until mixture comes to a boil. Boil for about 5 minutes. Lower heat and let the mixture cook until thick, about 1 hour. Stir frequently to prevent scorching. Mixture is done when bottom of the pan can be seen in the wake of the spoon. Remove bits and pieces of cloves and cinnamon before serving.

CALABAZA (*Pumpkin Pudding*) Serves 8–10

The Mexicans really have the Cinderella touch when it comes to pumpkin. In this case, of course, the lowly vegetable is transformed into a delightful dessert.

1 5–6-pound pumpkin
1 stick cinnamon
3 oranges, unpeeled and sliced thin
3 cups dark molasses (or you can use brown sugar: 1½ pounds, firmly packed, to every 2 pounds pumpkin)

1 teaspoon coriander
4 whole cloves
3 whole apples, unpeeled
½ cup raisins (optional)

Cut pumpkin into chunks and remove seeds but leave the skin intact. Put the pumpkin pieces into a heavy pot with water to cover; add the cinnamon, orange slices, molasses, coriander, and cloves. Simmer, covered, over a very low flame until almost tender. Add the apples and raisins and cook until apples are quite done but not too mushy. More water and molasses may be added during cooking, if necessary. Remove the cinnamon stick and cloves while pudding cools to keep it from getting too "hot." Cut apples into pieces when the dish is served. The dish is served cold with milk or cream in deep soup bowls.

VARIATIONS

1. Drill a hole in the pumpkin and pour into it as much rum or brandy as it will hold. Let it stand overnight. Cook the liquor-flavored pumpkin as in the previous recipe, using the liquor in place of the water. Some of the liquor will be absorbed as the pumpkin stands overnight, so you may have to add some water to cover, as in the preceding recipe.

2. Put pumpkin chunks in deep heavy kettle. Pack 4 cups of brown sugar solidly around it; cut up 3 oranges and put unpeeled orange slices here and there. In a little cheesecloth bag, put 1 cinnamon stick, 12 whole cloves, 1 teaspoon anise seeds, and 1 teaspoon coriander. Tie and place in the center of the kettle. Add 6 tablespoons of water and 2 tablespoons of rum. Cover tightly and cook over very low flame until pumpkin is tender and glazed. Remove pumpkin and keep warm. Cook syrup over low flame until very heavy and pour over pumpkin. Serve warm or cold.

PLATANOS CON RON (*Bananas with Rum*)
Serves 6

Some say that this dish originated in Zacatecas, a central state noted for its abundant fruits. The only reason we'd like to find out who created it is to say "thank you."

4 large bananas
⅓ cup sweet butter
½ cup sugar
1 cup heavy cream

¼ cup rum (or more to taste)
¾ teaspoon vanilla extract
Dash of ground cloves

Peel bananas and slice them in half lengthwise. Sauté them in butter until golden brown. Drain them on absorbent paper and place them on a platter. Cool. Sprinkle with one-half of the sugar. Whip cream until stiff and fold in the remaining sugar, rum, and vanilla. Cover bananas completely with this mixture. Chill. Serve sprinkled with ground cloves.

DULCE DE MANGO (*Mango Dessert*)   Serves 6

6 large ripe mangoes
1 cup water
1¾ cups sugar
Juice of 1 lemon

Peel and slice mangoes. Simmer 1 cup water with sugar and lemon over a low flame for about 30 minutes. Add mangoes to syrup and simmer gently until syrup is condensed to about half the amount you started with. Serve very cold.

COCADA (*Coconut Pudding*)   Serves 6–7

1 cup sugar
1 cup water
1 cup fresh or 4 ounces
  canned shredded coconut
Salt to taste

3¼ cups milk
2 tablespoons ground
  cinnamon
⅓ cup milk, ice-cold
3 egg yolks, well beaten

Combine the sugar and 1 cup water and boil for 15 minutes. Add coconut and salt to taste and cook until the syrup is absorbed. In another pan, bring the 3¼ cups milk to a boil with the cinnamon and salt. Add the coconut, reduce the heat, and stir constantly until mixture resembles custard. Mix the ice-cold milk with the eggs. Stir a little coconut mixture into eggs and cold milk and add the egg-milk mixture very gradually to pot. Continue to simmer, stirring until thick. Pour into a buttered dish. Cool. Refrigerate.

HUEVOS MOLES (*Egg Yolk Cream*)   Serves 6–8

1½ cups sugar
1 cup water
6 whole cloves
1 teaspoon ground
  cinnamon
4 tablespoons sherry
1 spongecake (prepare
  according to favorite
  recipe or buy one ready-
  made)

8 egg yolks, lightly beaten
  with a pinch of salt
½ stick cinnamon,
  chopped into little bits
¼ cup pine nuts, left
  whole
¼ cup raisins
¼ cup almonds, chopped

Boil the sugar with 1 cup water, cloves, and ground cinnamon for about 5 minutes. Remove from the flame and stir in the sherry. Slice spongecake and dip slices in this syrup, figuring a slice per person. Put each slice on a serving dish. Strain the remaining syrup and combine it with the lightly beaten egg yolks. Cook over a low flame, stirring constantly, until mixture thickens. Pour this custard over the cake slices. Decorate with bits of cinnamon, pine nuts, raisins, and almonds.

FLAN (*Mexican Custard*) Serves 6

*6 dabs brown sugar, about
 the size of walnuts
1 quart milk
½ cup sugar (¾ cup if
 you like your custard on the
 sweet side)
½ teaspoon ground
 cinnamon*

*¼ teaspoon salt
1 teaspoon vanilla extract
⅛ teaspoon grated lemon
 or orange rind
 (optional)
4 egg yolks, lightly beaten
2 egg whites, lightly
 beaten*

To caramelize custard cups—Put the dabs of brown sugar in the bottom of 6 individual cups, one to a cup. Place cups in hot oven. Move the cups from side to side as sugar melts so the surface of each cup is covered with melted brown sugar.

For custard—Combine the milk, sugar, cinnamon, salt, vanilla, and lemon rind and cook over a very low flame, stirring constantly, until mixture has reached a custard stage. Cool. Combine the lightly beaten yolks and whites and add to custard. Mix well.

Pour the custard into the little cups and place them in a larger pan containing hot water. (The Mexicans call this *baño de Maria,* or Mary's bath.) Bake in a slow oven (300°) for about 1 hour or until a knife inserted in the center of a cup comes out clean. Cool. Chill several hours before serving.

VARIATIONS

1. Pour 6 or 7 tablespoons of warmed brandy or rum over the cold flan at serving time and ignite when carrying to the table.

2. Coconut Flan: to basic recipe, add ½ cup grated canned coconut.

3. Pineapple Upside-down Flan: before brown sugar has a chance to cool in cups, add a tablespoon of well-drained crushed pineapple and a candied cherry to each cup. Or, use chunks of pineapple in the bottom to form a flower with cherry as center. Bake a little longer than basic flan.

FLAN DE ALMENDRAS (*Custard with Almonds*)
Serves 6–7

1 cup boiling water
1 can sweetened condensed
  milk (15-ounce size)
½ teaspoon vanilla
1 cup almonds, blanched,
  toasted, and ground

4 egg yolks
4 tablespoons brown sugar,
  firmly packed
½ cup (about) almonds,
  left whole

To 1 cup of boiling water add the condensed milk, vanilla, and ground almonds, and simmer for about 5 minutes. Cool. Add egg yolks, a little bit at a time, stirring constantly until thickened. Put brown sugar in baking dish or individual cups and melt to coat dish or cups as in basic Flan* recipe. Cool slightly. Fill dish with custard, place in a larger pan of hot water, and bake in a 300° oven for about ½ hour or until silver knife blade emerges clean when dipped into custard. Chill thoroughly and serve ice-cold. Decorate with whole almonds before serving.

VARIATIONS

1. Use strong coffee for one-half of the liquid.

2. Use ground pine nuts, pecans, or walnuts instead of almonds.

3. Use 2 tablespoons of cocoa mixed with the ground almonds in the first step of the recipe. Or, add a combination of cocoa and strong coffee for a mocha taste.

4. Flans can also be topped with a dab of sweet whipped cream right before serving.

HUEVOS REALES (*Royal Eggs*)   Serves 6

A dish from Spain, but considered a national dessert in Mexico.

8 egg yolks
1¼ cups sugar
3 cloves
1 thick cinnamon stick
½ cup water

¼ cup sherry, rum, or
  brandy
5 tablespoons pine nuts
4 tablespoons raisins

Beat egg yolks until thick, pale, and lemon-colored. (Tradition calls for ½ hour of beating by hand, but we advise using an electric mixer.) Pour eggs into a buttered baking dish, set the pan in another pan of hot water, and bake in a moderate oven, 350°, until eggs are puffy, or for about 30 minutes. While the eggs are baking, make a syrup by combining the sugar, cloves, and cinnamon stick with about ½ cup water and boil until sugar is dissolved—about 5 minutes. Discard cinnamon stick and cloves. Add sherry, rum, or brandy. Cut eggs into squares or triangles and let them soak in the hot syrup until cold—at least 2 hours. Serve garnished with nuts and raisins.

CHONGOS (*Little Knots*)   Serves 6

This delicate dessert comes from Zamora, a little town not far from Guadalajara. Chongos are used for fiestas and everyday fare.

4 cups milk
½ teaspoon vanilla extract
1 egg yolk, beaten lightly
2 junket tablets
3 tablespoons water
2 cups white sugar

2 tablespoons brown sugar,
  firmly packed
1 cup water
1 teaspoon ground
  cinnamon
Pinch of salt

Heat milk enough to take the chill off and stir in the vanilla. Add the egg yolk and strain. Dissolve the junket tablets in 3 tablespoons of cold water and combine this mixture with egg-and-milk mixture. Stir and let stand unrefrigerated until junket sets, about 20 minutes or more. Cut the junket mixture into squares about 2 inches in diameter. Carefully place the squares one at a time in a deep saucepan, separating one from another, and cook over a low flame.

Mix the sugars with the cinnamon and salt and 1 cup of water in a separate bowl. When junket squares start bubbling around the edges, add 1 cup of the mixture, pouring it very carefully around the squares so you don't break them. Continue cooking on a very low flame and add more syrup to the squares as the mixture in the pan thickens; do this until all the syrup has been added. Simmer about 35 minutes or more, or until the syrup is very thick. Let cool. Remove to individual plates and refrigerate. Serve ice-cold.

QUESO DE ALMENDRAS (*Almond Cheese*)
Serves 6

The Spaniards brought almonds to Mexico, but it was the Mexicans who created this delicious mock cheese from them.

¾ pound almonds, blanched and ground
1 teaspoon vanilla
1 egg white
6 egg yolks, lightly beaten
1½ cups sugar
1 cup water
Freshly ground cinnamon, if possible

Grind the almonds well and mix with vanilla, egg white, and yolks to make a paste. Boil the sugar with 1 cup of water until it reaches the soft-ball stage when a bit is dropped into a cup of cold water (236° on candy thermometer). Remove from the flame and combine with ground almond-egg paste. Cook this mixture over a very low flame, stirring constantly, until bottom of the pan can be seen in the wake of the spoon. Remove from the fire and beat into a paste. Grind again if mixture is not completely smooth. Line a mold with wax paper and pour in mixture. Shape it to resemble a round cheese ball. Let cool, remove from mold, remove the paper, and dust with ground cinnamon until cheese is covered completely. Cut into small wedges when serving and accompany with fruit, most especially apples, and thin salted crackers.

BUDIN DE VIRREY (*Viceroy's Pudding*)
Serves 8–10

3 cups granulated sugar
1 cup water
16 egg yolks, lightly
    beaten
1 teaspoon ground
    cinnamon
¼ cup rum
1 cup heavy sweet cream
5 egg whites

1 cup confectioners' sugar
1 spongecake, about 1
    pound, cut into thin
    slices (*prepare according*
    to favorite recipe or use
    ready-made cake)
¼ cup grated unsweetened
    chocolate

Boil the granulated sugar in a cup of water until it reaches a thin-thread stage when exposed to the air (230°–234° on thermometer). Remove from heat, cool, and add the lightly beaten egg yolks and cinnamon. Cook mixture over a low flame, stirring constantly, until thick. Remove from the stove and add the rum. Beat the heavy cream in a chilled bowl until it stands in peaks. Beat the egg whites, along with the confectioners' sugar, until stiff and mixture stands in peaks. Fold whipped cream into egg white mixture. In your prettiest serving dish— a fairly deep one—arrange a layer of cake slices, follow with a layer of egg yolk cream, another layer of cake, a layer of whipped cream, and so on until all the ingredients are used up. Top with chocolate.

DULCE DE ALMENDRA (*Almond Dessert*)
Serves 8–10

This dish was created in a convent near Puebla. At one time people from all over Mexico used to send to the convent for Dulce de Almendra to give to friends on special occasions.

3 egg yolks, lightly beaten with a pinch of salt and ½ teaspoon vanilla
1½ cups shelled almonds, blanched and ground
3 cups sugar

1 cup water
⅔ cup sweet dessert wine
1 spongecake, sliced (prepare according to your favorite recipe or use ready-made cake)

Mix together the egg yolks and almonds and let stand while you boil the sugar in 1 cup of water for 5 minutes. Remove syrup from stove and divide into 2 equal parts. To one-half of the syrup add the dessert wine; to the other part add the almonds and eggs. Cook the almond syrup very slowly, stirring constantly, until thick and custardy. Dip the cake slices in the wine syrup mixture and place in alternate layers with the almond custard in a greased baking dish. The top layer should be made of the almond custard. Bake in a 300° oven until the top layer is golden, about ½ hour. Serve hot or cold, but *do not refrigerate*. Keep overnight.

MANZANA DE MOCTEZUMA
(*Apples with Custard*)   Serves 6

This dish is best if made with firm, hard, green cooking apples. It is popular in Moctezuma's old "home town," Mexico City.

6 green apples
1 cup sugar
½ cup water
1 tablespoon lemon juice
4 tablespoons strawberry
   jam
1 tablespoon brandy

2 tablespoons butter
3 eggs, beaten
1 pint milk
1 teaspoon vanilla
¼ cup ladyfingers,
   crumbled

Peel and core the apples. Boil together ½ cup sugar, ½ cup water, and lemon juice. Add the apples and simmer until almost tender. Remove apples to a greased baking dish and fill the cavities with jam, which has been mixed with the brandy. Top each apple with a bit of the butter. Mix together the eggs and remaining sugar. Add the milk, vanilla, and cookie crumbs. Mix and pour around the apples. Bake in a slow oven (300°) for about 1 hour or until custard is set.

CELAYA CAJETA (*Caramel Sauce*)
Yield: 2 quarts

This is a specialty from the state of Guanajuato. It is shipped from there all over the Republic in decorative little wooden boxes.

¼ teaspoon baking soda
1½ quarts goat's milk[1]
4 tablespoons cornstarch
1½ quarts cow's milk
3 cups sugar

1 teaspoon ground
   cinnamon (*add more if
   you want a more
   definite spicy taste*)

[1] Cow's milk can be used.

Dissolve the soda in 1 cup of the goat's milk and strain. Dissolve the cornstarch in a cup of cow's milk and strain. Combine the rest of the milk and heat to boiling point. Add the milks in which the cornstarch and soda were dissolved. Add the sugar and cinnamon and continue cooking. Stir constantly with a wooden spoon until mixture thickens and the bottom of the pan can be seen in the wake of the spoon. Remove from the flame and pour into a large serving dish.

VARIATION

Prepare as above, but add 5 tablespoons of rum when mixture is almost done, or at about the time that the bottom of the pan can be seen.

Serving suggestions – this caramel sauce is eaten plain, spread on bread, or poured over ice cream. In sophisticated homes the sauce is used as topping on crepes and further garnished with chopped walnuts or confectioners' sugar.

ARROZ DELICIA *(Rice Delight)*   Serves 8–10

The name of the state of Guerrero may not mean too much to you, but the name of a place in that state, Acapulco, immediately evokes an image of one of the most famous beach resorts in the world . . . surrounded by coconut palms which yield the fruits for this dessert.

2 cups shredded coconut (fresh, if possible)	1 stick cinnamon
	2 cups water
1 quart milk (or part coconut milk and part cow's milk to make up a quart)	1¼ cups sugar
	2 egg yolks, lightly beaten
	½ cup raisins
⅝ cup rice	¼ cup citron, chopped
	¼ cup chopped nuts

Grind the coconut and mix it in the milk. Strain this mixture. Soak the rice in hot water for 15 minutes; drain. Rinse in cold water. Cook rice and cinnamon in the water until the liquid has been absorbed. Add the sugar and the coconut-and-milk mixture. Keep cooking until the rice is tender. Stir in the lightly beaten egg yolks a little at a time. Allow mixture to boil up once, remove cinnamon stick, and pour into sherbert dishes or sauce plates. Sprinkle with the raisins, citron, and chopped nuts.

CAPIROTADA (*Bread Pudding*)   Serves 6

This is very popular for Lent.

8–9 slices white bread or toast (the equivalent in poundcake or spongecake can be used)
¾ cup lard or other shortening
1 stick cinnamon, about 2 inches long
1 cup brown sugar, firmly packed
⅛ teaspoon ground cloves

½ cup water
3 ounces mild Cheddar cheese, crumbled
1 apple, peeled, cored, and sliced
½ cup chopped nuts
¼ stick butter, more or less
1 teaspoon ground cinnamon

Sauté the bread in the shortening. Cook together the cinnamon, sugar, cloves, and ½ cup of water until thickened, about 5 minutes. Discard the cinnamon stick. In a greased baking dish arrange a layer of bread, douse it with syrup, and dot it with cheese, apples, nuts, and bits of butter. Top this with another layer of bread and add syrup and cheese, apples, nuts, and butter as described above until you have used up all of the ingredients. Brown in a slow oven (300°) for about 30 minutes. Dust with ground cinnamon and serve hot.

VARIATION 1.

1 medium-sized onion
2 small tomatoes, peeled and chopped
½ cup raisins

Following the above recipe, make a syrup of sugar, water, and cinnamon. Discard the cinnamon stick and add the onion and tomato. Strain the syrup. Then arrange in a baking dish in layers starting with the bread and going on as in the above. Raisins are sprinkled as layers are made.

VARIATION 2.

To make this dish as in Guadalajara, use the basic recipe but substitute molasses for the sugar and, instead of cloves, use the juice of 1 lemon and ¾ teaspoon anise seed. Following the basic recipe, make the syrup out of the molasses, lemon juice, and spices. When pudding is piping hot, pour a heavy sweet wine over it. Serve right away.

DULCE DEL SUR (*Southern Sweet*)   Serves 6

1 stick butter	½ cup flour, sifted
½ cup powdered sugar	1 teaspoon baking powder
1 teaspoon cinnamon	¼ teaspoon salt
Grated rinds of ½ lime and ½ lemon	2 tablespoons chopped raisins
2 eggs	2 tablespoons chopped pecans
⅓ cup yellow corn meal, uncooked	½ cup heavy cream

Cream butter, sugar, cinnamon, and lemon and lime rinds; beat in eggs. Sift dry ingredients into the cream mixture; add raisins, nuts, and cream. Mix into a smooth batter and pour into 6 buttered custard cups. Bake in a 350° oven for 20 minutes or until done. Turn out into dessert plates and serve plain or with the following sauce:

1 egg	½ cup milk
½ cup sugar	½ cup cream
1 teaspoon cornstarch	2 tablespoons rum

Beat egg, sugar, cornstarch, milk, and cream. Cook over a slow flame, stirring constantly, until slightly thickened. This should take about 5 or 10 minutes. Add the rum.

VARIATION

You can also dust Southern Sweet with confectioners' sugar before it is served, rather than using the above sauce.

DULCE DE CAMOTE Y PINA
(Sweet Potato and Pineapple Dessert)   Yield: 12 servings

2 pounds sweet potatoes, cooked	1 pint heavy cream, whipped
2 pounds sugar	¼ cup almonds
¼ teaspoon salt	¼ cup raisins
½ cup water	Cinnamon
2 cups fresh or canned pineapple, ground	

Peel and grind the sweet potatoes. Heat together the sugar, salt, and ½ cup water and cook until sugar is completely dissolved. Add the mashed potatoes and simmer 15 minutes or more, stirring constantly. Add the pineapple and simmer until mixture is thick and the bottom of the pan can be seen in the wake of the spoon. Remove from flame. Cool and mold into a loaf. Serve garnished with a topping of sweetened whipped cream, almonds, raisins, and cinnamon. Makes about 3 pounds of paste.

NOTE: If canned pineapple is used, drain well and substitute ¼ cup pineapple juice for half of the water.

PASTEL HELADO *(Iced Pudding)*   Serves 8–10

Señora Reina Fernandez de Villagómez of Guadalajara was kind enough to tell us about this favorite dessert recipe.

100 vanilla wafers (or comparable number ladyfingers)
1 package raspberry or strawberry gelatin
1 package chocolate or butterscotch pudding

¼ cup fresh cream
2 tablespoons sugar
½ teaspoon vanilla extract
Small amount of grated coconut

Cover the bottom and sides of a 9-inch ring mold with heavy wax paper, allowing enough for a small overlap at the top. Place wafers on the bottom and sides of the mold so that they are completely covered and the wax paper cannot be seen anywhere.

Prepare the gelatin and pudding according to package directions. When the mixtures are almost firm, pour one-half of the gelatin over the wafers. Place another layer of wafers on top of this. Place one-half of the pudding on the wafers. Repeat layers beginning with covering the wafers until ingredients are used up. Whip the cream with the sugar till stiff but not dry; add the vanilla. Pour over the pudding and gelatin. Sprinkle with coconut. Refrigerate until firm.

Out of the simplest ingredients Mexicans create some of their most delicious sweets. The next two are examples of this. A word of warning: they take time, but the tasty results are well worth the efforts.

1.

DULCE DE CALABAZA *(Squash Sweet)*

1 squash, weighing about 1 pound (not too ripe)
½ tablespoon lime to 1 gallon of water

Sugar (2½ cups to 1½ cups water for each pound of squash)
½ teaspoon coriander
½ teaspoon cinnamon

Cut squash in half and remove all the seeds. Cut the squash into strips about 2×4 inches. Prepare a solution by boiling the lime in a gallon of water, stirring until it stops bubbling; allow it to settle until clear. Pour the clear lye solution over the squash strips, using just enough of the solution to cover the strips. Let stand about 8 hours or overnight. Remove the squash and wash it under cold tap water until all of the lime is out of it. Boil in fresh water until tender, but not soft. Dunk immediately into cold water. Combine the sugar and water in proportions described above, add the coriander and the cinnamon, and boil gently until the mixture thickens slightly. Add the squash and cook slowly, covered, until squash is brittle and syrup is very thick. This sweet will keep for several weeks if stored in a cool place.

2.

DULCE DE LIMONES (*Candied Limes*)
Yield: 2 dozen

2 dozen large limes
1½ cups sugar
½ teaspoon salt
Juice of 1 lemon

Scrape the limes to rough up the skin and create a texture which partly removes the outer skin. Slash each lime with a long vertical cut. Soak for three days in cold water to cover, changing the water in the morning and evening of each day. Each time the water is changed, squeeze the limes gently. After they've soaked for the allotted time, put the sugar, salt, lemon juice, and ¾ cup of water in a heavy kettle and bring to a boil. Add the limes and allow them to simmer about 15–20 minutes. Remove from the heat and let stand another 8 hours. Boil them again in the same syrup for about 15–20 minutes, and boil again for the third time after letting the limes stand another 8 hours. Limes should be transparent when done.

ATE DE GUAYABA (*Guava Paste*)
Yield: 2½ pounds

Believe it or not, this sweet is worth the trouble it takes to prepare it. Mexicans frequently make it one year and serve it the next.

2 large cans guavas (if fresh guavas are used, figure on 2 pounds)	*7 cups sugar Pinch of salt ¼ teaspoon cumin*

Cut guavas in half and remove the seeds. Place the seeds in a cup of water. Let seeds stand for 15 minutes. Grind the guavas. Strain the water from the seeds. Dispose of seeds and re-serve water. Mix guavas with the water and put in a heavy pot (copper, iron, or earthenware). Add sugar, salt, and cumin and place over a very low flame, stirring constantly with a wooden spoon until slightly thickened and the bottom of the pan can be seen in the wake of the spoon. Pour into a narrow pan about 1 inch deep and allow to harden, preferably in the sun, until it is completely dry on top. This can take 5 days to a week. The *ate* will keep for months if stored in a cool place, wrapped in foil, in an airtight container.

BOLITAS DE ALMENDRA (*Almond Candies*)
Yield: 1 dozen

A sweet from Durango.

1 cup almonds, blanched and ground ½ cup powdered sugar	*½ teaspoon vanilla 1 egg white, stiffly beaten*

Mix the ground nuts with the sugar and vanilla and add the stiffly beaten egg white. Form into small balls and bake on a buttered cookie sheet in a moderate oven for about 5 minutes.

PANOCHITAS DE CACAHUATE (*Peanut Balls*)
Yield: 2½ pounds

2 pounds peanuts, unsalted
  and skinned
4 cups sugar
2 cups water
4 egg yolks

1 tablespoon ground
  cinnamon
½ teaspoon salt
½ teaspoon vanilla
Powdered sugar

Roast the peanuts lightly in the oven; cool and grind. Boil the sugar with 2 cups of water till mixture forms a hard ball in cold water (240°). Add the ground peanuts and continue cooking, stirring constantly, until bottom of the pan can be seen in the wake of the spoon. Remove from flame. Add the egg yolks, cinnamon, salt, and vanilla and beat the mixture into a paste. Press mixture into small balls with wooden paddles moistened in cold water. Arrange on wax paper-lined tray and dust with powdered sugar. Serve when dry.

DULCE DE NUECES OBSCURAS
(*Mixed Nut Candy*) Yield: 1½ dozen

2 cups brown sugar
½ cup water
1 tablespoon vinegar
1 tablespoon butter

1 cup assorted nut meats,
  roughly chopped
1 teaspoon almond extract

Mix sugar, ½ cup water, vinegar, and butter. Boil until syrup forms a thin thread when dropped from a spoon, or has reached 233° on candy thermometer. Cool slightly, add nuts and almond extract, and beat until creamy. Drop from tip of spoon on oiled paper or pour into buttered pan and cut into squares.

YEMITAS (*Little Egg Yolk Candies*)
Yield: 1½ pounds

2¼ cups sugar
1 cup water
10 egg yolks, beaten
  slightly

2 tablespoons granulated
  sugar
1½ teaspoons ground
  cinnamon

Stir sugar into a cup of water and boil until mixture reaches
236° on the candy thermometer or the soft-ball stage in cold
water. Remove and cool until comfortable to the touch. Add
egg yolks, stirring constantly. Cook over a very low flame, stirring all the while, until mixture forms a paste. This should
take around 15–20 minutes. Pour into a shallow dish and cool.
Mold into little balls the size and shape of an egg yolk. Combine the extra sugar with the cinnamon and roll each yolk in
this mixture.

HELADO DE NARANJA Y CIRUELA
(*Orange and Prune Ice Cream*)   Serves 5–6

This is a kind of mock ice cream. We're not sure it's purely
Mexican, but it's very good and we first ate it in Mexico.

1 egg white, stiffly beaten
½ cup sugar
¾ cup prune pulp
  (*cooked or canned
  prunes which have been
  pushed through strainer*)
½ cup orange juice, fresh
  or frozen

1 tablespoon lemon juice
1 tablespoon lime juice
½ teaspoon grated orange
  peel
1 cup heavy cream,
  whipped

Beat the egg white with the sugar; add the prune pulp and
mix well. Add the orange juice, lemon and lime juices, and the

orange peel. Fold in the whipped cream. Freeze in refrigerator tray about 3–4 hours.

NIEVE DE VINO (*Wine Ice*) Serves 8–10

1½ cups sugar
½ cup water
4 cups, or 1 quart, plain
  sparkling soda

1 cup red or white wine
Juice of 1 large lemon

Boil the sugar and ½ cup of water for about 5 minutes or until sugar is dissolved. Strain through cheesecloth, which has been folded several times, and cool. Add the sparkling water, wine, and lemon juice. Freeze for several hours or until serving time.

NOTE: If white wine is used, a few drops of food coloring can impart to it any color you'd like . . . perhaps to match or contrast with the *décor.*

PLATON DE FRUTA FRESCA
(*Fresh Fruit Platter*) Serves 6–8

To prepare a Mexican fruit platter, you'll need:

12–15 fresh strawberries
1 large orange
1 fresh pineapple
1 dozen long strips
  watermelon
1 dozen long strips
  cantaloupe, casaba, or
  other melon

½ cup fresh lime juice
½ cup grated fresh
  coconut

Clean the strawberries, but do not remove stems. Peel the orange and cut into thin slices. Cut the pineapple into quarters, taking care to leave on the green spikes. With a sharp, pointed knife cut the pineapple meat away from each section and then cut it into cubes, keeping it on the shell. Arrange the 4 quarters of pineapple on a round plate. Place the strawberries on toothpicks and decorate the pineapple with them here and there by inserting them in the pineapple chunks. Place orange slices on the empty spots on the platter. On top of them arrange the strips of melon, alternating the watermelon with the other type. Cover with lime juice and sprinkle with coconut.

Brebajes

❖

(BEVERAGES)

In Mexico you can almost drink your way through the alphabet —at least from *A* to *X*—delightfully.

We won't attempt to cover all the letters here, but we will start with *atoles*. These are gruels which are adored by both young and old. They can be made with fresh fruit, such as Atole de Fresa,* or nuts and coconut, as in Atole de Coco.* There are also marvelous beers which make drinking water for thirst-quenching purposes a thing of the past. The Mexicans make their own very good brandy.

C is for chocolate and coffee. The chocolate is flavored with cinnamon and the coffee is potent and sweet. To skip along, rum is used to make Daiquiris* and Rompope,* an eggnog. Tequila is the drink most frequently served at cocktail time. It is drunk with lime and salt on the side, or mixed with other ingredients to form Margaritas* or other drinks.

The country produces its own wine and there is a famous wine punch called Sangría.* There are excellent Mexican cordials, including the one we mentioned in the introduction, Xtabentum, which brings us to *X* and our drink suggestions.

ATOLE DE COCO (*Coconut Gruel*)   Serves 6–7

¼ cup flour
Dash of salt
2 cups water
1 small fresh coconut,
  grated extra-fine
4 cups milk (or enough
  milk and coconut milk
  to make a quart)

1⅛ cups sugar
2 teaspoons cinnamon
Dash of vanilla

Mix the flour, salt, and 2 cups of water in a saucepan. Simmer, stirring constantly, until mixture is thick. Combine coconut, milk, sugar, cinnamon, and vanilla. Add to the flour and water. Cook on a low heat, stirring constantly, until thickened. Strain. Serve hot.

ATOLE DE FRESA (*Strawberry Gruel*) Serves 7–8

1½ cups whole strawberries
½ cup masa or nixtamalina (special Mexican corn meal available at fine food stores)
1 tablespoon ground cinnamon

2 cups water
¾ cup sugar
3 cups milk
Dash of vanilla
Small amount red food coloring
1 cup sweet cream
3 egg yolks

Crush the berries. Mix the masa or *nixtamalina* with the cinnamon and 2 cups of water. Simmer, stirring constantly, until thickened. Remove from stove. Dissolve the sugar in the milk. Add to masa. Add the vanilla, crushed strawberries, and a few drops of food coloring. Add cream and mix well. Return to the stove and simmer again, stirring until thick. Remove from heat. Beat in egg yolks, one at a time, beating after each addition. Return to stove. Heat to boiling point. Serve immediately.

VARIATIONS

1. Substitute 8 tablespoons blanched ground almonds for the strawberries and omit the food coloring.

2. Use raspberries instead of strawberries and add red food coloring.

CAFE (*Coffee*)

The Mexicans like their coffee very strong and rather thick. In the morning, it is served *con leche,* or with milk—very strong coffee in a pot with a jug of warm milk beside it. The milk is used to dilute the coffee essence, and there you have it—*café con leche.*

In the evening, small cups of coffee are sweetened with sugar and served piping hot. Sometimes the evening coffee is flavored with Mexican chocolate and this is sweetened when you buy it. The addition of chocolate makes a rich, thick drink, and about all you can take of it is a tiny cup. At home you can do this by melting a small amount of grated Mexican chocolate (available in Mexican food stores) or sweetened American chocolate into your strongest brew of coffee. Be sure and serve it hot.

Ranch-style Coffee–or Café de Olla–is made with *piloncillo* (brown loaf sugar). Cinnamon and cloves are added for taste. As it cooks, a red-hot coal is popped into the brew and left to settle with the grounds. It's served in little clay mugs.

TE (*Tea*)

If you are wondering what kinds of tea the Mexicans use, here is a partial list of the teas you might find in a well-stocked Mexican pantry.

Hawthorn Cinnamon–used for curing coughs
Orange Leaf–used as a tranquilizer, a sort of "Miltown" among teas
Corn Silk–for kidney ailments
Cedar–for the stomach
Bark and Root of Oak–for strengthening the teeth
Asafetida–when he says: "It's not like Mother used to make," you serve him this tea . . . for his temper

And, there are a dozen or so more, including jasmine and artichoke tea. We can understand about the jasmine . . . the flower has petals, but how in the world would you put an artichoke in a tea bag?

CHOCOLATE MEXICANO (*Mexican Chocolate*)
Serves 6

The anecdotes surrounding Mexican chocolate are many and nearly as rich as the beverage itself. But the one which we find the most amusing of all concerns the early Spanish in Mexico who liked chocolate so much that they drank it all day long at home, and sipped it at church as well. There were decrees, sermons, edicts, and proclamations to put an end to all this, but the people paid no attention and went right on drinking their chocolate during the sermons as before. Indeed, a viceroy named Mancera was so troubled by the inconvenience of having to put his cup and saucer down when services required him to kneel, that he rose to the occasion and invented a cup and saucer which could be handled comfortably while kneeling or standing. These *mancerinas* are no longer used in church, but there are many old ones to be found in traditional Mexican homes, and there are new ones too. They are made in Europe and are purchased as curiosities for china cabinets. When you taste your first sip of Mexican chocolate you'll become pleasantly addicted, just as the Spanish did years and years ago. We warn you.

4 ounces Mexican chocolate (or 4 ounces sweet American chocolate)
4 cups milk
1 teaspoon ground cinnamon (Mexican chocolate has a cinnamon flavor to it, but some people like to add a touch more. You'll need it, of course, with American chocolate)

Combine all and cook over a low heat, stirring constantly, until mixture is blended and all the chocolate has melted. Beat to a froth before serving.

It's fun to do as the Mexicans do when serving chocolate. Pour it in a large earthenware jug and bring it to the table steaming and foaming. The Mexicans use a *molinillo* (wooden beater) to whip their chocolate. Some Mexican specialty stores carry them and they make nice additions to kitchen gadget collections. If you don't have a *molinillo,* use a hand beater and whip like blazes.

AGUA DE TAMARINDO *(Tamarind "Water")*
Yield: almost 5 quarts

½ pound tamarinds (a Mexican fruit available at most Mexican food stores)
4 quarts water
1 cup orange juice, fresh, frozen, or canned

2 cups fresh pineapple, pulverized
1 thick cinnamon stick
6 whole cloves, slightly bruised
2 cups sugar

Wash and peel the tamarinds. Add them to 4 quarts of water and the rest of the ingredients. Place all in a large earthenware jug; cover tightly and let stand 72 hours in refrigerator. Strain and add more sugar if necessary. Serve very cold.

CHICHA DE FRUTAS *(Fruit Punch)*
Yield: 2 quarts

Sprig of fresh mint (if available)
8 tablespoons very fine granulated sugar
1 cup water
2 cinnamon sticks
15 cloves
1 no. 3 can pineapple juice and 1 10-ounce can pineapple juice

1¾ cup orange juice, fresh, frozen, or canned
½ cup lemon juice
¼ cup lime juice
Pineapple or other fruit ice

Muddle the mint in one-quarter of the sugar for a few minutes. Shake the sugar particles off the mint and discard the sprig. Combine the sugar with 1 cup of water, cinnamon sticks, and cloves and simmer for about ½ hour. Strain through cheesecloth. Add the juices. Mix well. Serve very cold with a float of pineapple, orange, raspberry, or other favorite ice.

PONCHE DE CHAMPAGNE *(Champagne Punch)*
Serves 12–15

1 large fresh pineapple
Sugar
¾ cup fresh lemon juice, strained
1½ cups light rum

1 pint brandy
¾ cup orange curaçao
4 quarts dry champagne
1 orange, sliced thin

Peel and slice the pineapple. Put the slices, all except the one reserved for chunks, into a punch bowl. Sprinkle lightly with granulated sugar. Add the lemon juice, rum, brandy, and curaçao. Mix to blend. Put a large chunk of ice in the bowl and slowly add the champagne. Stir gently. Garnish with orange slices and pineapple chunks.

NOTE: The pineapple in the bottom of the bowl makes delicious eating for late-staying guests or just the family.

ROMPOPE (*Eggnog*)   Yield: 1 quart

10 egg yolks
4 cups milk
¾ cup sugar
1 thick cinnamon stick

4 tablespoons almonds,
blanched and ground
1 cup brandy or rum

Beat yolks until thick and lemon-colored and set aside. Combine the milk, sugar, and cinnamon in the top of a double boiler and bring to the boiling point, stirring frequently. Reduce heat and cook another 10 minutes, stirring all the while. Remove from heat and stir gently until mixture is lukewarm. (If a coating forms on the milk because you haven't been too vigilant about stirring, strain through cheesecloth.) Add beaten yolks and almonds. Cook once more over hot water in a double boiler and cool again, stirring often. When liquid is cool, add the brandy or rum. Remove the cinnamon stick. Keep in the refrigerator for about 24 hours before serving.

NOTE: Rompope is traditionally made with brandy, but we find rum just as tasty.

SANGRITA   Yield: 1 quart

Sangrita is used as a chaser with tequila, and is a sort of Mexican version of a Bloody Mary, literally meaning "little blood." However, with a Bloody Mary the juice and the spirits are mixed; with Sangrita the tequila and juice are never combined, but served in two glasses slightly larger than shot size. The technique is to take a sip of the tequila, then a sip of the sangrita, and a taste of fresh lime from the slice you are holding in your hand. Let's see now: one glass of sangrita, one glass of tequila—that's one in either hand—so you'll need a third hand for the lime. Never mind, have enough of these and you'll think you have three hands.

2½ pounds tomatoes	*1 onion*
4 oranges	*1 teaspoon sugar*
1 lemon	*Tabasco*
2 limes	*Salt to taste (or served on*
5 hot green chilies (or	*the side, as suggested*
chili powder, about 4–	*below)*
5 tablespoons for a very	
hot drink)	

Parboil the tomatoes; peel them. Grind and strain the pulp to get the juice. Add the juice of the oranges, lemon, and limes. Grind the chilies and onion very fine and add, along with the sugar. Add the Tabasco to taste. Mix well. Chill until very cold. Strain. Serve with tequila and slices of lime. Salt is sometimes served along with the lime too.

NOTE: Lazy folks like us use canned tomato juice and add the seasonings to it, including the juices. But don't tell a good Mexican bartender, please!

BERTA

This is a collins from Taxco, the silver center of Mexico. To make this drink you have to concoct a simple syrup that is as simple to make as it sounds:

Combine equal parts of sugar and water and cook until clear. Cool well. Make more than you need; you can use it for other drinks too.

FOR THE DRINK

1 jigger tequila   *1 jigger simple syrup*
1 jigger lime or lemon   *Charged water*
juice

Combine all but the charged water and pour into a tall glass with lots of ice. Fill to the brim with charged water. (Some people make this drink frothy by adding an egg white to the simple syrup after it's cool and shaking the drink before the soda is added.)

SANGRIA *(Wine Drink)*   Serves 6–8

There is a very beautiful toast which we associate with this drink. It goes:

> *"Salud, dinero, y amor,*
> *Y tiempo para gustarlos."*
> (Health, money, and love,
> And the time to enjoy them.)

⅔ cup freshly squeezed   *1 bottle (⅘ quart)*
lemon juice, strained   *Mexican dry red wine*
¼ cup freshly squeezed   *or other dry red wine*
orange juice, strained   *of the Burgundy type.*
8 tablespoons sugar

Mix the juices with the sugar until the sugar dissolves. Fill a pitcher about one-half full of ice cubes and pour in the juices and the wine. Stir well to blend.

NOTE: You can toss in a few slices of lemon and orange for color right before serving, if you like.

COCTEL DE PINA (*Pineapple Cocktail*)
Yield: 8–10 servings

A very nice gentleman, Señor Luis Márguez Romay, contributed this drink, which is sure to make a hit at your next party.

1 bottle tequila
1 fresh pineapple, crushed
½ cup sugar

Mix all and strain. Chill before serving.

DAIQUIRI

1½ ounces white rum
Juice of ½ lime
1 scant bar spoon sugar

Combine all and shake with cracked ice until shaker frosts. Strain into cocktail glass.

COCO CON RON (*Rum and Coconut Milk*)

Very good if you are going native at a beach party.

1 whole fresh coconut   *Ice*
Rum   *Soda*

Drill holes in coconut, pour out the milk and reserve. Measure milk and add an equal amount of light rum. Pour over ice cubes in a tall glass and add a small amount of soda.

NOTE: For suggestions of what to do with the coconut meat, see the dessert section of this book.

TEPACHE (*Pineapple "Cider"*)   Yield: 4 quarts

A drink from Jalisco . . . with a kick.

1 large fresh pineapple   *1 pound barley*
1 2-inch stick cinnamon   *2 pounds brown sugar*
10 cloves   *Water*
5 anise seeds

Wash the pineapple, peel, and grind it. Combine the peel, ground pineapple, and spices with 12 cups of water. Let the mixture stand in an earthenware jug for 48 hours. Cook the barley in 4 cups of water until the grains pop open. Cool. Add to the pineapple along with the brown sugar. Mix well. Let stand in crock at room temperature until it ferments. In warm weather this will take 48–72 hours; in cooler weather, a week or more. Strain and serve over crushed ice.

NOTE: Do not use a metal pot when making this drink.

EL SUENO (*The Dream*)

Over 1 scoop of lemon ice pour 1 jigger of rum. Stir together and serve in your prettiest cocktail glass with a short straw plunged into the ice.

MARGARITA

Margarita means daisy, so we sometimes serve this drink with little daisies wound around the stem of the cocktail glass.

1 ounce tequila   *Juice of ½ fresh lime*
Dash of Cointreau   *Coarse salt*

Pour tequila, Cointreau, and lime juice over crushed ice. Stir and serve in a cocktail glass, the rim of which has been moistened with lime juice and twirled in coarse salt.

TEQUILA SOUR

1 ounce simple syrup (see recipe for Berta*)
2 ounces lemon juice

8 ounces tequila
Orange slice, optional
Cherry, optional

Blend all over ice cubes. Strain and pour into sour glasses Decorate with orange slice and cherry, if so desired.

NOTE: You can make a rum sour by substituting light rum for the tequila.

MAYA

1 ounce honey
4 ounces rum

½ ounce lime juice
½ ounce lemon juice

Combine all; stir well. Add ice and shake. Serve in cocktail glass.

TEQUILA MARTINI

1 part vermouth
3 parts tequila

Dash of Pernod
Twist of orange rind

Stir all but rind in a tall glass with ice cubes or broken ice. Strain into a cocktail glass. Squeeze orange rind over the drink and drop it into the drink.

BLACK CHARRO

Mix equal parts of Kahlúa (coffee liqueur) and tequila and serve on the rocks.

AZTECA

¾ part white crème de menthe
¼ part Kahlúa (coffee liqueur)

Pour the crème de menthe over ice in an Old Fashioned glass and top with coffee liqueur.

EL DIABLO (The Devil)

⅔ part brandy
⅓ part white crème de menthe
Red chili powder

Combine the brandy and crème de menthe in shaker loaded with ice. Shake well. Strain and serve with the chili powder sprinkled on top.

BESO DE ANGEL (Angel's Kiss)

Fill a liqueur glass three-quarters full of Kahlúa (coffee liqueur) and carefully float heavy cream to the rim of the glass.

Fiestas

❖

Mexico is a country of fiestas and in our introduction we described a few of them. Now we are going to add some of the special foods which go with these special days and a few notes of interest and recipes associated with other holidays. We are only highlighting a few of the special days in Mexico here. To cover all of them, we'd have to write a book, for in Mexico every day there is a celebration somewhere and a special dish to go with it.

But, before we get on with the holidays, there is a festival custom in the Yucatán worth remembering. Should you ever be in Mérida or another city in that region and you see a wedding party, join right in! You'll be asked to pay a dollar and you'll be free to mingle with the guests and sample all the wedding foods. It's fun and a splendid way to taste native cuisine.

And now for some fiestas for everyone:

NAVIDAD
(*Christmas*)

Navidad is probably the happiest and most colorful of all Mexican festivals. We went into detail about the *posadas* associated with it in our introduction, so we'll skip right into the foods here.

ENSALADA DE NOCHEBUENA
(*Christmas Eve Salad*)   Serves 6

2 beets, cooked and sliced
¾ cup pineapple (fresh, preferably, but canned or frozen can be used)
1 apple, cored and peeled
2 oranges, peeled and sectioned (or 1 orange and 2 small tangerines)
1 banana, sliced
Favorite French dressing, sweetened with sugar to taste; or mayonnaise, thinned with a little cream

Seeds of 1 pomegranate
½ cup peanuts or walnuts, chopped coarsely
2 carrots, cut in strips
Romaine or other tart lettuce, washed well and separated with leaves left whole

Mix the first 5 ingredients. Toss with either of the dressings mentioned above and garnish with pomegranate seeds, nuts, and carrot strips. Serve on a bed of romaine or other tart lettuce.

The traditional recipe for Christmas salad does not call for a dressing—just sugar or small sugar candies. It also requires the jicama, a vegetable that tastes somewhat like a sweet turnip. It is virtually impossible to find at your local store, so we've just left it out.

NOTE: Dressings for Stuffed Avocados I and II* are good with this salad too!

Among the Mexican Christmas treats are *buñuelos* (fritters), which we've eaten at other times of the year but they are especially associated with Oaxaca and the Christmas season. These syrup-soaked fritters are eaten on Oaxaca's Radish Night when the whole town is gaily decorated with carved figures all made out of radishes. The custom is to eat the sweet and smash the plate on which it was served. For obvious reasons, in "Americanizing" this dish, we suggest the use of paper plates.

BUNUELOS *(Fritters)*   Serves 8

> ½ tablespoon anise seed
> ½ cup water
> 2 eggs, beaten
> ½ cup milk
>
> 4 cups flour
> 1 teaspoon baking powder
> ¾ teaspoon salt

Boil ½ tablespoon anise seed in ½ cup of water for 5 minutes. Let cool. Strain, but reserve water. Blend together the eggs, milk, and anise water. Sift the dry ingredients and add to the eggs, milk, and anise water. Knead well. Roll dough out as thin as possible on a lightly floured board. Cut into rounds about 6 inches in diameter. Fry in hot fat (370°) until they are a light golden brown. Drain and serve covered with either of the following syrups.

SYRUP I

> ½ pound piloncillo (*brown*
> *unrefined sugar—usually*
> *comes in small loaves*),
> *or substitute 6*
> *tablespoons brown sugar*
> *moistened to a damp*
> *consistency with dark*
> *molasses*
>
> 1 cup water
> ½ tablespoon anise seed
> ¼ cup candy sprinkles

Boil the *piloncillo* or brown sugar and molasses mixture with 1 cup of water and the anise seed until thick. Strain, pour over the fritters, and decorate with candy sprinkles.

SYRUP II

⅓ *cup sugar*	½ *teaspoon cinnamon*
½ *cup water*	¼ *teaspoon ground cloves*
½ *cup white wine*	

Combine all ingredients and boil slowly until syrup is formed.

NOTE: Buñuelos can be frozen, without the syrup topping. Wrap each one separately. Heat before serving to make them crispy.

TORREJAS DE COCO
(*Cake Slices in Coconut Syrup*) Serves 6

Still another Christmas sweet . . . .

1½ *cups sugar*	¼ *cup butter*
Water, as directed	¼ *cup sherry*
1 *4-ounce can shredded coconut, or equivalent in fresh*	1 *stick cinnamon, about 2 inches long*
3 *eggs, beaten lightly*	3 *cloves*
¼ *teaspoon salt*	3–4 *candied figs, chopped*
12 *slices poundcake, cut about ¼-inch thick (make according to your favorite recipe or buy cake ready-made)*	9 *candied cherries*
	2 *tablespoons candied citron, chopped*

Cook sugar (reserve ½ cup for later) in ½ cup water for about 3 minutes. Add the shredded coconut and cook until the moisture is absorbed and the coconut is dry. Remove from stove and cool.

To the lightly beaten eggs add the salt and beat again lightly or until blended. Spread some of the coconut mixture on a slice of cake and top sandwich-fashion with another slice. Dip the cake sandwiches in the eggs and sauté in butter, turning until cake slices are golden brown.

Combine remaining sugar with 1 cup of water, add the sherry, cinnamon, and cloves and simmer together for about 5 minutes. Gently lower cake slices into syrup and simmer 4 or 5 minutes. Serve in sauce dishes with some syrup on each cake sandwich. Trim with chopped figs, cherries, and citron.

NOTE: This dish can be made without coconut. If so, use 6 cake slices about ¾ inch thick. Start by dipping them into beaten eggs. You can garnish this dish with pine nuts and raisins instead of figs, cherries, and citron. Use about ¼ cup of each.

BUDIN DE NAVIDAD (*Christmas Pudding*)
Serves 12–15

2 tablespoons unflavored gelatin	6 eggs, separated
1½ cups sugar	1 cup heavy cream
½ cup flour	1½ teaspoons almond extract
3½ cups milk	½ teaspoon vanilla
Pinch of salt	Red and green colorings

Combine the gelatin with ½ cup sugar and the flour. Put into a saucepan and gradually stir in the milk. Cook over a low flame, stirring constantly, until mixture thickens and reaches boiling point. Remove from stove. Let stand until cool. Beat until smooth.

Add salt to egg whites. Beat the whites until nearly stiff and standing in peaks. Add 1 cup of sugar, a little bit at a time, beating to form a glossy meringue. Beat heavy cream until stiff. Add the extracts to cream. Fold cream into meringue. Fold carefully into gelatin custard. Divide into 3 parts. To part one, add a few drops of red coloring. To part two, add a few drops of green. Leave the third portion as is. Lightly oil a 9×12-inch pan. Pour in green custard; pour in white custard carefully over green; top with dark pink. Chill 5 hours or until firm.

SAUCE

Mix egg yolks with ⅓ cup sugar, ¼ teaspoon salt, and 2¼ cups scalded milk. Cook slowly in double boiler, stirring constantly, to form a light custard. It is done when mixture coats spoon. Add ¼ teaspoon vanilla extract. Cool.

Cut the pudding into serving portions, top with custard, and serve.

NOTE: This is not a traditional dish, but it's festive-looking and delicious.

FIESTA DE LOS SANTOS REYES
(*The Coming of the Kings*)

We explained a good deal about the Coming of the Kings, January 6, in our introduction. Here is the recipe for Rosca de Reyes, a coffeecake which is traditionally eaten on that day.

ROSCA DE REYES (*Coffeecake*)   Yield: 2 cakes

2 cakes yeast
2 tablespoons warm water
⅔ cup milk, heated to the boiling point
⅓ cup sugar
1 teaspoon vanilla
1 teaspoon salt
4 eggs, beaten until lemon-colored

⅓ cup butter, quite soft
5 cups flour, sifted
2 candied oranges, chopped
2 candied citrons, chopped
½ cup nuts, chopped
½ cup raisins, chopped
2 tiny china dolls
Granulated sugar

Dissolve the yeast in 2 tablespoons of warm water. Mix the hot milk, sugar, vanilla, and salt, stirring well. Cool until just warm. Add the dissolved yeast, 3 eggs, soft butter, and 1 cup of the flour. Next, add the rest of the flour, which has been mixed lightly with most of the candied fruits, nuts, and raisins. Mix to a firm dough. Knead on a lightly floured wooden surface until dough is very smooth. Cover with cloth; let stand 30 minutes. Divide dough and form 2 rings and place them on 2 greased baking sheets or ring molds. In each ring insert a china doll so that it does not show. Cover with cloth and let dough rise until both rings are double in bulk. This will take about 1 hour or more. Brush rings lightly with the remaining beaten egg; decorate here and there with remaining chunks of candied fruit. Snip the surface of the dough lightly and sprinkle incisions with granulated sugar. Bake at 375° for about ½ hour or until bread is well done and brown. Let it get cold before cutting.

NOTE: You can make these jelly-roll-fashion too. When adding second portion of flour, do not add chopped fruits. Knead; cover and let stand. Roll out; sprinkle chopped fruits on dough. Roll up as jelly roll and proceed as directed.

VIERNES DE DOLORES
(*Friday of Seven Sorrows*)

Seven days before Good Friday, lots of people celebrate the Day of Seven Sorrows by going off to Xochimilco, called the Venice of Mexico because of the many canals, man-made lakes, and the profusion of flowers. On this special day, the floating gardens look more festive than ever. People wear wreaths of flowers in their hair, and the canoes are bright with fresh blossoms. Prizes are awarded for the most beautiful boat, the best singer, the outstanding musician, and the most spirited dancers. But, we think that they've forgotten one prize . . . for this delicious chocolate drink.

CHAMPURRADO Serves 6

5 tablespoons masa or
nixtamalina (*Mexican
corn meal, available in
most specialty food
stores*), or 3¼
tablespoons cornstarch
3 cups water
2 tablespoons sugar
1 teaspoon vanilla

½ teaspoon salt
2 squares Mexican
chocolate, grated (*or 3
ounces Dutch chocolate
plus 1½ teaspoons
ground cinnamon*)
½ pint milk
Heavy whipped cream
(*optional*)

Blend the corn meal or the cornstarch with 3 cups of water.
Strain. Bring to a boil, stirring constantly. Add the sugar,
vanilla, salt, and, lastly, the chocolate, gradually, and continue
to cook, stirring constantly. Add milk and stir until chocolate
is creamy and thick. Top with whipped cream.

NOTE: We also like to spike this drink by adding about ¼ cup
of rum to it and decreasing the water to 2¾ cups. We stir in
the rum at the end, so the flavor doesn't disappear. For the
purists, we also add that the whipped cream is not traditional
—just a tasty addition.

CUARESMA
(*Lent*)

During Lent, everyone enjoys the following dish.

TORTILLAS DE VIGILIA
(*Onion and Cheese Tortillas*)   Yield: 12

6 tablespoons oil
1 8-ounce can whole
   tomatoes, chopped
1 very small onion,
   minced
2 bell peppers, peeled and
   chopped
¾ cup mild Cheddar
   cheese, grated

1 teaspoon salt
Dash of cayenne pepper
½ teaspoon freshly ground
   pepper
1¾ cups cream
1 dozen Tortillas*

In one-half of the oil sauté the tomatoes, onions, and peppers until softened. Add three-quarters of the cheese, salt, cayenne and ground pepper, and cream and simmer—but do not boil— about 10 minutes. Remove from the stove and keep warm. Sauté the tortillas in the rest of the oil until they are crisp and brown. Drain on absorbent paper. Continue to cook sauce until quite thick, stirring constantly. Top the toasted tortillas (*tostadas*) with the sauce and the remaining cheese. Figure on 2 to a person.

Capirotada* (Bread Pudding) is also popular at this time of year.

DIA DE SAN JUAN
(*St. John's Day*)

This holiday is celebrated June 24 and is associated, in terms of food, with fresh fruit. In many places in Mexico people make it a point to eat pears on this day. In Tehuantepec, Oaxaca, which is famous for its beautiful women, the day is celebrated by having the women climb to the top of the belfry carrying large platters of fruit for a *tirada,* which means they throw the fruit right off the bell tower . . . and there are usually coconuts among the delicacies. Lots of people spend their time swimming on this holiday. We can understand this, especially if you are hit by a piece of ripe fruit in Tehuantepec. The belief is that the water on this day will make you more beautiful and pure.

DIA DE SAN AGUSTIN
(*St. Augustine's Day*)

As we said, somewhere in Mexico every day there is a special festival. A good example of this is the feast of St. Augustine, August 28. It is observed in Puebla, and the following dish is associated with it.

CHILES EN NOGADA
(*Chili Peppers in Walnut Sauce*)   Serves 7

SAUCE

50 walnuts, shelled
Milk to cover walnuts
4 ounces goat's milk cheese (if not available, use 1 3-ounce package cream cheese)

Hard roll, soaked in small amount milk
Salt and pepper to taste
Dash of cinnamon
7 bell peppers

STUFFING

½ cup olive oil
½ pound pork, ground
½ pound beef, ground
(*all beef or pork may be used*)
3 tomatoes, peeled and chopped (*or 1 8-ounce can*)
½ onion, minced
1 clove of garlic, crushed
½ cup almonds, blanched and chopped
½ cup raisins, plumped in a small amount water

¼ teaspoon saffron
2 peaches, peeled and chopped
2 pears, peeled and chopped
Salt and pepper to taste
¾ cup flour, sifted
1 teaspoon cinnamon
½ teaspoon cloves
2 teaspoons sugar
2 large eggs, beaten lightly

GARNISHES

Pomegranate seeds and parsley, chopped

Soak the walnuts in the milk long enough to loosen the skins. Then remove the skins. Grind the walnuts, cheese, hard roll in milk together to make a sauce. Sauce should be thin enough to pour; add a bit more milk if necessary. Season the sauce with salt, pepper, and a dash of cinnamon. Plunge the peppers into boiling water for a few minutes. Remove tops and take out seeds, being careful to leave peppers whole for stuffing.

For stuffing: Heat the oil, add the meat, and brown. Add the tomatoes, onion, and garlic, and cook, covered, to blend flavors for a few minutes. Add the almonds, raisins, saffron, and chopped fruits. Season to taste with salt and pepper and let cook until thick. Stuff the peppers with the meat. Dip them in mixture of sifted flour, cinnamon, cloves, and sugar. Beat the eggs and dip the peppers in the eggs. Sprinkle again with the flour and condiments. Fry in hot fat at 375° until browned. Drain on absorbent paper. Serve with cold sauce, garnished with pomegranate seeds and parsley.

DIA DE LOS MUERTOS
(*Day of the Dead*)

November 2. This is the Mexican version of All Saints' Day and the shops are full of sugar skulls, skeletons, and other bizarre sweets. They start to grin wildly from the windows around October 15, and vanish from sight after the holiday. The Day of the Dead is celebrated all over the country, but it is in Janitzio, the small island in Lake Pâtzcuaro, where it takes its most interesting and unusual form. There, two days prior to the second day of November, all the men go off in canoes to hunt ducks . . . which they do with harpoons, not guns. On the day of the festival they return home and the women make some delicious dishes out of the fresh ducks. The men stay home and eat, while the women, bearing candles, take their duck delicacies to the cemetery and keep watch all night. The candles remain lit, making a cluster of flickering lights which can be seen clear across the lake. The men and women get together in the morning and eat Pan de Muertos. The bread is usually decorated with "bones," "tears," and "knobs," and is topped with pink sugar.

PAN DE MUERTOS (*Bread of the Dead*)
Yield: 2 loaves

1 cake yeast
3 cups flour
⅓ cup sugar
½ teaspoon salt
6 eggs, separated
1 tablespoon orange extract

1 stick butter
2 tablespoons anise extract
1 tablespoon grated orange rind

TOPPING

½ cup sugar
½ cup water
Granulated sugar, tossed lightly with a tiny amount of red
   food coloring

Dissolve the yeast in a ¼ cup warm water and mix it with
½ cup flour. Let stand in a warm place for 15 minutes or
until it doubles in size. Sift the remaining dry ingredients 4
times. Place in a large bowl and make a deep depression in
the flour. Add the egg yolks and orange extract; cut in butter;
add anise and orange rind. Mix well and add enough egg whites
to form a soft dough. Pound the dough against a lightly
floured wooden surface until it bubbles and does not stick. Put
the dough in a lightly greased bowl, cover it with a cloth, and
let it stand until it doubles in bulk, or about 1–1½ hours.
Knead and shape into 2 round loaves, but reserve some dough
for the crossbones, tears, and knobs. Attach these to the loaves.
Let breads rise on a greased baking sheet until double in bulk.
When breads have risen properly, bake at 375° for about ½
hour or until done. Cool.

For Topping: Cook ½ cup sugar and ½ cup water together
to form a thick syrup. Brush syrup over breads and dust with
colored granulated sugar. Wait a few minutes and dust with more
sugar. Cut when cold.

NOTE: To make crossbones, tears, and knobs, just divide
dough and roll with palms of hands to get desired shape. You
can make these breads with only two teardrops, attractively,
too.

Index

❖